TALES
FROM THE
BIG TRAILS

TALES
FROM THE
BIG TRAILS

A FORTY-YEAR QUEST TO WALK
THE ICONIC LONG-DISTANCE TRAILS OF
ENGLAND, SCOTLAND AND WALES

MARTYN HOWE

Vertebrate Publishing, Sheffield
www.v-publishing.co.uk

TALES
FROM THE
BIG TRAILS

MARTYN HOWE

First published in 2021 by Vertebrate Publishing.

VERTEBRATE PUBLISHING
Omega Court, 352 Cemetery Road, Sheffield S11 8FT, United Kingdom.
www.v-publishing.co.uk

Excerpt from 'On Scratchbury Camp' by Siegfried Sassoon
reproduced by kind permission of the Estate of George Sassoon.

Excerpts from 'The Waste Land Part III – the Fire Sermon' and *Four Quartets*
by T.S. Eliot reproduced by kind permission of Faber & Faber.

'Rain' by Simon Armitage reproduced by kind permission of Faber & Faber.

The author would also like to thank Dan Maier (via the Curtis Brown literary and talent agency), Ian McMillan, the Battle of Britain Memorial Trust CIO (for 'Our Wall' by William L.B. Walker), John Wedgwood Clarke, Tom Bryan and Hugh Lupton for their kind permission to quote from their work.

We would like to thank Natural England and NatureScot for granting permission to feature the acorn and thistle icons on the cover.

A CIP catalogue record for this book is available from the British Library.

ISBN: 978-1-83981-058-9 (Paperback)
ISBN: 978-1-83981-059-6 (Ebook)

10 9 8 7 6 5 4 3 2 1

Design by Jane Beagley, Vertebrate Publishing.
Production by Cameron Bonser, Vertebrate Publishing.
www.v-publishing.co.uk

Vertebrate Publishing is committed to printing on paper from sustainable sources.

MIX
Paper from
responsible sources
FSC® C018072

Printed and bound in Great Britain by Clays Ltd, Elcograf S.p.A.

To my wife, Alison,
for encouraging me to live my dreams.

CONTENTS

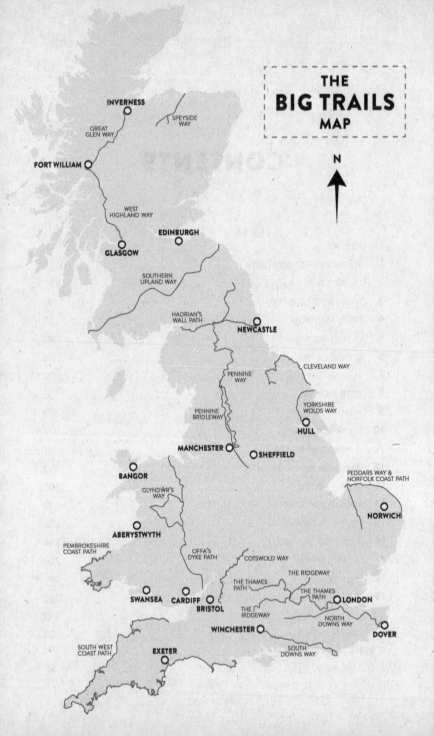

INTRODUCTION

The British Isles are blessed with a vast network of walking trails and paths, more than anyone could walk in a lifetime. Lying between fifty and sixty-one degrees latitude and exposed to the Gulf Stream, the temperate climate and coastal disposition make this a unique landscape on planet Earth. Run your finger around a globe, and you would be hard pressed to find another place where sea, land, people and weather combine to make walking so pleasant.

In the 1960s, ramblers with foresight and ambition fought to develop a long-distance network, funded and maintained by governments to a minimum standard. There are now eleven National Trails in England and four in Wales, overseen by Natural England and Natural Resources Wales. Lobbying and campaigning continue to protect our rights to walk in the countryside; the network is growing still as the England Coast Path approaches completion and plans develop to open more long-distance trails. These fifteen (soon to be sixteen) paths are waymarked with the acorn symbol. In Scotland, you can spend a lifetime walking in the most stunning landscapes in the world. Scotland's Great Trails are a growing network of routes for paddlers, cyclists, horse riders and backpackers. Within this network are four designated long-distance routes, equivalent to the National Trails in England and Wales, waymarked by a white thistle symbol. Together these routes in England, Scotland and Wales make up the nineteen iconic national trails that formed the basis of my journey.

These same paths are listed in the Long Distance Walkers Association's (LDWA) Diamond Award challenge, which has been completed by fewer than sixty walkers since its inception in 2009 and is a distance of 3,029 miles by their reckoning. The distances quoted at the beginning of each chapter reflect the mileage I noted at the time of the walk and may differ from those quoted in guidebooks. A path may have optional routes (such as the North Downs Way alternative route via Canterbury), ferry crossings, extensions and alterations. In reality I have walked further: seeking accommodation off the main route, and getting lost more often than I would like to admit.

These paths are challenging adventures, passing through diverse landscapes: you will encounter stunning coastal paths, remote wilderness, moorlands, woodlands and ancient ways that have been in continuous use for millennia. Perhaps more importantly, you will discover unique cultures, communities, people and heritage in a land with unparalleled global influence. All of this will be washed with changing weather conditions, which will dishearten you on one day but bring joy the next. This richness stimulates the senses; you tune into the landscape and observe patterns and behaviours, often triggered by increasing recognition of birdsong and natural sounds. The repetitive motion of walking leads to a meditative state that resonates in harmony with your environment. More than this, I have developed empathy and listening skills from all the beautiful people I have met. I understand how important it is to get outside my privileged bubble and interact with communities with different perspectives and situations to my own, often ones I envy, from all of which I learn.

These observations were the last thing on my mind when I walked from Fishguard to St Davids in Pembrokeshire when I was fifteen. As a young boy, my sense of adventure had already developed with numerous wild-camping experiences, encouraged by parents who would kick me out of the back door on a Friday night to go exploring. You might think that irresponsible, but I lived in a place and a time where that was considered normal.

During my working years, those seeds of adventure lay dormant and were awakened in later life, watered by a change in circumstance. While I walked these trails, both my parents and younger brother succumbed to cancer, and my full-time career faltered. These life-changing events led me to re-evaluate my place in the world. I started freelance work, giving up corporate life trappings in exchange for that most precious resource: time.

This publication is not a guidebook – there are many of those on the bookshelves – yet anyone with essential map-reading and travel-planning skills can walk these trails. Even those with a basic fitness level can start with more accessible routes, taking one day at a time. It does, however, come with a warning: this passion is addictive and leads to an ever-increasing upward spiral of ambition. I now find myself walking further and longer, through wilderness areas with no support or comfort, for up to a month. I have recently completed the Wales Coast Path and will walk the England Coast Path in stages. Finally, I plan to walk the Scottish National Trail (devised by Cameron McNeish in 2012) – perhaps the ultimate backpacking route in the British Isles. I am sure this will only lead to further adventure on foot, or by bike.

This journey is not complete, for I have become addicted to walking and adventure in the outdoors. As I reach the end of a path, I am planning the next. The challenges become more ambitious, as my experience develops, to manage my physical resources and overcome doubt. Yet I still have a stomach full of butterflies every time I step aboard the train to reach the trailhead. Is this fear, or is this excitement? I still don't know, but I feel as if I am living.

To quote Gwyn Thomas, 'the beauty is in the walking; we are betrayed by destinations'.

My journey did not start as a tick list, but it grew into one; my right-hemisphere-dominant brain demanded it, yet my left hemisphere benefited from it. Now I realise the wisdom of that quotation, and I feel a better person for it.

1

PEMBROKESHIRE COAST PATH

Distance: 186 miles
Days to complete: 10 days
Mileage so far: 0 miles

WHERE IT ALL BEGINS

The distance is nothing; it is only the first step that is difficult.
– Madame du Deffand

I still cannot believe I walked my first National Trail aged fifteen. With a friend, I caught a long-haul coach service to Fishguard, of a design you find in a *Carry On* movie c.1960s, with curved windows. We carried enormous aluminium-framed fluorescent backpacks, stuffed with tatty army sleeping bags, tents and clothing. We wore two or three pairs of socks, to compensate for the oversized boots we had borrowed from our fathers. Other heavy items included a brass Primus stove and a pint of paraffin – a dangerous combination we had taken months to master. We walked south to St Davids, wild camping and using youth hostels, and returned home after a week, alive and with memories that remain for a lifetime – the birth of my wanderlust.

Almost thirty years later, an opportunity to walk a long-distance path arose when a one-month window opened between employments. What should I do? My wife and I regularly walked, particularly in Wales, and we happened to be in Pembrokeshire when I picked up a leaflet about the coast path. I reconnected with my youth and started planning in earnest. I would walk south from St Dogmaels to Amroth. I had a tent, backpack, sleeping bag and boots. All I needed was a train ticket to Camarthen to connect with a bus service to Cardigan.

I'm reading Nick Crane's *Clear Waters Rising* for inspiration as the train rattles into Cardiff. He has somehow managed to negotiate a year away from his new bride to walk from Santiago de Compostela to Istanbul. My wife asked me to complete a list of tasks on my return in exchange for two weeks in Wales. It seemed a fair price to pay. Over the years, I will become eternally grateful for her understanding, as the most valuable asset for long-distance walking is time.

I'm the only person on the bus north, save for a young lad who is listening to Avril Lavigne's 'Skater Boy' at full volume on his headphones, repeatedly. Smartphones are yet to take hold, but the signs of addiction are there. I'm carrying a battered 35mm camera, two rolls of film and a Nokia candy bar phone with an annoying extended aerial. My pack is full of maps of varying vintage, and I thought to bring a Sony Walkman too. All of these functions will combine into a single device in a few years, to create a gadget of incredible utility.

The walk to Poppit Sands youth hostel alongside the Afon Teifi estuary introduces the coastline ahead. Although I'm carrying an evening meal, I can't pass Bowen's Fish & Chip Shop in St Dogmaels, just a few yards from the start of the path. I hear Welsh spoken for the first time in years as locals order their fish suppers, their accents in contrast to a distinct south-east England cadence at the hostel. A large group of birdwatchers are settling in for a week, a clique who are keeping conversations private, as if some rare bird sighting must remain a secret. I overhear a few words.

'I just got a pager message. Manx shearwaters at Strumble Head.'

'Any Cory's or sooties?' asks a woman.

'No. No news.'

'I'd love to see a migrating skua this week,' adds another.

I'm a morning person, up with the larks and eager to start the day. The nights are beginning to draw in now it is mid-September. Now you can catch the golden-hour light at a reasonable time. The heather is turning auburn, a reddish-brown hue that marks the coastal boundary between sea and farmland. I turn south-west at Cemaes Head towards dramatic folded cliff formations overlooking the Irish Sea. My urban mind is shaken free and refreshed with new stimuli. A natural canvas replaces commerce and industry, mechanical sounds fade to birdsong and breaking waves, new smells invade my nasal receptors, and the hairs on my arms bristle in the breeze.

I can hear seals in the bays and cautiously peer over the cliff edge to see them basking next to newborn pups wearing their white fur coats, an Ice Age remnant designed to camouflage them in the ice and snow. A peregrine falcon glides along the cliff edge, waiting to dive upon an unsuspecting victim. Fulmars quarrel and circle, unconcerned by my presence, using their webbed feet as airbrakes to land on their nests. I have to stop and observe; the narrow nine-inch track, carved with average-sized boots, requires concentration and balance to walk (I'm size twelve). I am reassured by a sturdy walking pole, ready to arrest a fall. These cliffs are exposed and can be dangerous.

My body needs to adjust to a new exercise regime. I hope to cover fifteen to eighteen miles a day to synchronise with overnight accommodation. The first campsite is by the shore, near Parrog, and I pitch for the night. I cook the meal I have carried from Cardigan and take a stroll on the beach. Thousands upon thousands of *Velella velella* (sail-by-the-wind) hydrozoa cover the sands. They are little blue jellyfish-like creatures with protruding twisted yin-yang sails attached to a body that looks like a Fresnel lens. They have been blown ashore by recent gales and lie forlorn, like aliens from another planet. They will feature on almost every beach I walk on in the coming weeks.

Cwm-yr-Eglwys, a few miles west, is home for a ruined church, once the focus of a small fishing community. It shelters in the lee of Dinas Island, a large hill almost separated from the mainland, rising to 142 metres. An Ordnance Survey trig pillar provides just enough shelter from the wind to sit and scan the views east and west. I can see Fishguard harbour in the distance, confirmed when the DFDS ferry departs for Ireland. It only takes a few hours to reach the breakwater, to stop for lunch by a camping spot we first used twenty-five years ago; it remains unchanged. I cannot imagine the sight of two gangly teenagers huddled inside a white canvas pup tent, trying to light a paraffin stove to cook a tin of beans. What were we doing? How did we survive?

The dockside is busy with lorries, cars and vans running up the ramps into the bowels of another enormous ferry, loading with astonishing efficiency. The French army, however, did not disembark as effectively in 1797 when they sought to land an invasion force a few miles further west. The coastline is rugged and exposed, so it is a wonder that they managed to land any men or arms. They mistook the local womenfolk (who had gathered in numbers) as the local militia; dressed in traditional red shawls and black hats, they precipitated a surrender at Fishguard. So ended the last land invasion of the British Isles.

I make steady progress to Strumble Head, where I meet the birdwatchers from the hostel. Their binoculars and telescopes point seaward as they count migrating shearwaters. The wind has strengthened to force 7. The gusts make landfall, loaded with rain, and I have to cling to the path. I decide against waterproof leggings, which can act like a greased sledge on wet grass – not a safe combination. It is a long way down to the rocky shoreline, and I do not want to join the seals for a swim. The conditions are like a washing machine on an endless rinse/spin cycle; it floods every crevice of my body with clean, cold rainwater.

> Sun, wind, and cloud shall fail not from the face of it,
> Stinging, ringing spindrift, nor the fulmar flying free;
> And the ships shall go abroad
> To the glory of the Lord
> Who heard the silly sailor-folk and gave them back their sea!
> – Rudyard Kipling, from 'The Last Chantey' (1893)

I am soaked and shivering as I reach Pwll Deri hostel at 4 p.m. and wait an hour for it to open. I hear the latch unlock and the door creak open. A beautiful warden smiles at me like an angel from heaven.

'Hello,' I mutter.

'Come in, come in. You should have knocked earlier,' she says with a radiant smile. 'Here's a key; you can fill out the paperwork later. Get changed. I'll get the kettle going.'

After a shower, warm clothing and a meal, I sit in the common room overlooking a wild seascape out of the bay window. This view is one of the best from a youth hostel in Wales, made all the more pleasant with added conversation, over endless cups of tea, with fellow guests and a knowledgeable warden.

'Can you see the falcon hunting?'

'Look at the harbour porpoises below, bay residents we see often,' says the warden.

'Jeez, look at the size of that black-backed gull!'

'Did you see any shearwaters at Strumble Head?' I ask.

'Not many, you need to go to Skomer Island further south to see them at dusk.'

'Anyone for another pot of tea?' asks someone, holding a mug aloft.

These beautiful shearwaters spend most of their time at sea; migrating as far south as Argentina in the winter months, they shear as if cutting the wave tops, yet miss the crest by centimetres. Young chicks born in Wales will fledge from their burrows in late August, and commence an astonishing 7,000-mile journey south. Once known as Manx puffins, Manx shearwaters (scientific name, *Puffinus puffinus*) belong to Procellariidae, a family of birds (including albatross and fulmars) that have an acute sense of smell to guide them to their diet of sand eels, herrings and sardines. There are concerns that the volume of plastic in the sea floods their nostrils with unusual odours, upsetting their ability to navigate and hunt. Colonies raft in huge numbers at sunset, before coming ashore at night to avoid predation by large gulls. They cannot run; they overbalance on legs designed to paddle at sea and must sledge into their burrows. Somehow they survive, with approximately seventy per cent of breeding pairs raising healthy chicks, which can live to over fifty years old. I'd love to see one.

Len's Radio Pembroke '10 past forecast' says the gale has run its course and the weather will improve. I am chuffed at having completed a twenty-mile day in rough conditions and step out early for another day on the Pembrokeshire Coast Path. The following section is remote and challenging, with only a few amenities until you reach St Davids. Large numbers of seals are in the bays. If you can't see them, you can hear them call; sometimes you can smell their fishy odour too. The sea state has eased, and I can relax into a steady pace and enjoy the views. This section is a rugged, beautiful coastline, considered by many to be the best in Britain. The heather has turned an auburn-purple-brown, and the seas are deep blue. The cliff faces look frightening: dark, weathered and riven with fractures. A black lichen marks the tidal level, a measure of the average high-water mark, frequently washed by freak waves. Rocks lie on the heather, thrown there during the most violent storms. Some are so large you could not pick them up with one hand.

I meet very few walkers on the path, even as I reach St Davids Head, which has the feel of a high mountain to it. Ancient forts and burial chambers litter the windswept landscape. It is a great place to relax and watch the world go by, nestled behind a rock boulder, seeing more detail if you have patience. Harbour porpoises reveal themselves offshore, gannets dive for fish, buzzards and peregrines hunt for prey, an occasional rabbit makes a run for cover. After an hour I head east to see surfers riding the swell that is falling on to Whitesands Bay. They are probably counting in sevens, waiting for the perfect wave. This mathematical harmony derives from an unknown law of fluid and wind mechanics; the sequence settles into patterns after an argument across the Atlantic. I walk inland to the hostel and settle down into the Stables with a couple of German lads. The girls are in the Cowshed, both dorms having been converted from their former farm use. It is cosy, warm and friendly, just as it should be – a welcome break from the elements.

The weather clears, but the southwesterlies still have plenty of puff. The wind faces the tide in Ramsey Sound, creating dramatic standing waves near The Bitches rocks. Only the porpoises and huge RIB tour boats, launched from the lifeboat station, brave the conditions. I'd like to linger, but I keep moving at a relaxed, modest pace, now with the wind behind me. The coastal path is well used, with numerous walkers taking a circular route from St Davids and using a popular bus service to return. I bury myself inside a cafe at Solva, even though most of the customers are outside. I overdose on calories and spend the next hour shaking off a food coma as I walk, resisting a short rest on the grass which could quickly turn into a long snooze.

Newgale beach is wild, with long ribbons of surf rolling up the sand. The fishermen have their waders on and are pulling lures through the shallows, hoping to hook a sizeable sea bass. I stop to watch, checking my map, and decide to stay at the campsite behind the huge shingle banks. It takes two mugs of hot rooibos tea to wash down a cold, tasteless pasty after a cold shower. The site is exhausted after a busy summer and needs an overhaul. I am asleep as the sun sets and wake as it rises, my body clock now synchronised to autumn daylight hours.

More often than not, I can complete the day's walking in the morning, rising early and full of energy. I am positively yomping along the path today, my fitness levels improving, and my backpack empty of food. I had a relaxing day yesterday, but now I am competitively chasing down walkers I can see ahead. There is no rhyme or reason for this behaviour. I just follow my mood. The walker in front has slung a coat over his backpack, which comes loose and falls to the path unnoticed. I reach it, to find pockets full of keys and a wallet. Instead of running to catch up, I blow my loudest rock-concert whistle, which registers in his ears after the third attempt. Waving his coat, we meet along the path.

'You dropped this, I believe.'

'Oh, gosh, thank you, that would have spoiled my day!' he replies.

'That is a large backpack, are you walking the coast path?'

We drop into a conversation as we reach Martin's Haven; the usual questions emerge.

'Why are you doing this?'

'What's the best bit?'

'How many miles a day are you walking?'

'How heavy is your pack?'

'Are you walking for a charity?'

I do not have rehearsed answers, but the questions make me think about the walk and the reasons I am doing it. I too ask the same of other long-distance walkers and have never had a satisfactory answer to the first question, until I met a young woman in Scotland on the Speyside Way, some ten years later.

'It makes me happy,' she declared proudly.

She is right, of course, and this will become my stock answer in a decade. 'The best bit … ' question I refuse to answer. I can only conclude that the entirety of the endeavour is the highlight, the diversity of the walk, the ups and downs, the rain and sun, happy days and sad; all these dimensions are unfiltered and real. This wider perspective is like reading a book, not a chapter or paragraph – experiences that combine into a beautiful story.

I scoff a sandwich on the beach and spot a lone seal pup hidden in the rocks. Its mother is just offshore, warily checking the many onlookers watching it from the cliff edge. I remain still and silent, having stumbled a little too close, eagerly popping the remains of a tuna sandwich in my mouth, daftly thinking the smell will attract the pup towards me. It rolls with the occasional breaking wave before settling comfortably, its eyes resting shut to daydream. I walk around the headland for a better view of Skomer Island, famous for its breeding bird populations: shearwaters, guillemots, razorbills, fulmars and endless burrows of puffins numbering in their tens of thousands. A good pair of binoculars would enhance the experience, but I dare not introduce any more weight into my pack. I make a note to return and join the many daytrippers to take a walk around the island, maybe in spring when the breeding season starts.

The youth hostel is just around the corner and a welcome sight. I am sharing the dorm with Ron, also walking the Pembrokeshire

Coast Path. He is seventy-eight and has spent ten days getting to this point from Cardigan. Our conversation connects easily; we both need to say little to express our experiences on the path, yet our words unlock vivid images and memories. We are joined by a couple from Ireland, driving around the coast, beachcombing. Their 1960s Land Rover is packed with flotsam and jetsam, and the roof rack loaded with twisted driftwood, secured with fishing nets and rope, which they will later work into sculptures and art. They place a bottle of Bushmills on the table, and we drift into easy conversation about our adventures, scheming and dreaming – inspiring each other to ambitious challenges.

'New Zealand is a wonderful place – have you been?'

'Yes, in the late nineties,' I answer, 'for work and pleasure. I had an opportunity to support a business. The locals spent time showing me around. The landscape is stunning, and many areas remind me of Wales. Why are you spending time beachcombing?'

'We were fed up with our jobs, so we bought Bessie (the Land Rover), scraped our savings together and set out to see where it would take us.'

'That's a relaxing way to spend your time. Have you seen the funny jellyfish?'

At breakfast, I tune the kitchen radio to the '10 past forecast', which is remarkably accurate compared to the landlubber briefing on national radio. Ron and I set out together.

'You go ahead, lad. Maybe we'll meet up again.'

I'd love to walk with him, but I find a slower pace exhausting. I need to find a natural rhythm and stride that suits my tall frame. Walking on, I soon reach St Ann's Head. Huge swells enter Milford Haven, coloured with blue waves and troughs topped with pure white breakers from a force 7–8 gale. Persil-white gannets cut and shear through the wind without effort, rising and falling along the undulations. They ascend when they detect a meal, to fold their wings and dive arrow-straight into the sea, sometimes emerging with a flapping mackerel. You would think the sea would overwhelm them, yet they casually take off after swallowing the fish, with a few strong beats of their six-foot wings.

Tugs and pilot boats face square on into the raging sea, seeking to guide tankers to the oil terminals. They rise precipitously to the crest of a swell, before crashing spectacularly into the troughs, covering the entire vessel in spray. They are needed, as the *Sea Empress* hit mid-channel rocks here in 1996, disgorging 72,000 tons of crude oil. The impact would cost £120 million to clean up but, more importantly, the effect on wildlife was devastating and would take time (not money) to recover – a shocking tragedy. Nature has evolved over aeons to master its environment; man can destroy it in a moment.

I walk into the sailing club cafe half an hour later, to meet Ron again, tucking into a full English breakfast! He has taken a shortcut from Westdale Bay, driven by hunger to the cafe.

'How did you pass me?'

'You young whippersnappers are not as fast as you think,' he jests. 'Besides, no need to rush; the tide is still in.' He points to the crossing we must both make to progress east, the sausage still attached to his fork. I order the same, and we carry on talking where we left off the night before. We walk together to the estuary crossing point. The tide has ebbed, permitting me to cross to the peninsula around St Ishmael's. Ron is not following; he has walked with me purely for a chat, returning to Dale to check in at a B&B. I up the pace to reach Sandy Haven to cross another estuary and reach a campsite on the opposite bank. No one is around, all the static homes are empty, and the caravans are parked and covered up. I pitch anyway, expecting the owner to turn up, but no one appears. The season has ended.

It is unlikely that anyone would consider the industrial land-scape of Milford Haven to be a tourist destination. Many walkers would choose to hop on a bus at this point, but I am keen to explore the oil refineries to see for myself the impact of man's addiction to energy. Huge silos of oil sit alongside the humming chemical plant machinery: pipes and pumps, tanks and chambers holding unknown processed liquids, flare towers burning off excess gases, and the whole facility secured with sturdy fencing. A tanker is docked alongside one of the many jetties, emptying its cargo through thick pipes. I am beginning to wish there was a ferry service from Angle to Dale (which there once used to be), but I have to walk to Cleddau Bridge, which spans the deeper reaches of Milford Haven. Were it not for this bridge, I'd have to walk even further into Haverfordwest and Narberth to reach Pembroke Dock, another thirty miles at least. This inlet (or Mil-*fjord*, not Mil-*ford* as you might expect) is one of Europe's largest natural deep-water harbours and has no natural crossing point. A local B&B is the only option; it has a bath and clean white sheets. The Indian restaurant has more than enough menu choices to keep me happy, and I order too much. I exceed my nutrition budget for the week in that one sitting.

A power station is a change of scenery, before another large oil refinery at Rhoscrowther. The industrial site consumes St Mary's Church at Pwllcrochan, built in 1342, possibly earlier. It is a friendless building, now managed and labelled as a facility asset by Texaco, and no longer used for its original religious purpose. Natural coastline scenery resumes. I wild camp on rough grass set back from the car park at West Angle Bay and lie down to sleep. Noisy cars are doing doughnuts, but do not stay long, perhaps driven away by a vast articulated lorry that arrives to occupy the central space. I soon realise it is full of sheep. The rear door lowers, and the driver has opened a gate to my field! Dozens of hungry sheep rush into the area and I fear they will eat my tent. I see the men trying to drive them to the field beyond.

'Can I help?' I ask, brandishing my walking pole, and hastily dressed commando-style in waterproofs and unlaced boots.

'Sure, take the left-hand side.'

After a few moments, we close the gate to the upper field. Their hyperactive collie has beaten three men in the sheep-moving competition. The weary woolly animals calm down after a long journey, munching an evening meal of fresh green grass.

'That's an unusual sight to see late at night; where have you come from?'

'We've driven down from the Lakes but got stuck in traffic. We're moving sheep to new pastures for the winter months.'

'Are you driving back home now?'

'No, we'll find a lay-by to sleep in and go back tomorrow. Thanks for your help,' they call as they climb back into the cab and head off. The collie sits proudly in the middle passenger seat, eyes forward, not knowing the meaning of rest, eager to seek out a wayward lamb to gather into the fold, or maybe just to get home.

I can lie in, timing my waking to a cafe opening time near the beach. A woman opens the door at 9 a.m.

'Looks like you could do with our special breakfast,' she insists.

'You read me like a book.'

'Eggs, bacon, sausages, beans, mushrooms, fried bread?'

'Everything,' I reply.

The meal is delicious, washed down with mugs of fragrant coffee. I order sandwiches to take away, and a slice of irresistible cake carefully packed to survive stuffing into my backpack.

I walk for an hour or so to Freshwater West beach, devoid of holidaymakers and surfers, even though the day is bright and sunny. It is a pity I can't continue around Linney Head, but the coast path has to divert inland around the Castlemartin firing ranges. On weekends I could cut through to the famous Green Bridge of Wales, but that too is closed. A long hard road walk is the only option, followed by a boundary fence walk into Bosherston. I can hear tanks moving in the fields behind the hedges, and I almost jump out of my skin as one passes close by, its enormous mass shaking the ground – a terrible earthquake-like experience.

My feet hurt from the hard tarmac walk, but I push on past the cafe in the village to Stackpole Warren and softer dunes. I can now eat that cake and soak my feet in the sea at Barafundle Bay, perhaps one of the prettiest beaches on the path. Those weird jellyfish still litter the sands and children poke them with sticks, collecting some to waft in front of their sleeping parents' noses.

It is a lazy few miles to the campsite in Freshwater East. The showers are so good I enter the cubicle in my base layers, a crude technique to wash both body and clothing. The sun allows me to air my sleeping bag and tent as I relax on the dry grass. There is a copy of *McCarthy's Bar* by Pete McCarthy in the information room, enough for a couple of hours' reading before I sleep. I was not to know that he would pass away a few weeks later. I'll miss his light-hearted take on life.

My legs are sore, which I later learn to be the first sign of shin splints. This affliction is caused by inflamed muscles straining against their protective sheath. I have walked more than 160 miles in nine days with a heavy backpack over rough coastal terrain. Fortunately, I do not have much further to go. The path conditions ease as I walk towards Tenby, past more military activity. Someone is launching drones into the sea and gunfire can be heard on the firing ranges. I lose sight of Caldey Island briefly until I reach the long beach that leads into Tenby, where I can just beat the tide to ascend steps into the town and settle into a cafe. The fish and chips will keep me satisfied for the rest of the day. It is only a short, yet hilly, walk to a campsite near Monkstone Point. I pitch my tent, pump up my air bed and unfurl my sleeping bag, to emerge to an offer of tea.

'Walked far? I'm sure you could do with a cuppa,' an elderly gent says. 'I'll stick the kettle on. Pop over to our caravan in five minutes.'

I tidy myself up and remove my muddy boots to step through the door, where I am met by his wife, cutting a slice of cake, and a Labrador, its tail wagging furiously, the motion transmitting to its shoulders. It is keen, and sniffs my socks and legs, no doubt encrusted with weeks' worth of coastal aromas (including dog smells undetectable by humans). After a pleasant hour's conversation it is time to leave, but the dog starts barking furiously.

'Down, Archie; stay!' the man shouts. 'Don't worry. He's a rescue puppy and hates it when people leave. We think it's due to some trauma when he was young.'

'Thank you so much for the tea and cake. A rare treat before bedtime. I'm sure he'll settle down in a moment.'

My gas canister will gasp its last butane breath the next morning, so that little gesture from a fellow camper means I can have a warm bowl of porridge, that essential meal that sets me up for the day. I sneak quietly away, in case Archie goes berserk. I run along the path to ensure I will arrive in time for a bus service from Amroth that will take me back to Tenby. Former railway tunnels help avoid a few steep climbs, until the final descent to the coast road and the Pembrokeshire Coast Path waymark that declares the 186-mile return to Cardigan. A plaque records a day in May 1970 when Wynford Vaughan-Thomas, a journalist, broadcaster and passionate advocate for the Welsh countryside, opened the route. I have no time to reflect, as I can see the bus and run to the shelter to board.

'Single to Tenby station, please,' I puff.

My walk is over, but both legs are stiff with pain. I can barely walk to the ticket office or board the train. I am expecting a rickety local service to take me to Cardiff, but instead, a gleaming Inter-City 125 sweeps into the station. I settle into a comfortable seat, opposite June, one of a group of walkers on their way back to London. She extracts my life story with skill, as we spend a few hours talking about our walks and love of Pembrokeshire.

'You look exhausted,' she starts, later followed by 'How many children? Where do you come from? How come you have time to spare?' I am too weak to resist her gentle questioning; I should have defended myself with a few questions of my own. I don't mind; it is nice to have company after the remote coastal paths.

I'm glowing on the outside, sunburnt on my ears and forearms. A white tan line bisects my hand (walking pole strap), and my legs are deep brown. I'm glowing on the inside too – a sense of achievement and a ten-day overdose of endorphins. Before I alight at Reading, I am already planning the next adventure, even though work intervenes for a few years.

The wanderlust that infected me has no cure.

2

THE RIDGEWAY

Distance: 86 miles
Days to complete: 5 days
Mileage so far: 186 miles

ANCIENT WAYS

All truly great thoughts are conceived while walking.
— Nietzsche

Traders and drovers have travelled along the elevated ridge connecting Dorset to Norfolk for at least 5,000 years. The Ridgeway is one of four paths that form the Greater Ridgeway, also known as the Greater Icknield Way (possibly derived from the word *Iceni*, a Norfolk tribe). How uncanny that this ancient route follows the boundary between chalk and greensand across England. You could almost use a British Geological Survey map for navigation. The greater journey starts in Lyme Regis, following the Wessex Ridgeway, the Ridgeway, the Icknield Way and Peddars Way to reach Hunstanton on the Norfolk coast, 362 miles away. The Ridgeway section is eighty-seven miles, an ideal distance to build my fitness and try out some new backpacking kit. I should be able to complete the trip in a week.

The Pembrokeshire Coast Path has taught me a great deal about what to take. This time I replace heavy items with lighter options and leave some things out altogether. I only need to carry one main meal and enough lunch to get me to the next village store, so this should be a lightweight expedition compared to longer unsupported journeys.

I set off in late August from Reading station, where I am fortunate enough to see a steam train pull into the central platform as I wait for a train to Swindon. I am utterly captivated by this living, breathing monster a few feet away.

'Any chance of a ride on the footplate?' I ask the driver, cheekily.

'Not a chance. Even the coaches are booked months in advance,' he says, smiling, pointing at his passenger carriages. Here stands a man who enjoys his work and understands the privilege of driving such an iconic machine. I would willingly have abandoned my trip and sold the contents of my backpack if he'd said yes. Passengers peer out of the windows, each smug-faced enthusiast anticipating an excellent lunch served on bone china with silver cutlery. Most have made an effort to dress in pre-war garb too.

'Off we go!' the driver says, hearing the station master's whistle. He touches his cap in my direction and pulls a large lever. Steam fills the pistons; a deep chuff-chuff increases in tempo. Slowly, the reciprocal motion of the connecting rods transmits energy to rotate the wheels. I can't help but wave, just like everyone else on the platform. I feel like an eight-year-old again.

My train arrives twenty minutes later, a modern InterCity 125, packed to the gunnels with passengers scoffing fast food or holding their styrofoam coffee mugs aloft. I squeeze onboard with my massive backpack to coughs of polite disapproval. Thankfully, I will soon exchange this discomfort for the open hills. A regular bus service takes me over the Marlborough Downs to Avebury, its location on my Ordnance Survey map hidden underneath a mesh of blue-boxed gothic script. Each cartographic symbol represents a Neolithic or Bronze Age site. I'd love to spend the night in a tent pitched in the centre of the stone circle, to trigger a spiritual experience with our ancestors, perhaps channelling their rituals – hopefully not sacrificial. Who knows what dreams I might have?

It is an opportunity to marvel at the standing stones that mark the ancient circles, ley lines and avenues. Further south you glimpse the mysterious Silbury Hill, the largest man-made mound in Europe. Crystal-clear chalk streams spouting from nearby springs influenced the decision to build in this area; this land was a cultural nexus of strategic significance. What a fitting start to a five-day walk.

The bus driver for the connecting service recognises a Ridgeway walker.

'Where's the nearest stop to the start of the Ridgeway?' I ask.

'No worries, mate [he is Australian]; I'll drop you off nearby.'

He kindly stops a few hundred yards from the starting point, as he turns south. I walk west to symbolically touch the fingerpost directing me to Ivinghoe Beacon (eighty-six miles north-west) and set off along the track. It is midday and time for a few handfuls of black-berries, ripe and delicious. Nothing beats freshly foraged food to brighten up your diet, as long as you don't eat too much of it.

Progressing into the Downs along Hackpen Hill, I approach Barbury Castle – my first encounter with an Iron Age hillfort. The views northwards are extensive, overlooking Swindon town – large enough to be a modern city. In the direction I am walking you can make out the sequence of hillforts to the north-west at Liddington and Uffington. This perspective brings a real sense of an ancient route. Your mind's eye sketches the vale with green forest and grassy hills, transporting yourself back in time to pre-history, joining soldiers, travellers and herdsmen in seeking the security of open downland.

The ancient way descends to Chiseldon, but the National Trail follows Smeathe's Ridge into Ogbourne St George – a village centred on a splendid seventeenth-century Jacobean manor house. Much as I would like to stay there, I will be camping at a small site masquerading as a stable yard. A young girl directs me to the paddock.

'You can pitch there. Water tap and loos are behind the stables. You'll have no trouble with the horses,' she says, grinning (maybe knowing most middle-aged men are terrified of the beasts).

It appears to be clean, so I pitch my tent, cook a meal and settle in for the night, only for the animals to start munching away at the turf nearby. Cattle I can cope with, but I am not that comfortable around horses – they are too intelligent and mischievous. The last one I met bit me. I don't want to add trampled and kicked to my list of equine experiences. It is reassuring to see a car battery connected to an electric fence, clicking high-tension pulses along the wires. It is also tempting to touch it to see if it works, but common sense overcomes my curiosity.

I wake with all limbs attached and make breakfast. I cannot find anyone to pay, so I drop a tenner through the letterbox. I know I have contributed to the site's upkeep in a small way; it is a change from the usual vanilla campsite experience, and the location suits my schedule perfectly. I head north towards Liddington Castle and the aural drone of the M4 motorway. I cross this modern Ridgeway, carrying heavy traffic between London and Wales. The elevated aspect amplifies the white noise of the traffic below, but the southern sunlit views more than compensate for that. My path is multi-use, and I pass several cyclists and horse riders enjoying a beautiful morning.

You reach the third Iron Age fort on the route at Uffington, marked by the famous White Horse carved into the green hillside, revealing the chalk bedrock. This stylised Celtic masterpiece of minimalist art dates from the late Bronze Age.

> *Before the gods that made the gods*
> *Had seen their sunrise pass,*
> *The White Horse of the White Horse Vale*
> *Was cut out of the grass.*

> – G.K. Chesterton,
> from 'The Ballad of the White Horse' (1911)

It has spawned many similar works, notably the Cerne Abbas Giant on the Wessex Ridgeway. Considered satirical art (drawn in the seventeenth century), it apparently depicts Oliver Cromwell with anatomically disproportionately large genitals, wielding a massive wooden club, although recent analysis suggests it was carved in the late Saxon period.

To the south are the Lambourn Downs, one of the largest centres for racehorse training in England. The area is a complex network of gallops and stables. To the north is the Vale of the White Horse and the River Thames beyond. I reach the Devil's Punchbowl, a spectacular dry valley feature set in the arable landscape, spoilt by the six large cooling towers of Didcot power station. This industrial eyesore will stay with me for a few days. Many people like brutalist architecture; I don't (although the first three towers were demolished in 2014, followed by the remainder in 2019, restoring the rural view).

I pass the fourth fort to reach Wantage youth hostel. I check in, pitching my tent before retiring for an evening meal – the usual wholesome fare, in the comfort of an indoor dining room. Quite a few walkers are staying in the dormitories, and we chat for a while in the common room. I explore the library and find an excellent book, *Round Britain Windsurf*, by Tim Batstone, who circumnavigated the British Isles in 1984 in ten weeks. Wow! I speed-read it from cover to cover, amazed at the sheer audacity of such an adventure; considering that windsurf technology was not at its height in the 1980s, this was quite an achievement, even by the standards of today.

Inspired, I return to my tent to find the camping field packed with enthusiastic scouts, pitching their tents. They are oblivious to their leader's helpful instructions. Before long, I am holding back my laughter at the sight of ten different geometric shapes derived from a standard-issue Vango tent. A dinner bell rings, and the scouts vanish, leaving repairs and laughter to the adults. 'Their first time camping?' I ask. They nod in agreement. Satiated, the scouts return at dusk, unable to contain their excitement of sleeping under canvas for the first time. I am too tired to worry about their loud, chattering noise and fall asleep. They can laugh at my snoring later; I'll never know.

The youth hostel concept started in Germany in 1909 and inspired the formation of a national hostel association in Britain twenty years later. By 1930, eleven affordable centres, located in areas of natural beauty, were full of young working people getting away from the depression-era inner-city life. After the Second World War, the properties increased to a peak of over 300, and were very popular with those of limited means. More recently, the Youth Hostels Association (YHA) has sold properties to maintain its financial viability. I have noticed (holiday season aside) that many guests are in their third age, retirees mostly, rekindling their youth or enjoying the simple pleasures of hostelling. I value the opportunity to meet like-minded people and to learn from their experiences and outlook on life. I also like to see the hostels used for their original purpose: to inspire children to start their lives of adventure; everyone should sleep outside in a tent at least once.

Being a lark, not an owl, I wake early and pack. Within a few minutes, I leave a scene of devastation, with boots, clothes, backpacks and extra bits of tent and poles strewn everywhere. It is a beautiful morning, the sun's angle revealing the texture of the landscape. The light casts surreal shadows across the vale, the dew has not yet cleared and the birds are in full song. If I sense a glorious day, an early start is always rewarded; sometimes I commence walking even before the sun has risen. Morning becomes midday, midday becomes afternoon.

> *Along the grave green downs, this idle afternoon,*
> *Shadows of loitering silver clouds, becalmed in blue,*
> *Bring, like unfoldment of a flower, the best of June.*
>
> *Shadows outspread in spacious movement, always you*
> *Have dappled the downs and valleys at this time of year,*
> *While larks, ascending shrill, praised freedom as they flew.*
> *Now, through that song, a fighter-squadron's drone I hear*
> *From Scratchbury Camp, whose turfed and cowslip'd*
> * rampart seems*
> *More hill than history, ageless and oblivion-blurred.*
> *– Siegfried Sassoon, from 'On Scratchbury Camp' (1942)[1]*

I follow Grim's Ditch, an enigmatic earthwork of unknown purpose, eastward to reach The Atomic (as it is known locally), a collection of buildings of the Atomic Energy Research Establishment (AERE) at Harwell. After a long decommissioning period it will become a business park, still with connections to the industry. The Anglo-Saxon word *grim* means 'unknown feature' – as unknown as the complexities of nuclear fission. Imagine explaining those concepts to Iron Age man, 2,500 years earlier, as he digs a mud ditch with spades and pickaxes.

I cross the A34 on to Blewbury Down and descend into Streatley and Goring. It is bin day, and the recycling boxes tell a story; volumes of empty champagne bottles stacked high can only mean one thing.

'Someone's had a good party,' I say to a neighbour, cutting the grass.

'Oh yes! Every summer is the same. A wedding this time, but usually a succession of barbecues,' he replies. 'It is all garden parties around here, you know.'

The bin men would make excellent anthropologists – sharp commentators on social status and the gossip in the area. You can tell a great deal from someone's rubbish. Sure enough, the recycling lorry appears, stopping to tip tons of heavy-rim glass into a hopper as it climbs up the street. They work diligently through boxloads of bottles.

Crossing the River Thames, I also pass a Thames Path National Trail acorn sign – a future walk. I make a note of the local store, which provides a decent lunch, only to find a very inviting flint-built Brakspear pub at South Stoke, a mile further. Very tempting, but likely to scupper my plans to reach Wallingford in good time. The Ridgeway follows the east bank, the Thames Path the west. I divert before another Grim's Ditch to the campsite at Crowmarsh Gifford. After pitching my tent and taking a quick shower, I walk across the bridge into Wallingford to stock up on food. The champagne has sold out in Waitrose; it must have been one hell of a party.

As its name suggests, Walling*ford* is one of many crossing points at the Goring Gap. Early travellers forded the river until a succession of bridges followed. The Normans added a castle in

1067, and for the next 600 years it defended this strategic route north to Oxford, until Cromwell dismantled the structure after the English Civil War. Even today, pillboxes remain on the river-banks, remnants of the Second World War defensive network. Wallingford has a reputation as the most besieged town in England, one of the last Royalist strongholds. Inspiration, apparently, for many of George R.R. Martin's bloodiest scenes in *Game of Thrones*.

After a lie-in, an ascent of the continuation of Grim's Ditch wakes me out of any slumber. I reach a golf course, where the lawn outside the clubhouse, beautifully kept, is covered in large white mushrooms. How they survived the groundsman's lawnmower is a mystery; they must grow in a few days. They look tasty, but I am not a mycologist (who would know if they are edible). The fields ahead are full of dozy pheasants, easily corralled along the hedgerow. This semi-domesticated bred-to-be-shot game bird must be no sport at all. Dinner could have been mushroom soup and a brace of ring-necked pheasants – a pleasant evening meal.

A muddy path descends steeply off the ridge to follow a heavily rutted track beneath the M40 motorway. These byways are used by motorised 4x4 vehicles, which makes life very difficult for a walker picking a path through the glutinous mud. I scoff a sand-wich standing up, as there is no place to rest. I keep going, reaching firmer tracks into Princes Risborough – a quintessential Chiltern town. I take a train home as there are no campsites or hostels nearby, and wild camping in an urban area is difficult. The return train fare is cheaper than staying in any B&B overnight.

I resist the temptation to pop down the pub for a celebratory pint before I finish the walk. So early to bed and early to rise. A good breakfast sees me return to the station carrying a light daypack.

The last section is a regular eighteen-mile training run for me, but usually in the opposite direction. It is quite a challenging day, with some tough climbs and rough, muddy paths to negotiate.

The ascent towards Whiteleaf Cross is strenuous, but the stunning reveal of the Three Hundreds of Aylesbury is unexpected.

It is strange what you see walking a path in a new direction. A 'hundred' is an ancient feudal division of land, usually a hundred homesteads or enough to provide a hundred men for war. With population growth, I suspect that several thousand men could answer a call to arms now if that enlistment method remained.

The views turn to woodland as you descend into Cadsden and the Plough, a pub frequented by prime ministers and foreign politicians alike. A recent visit by the Chinese President Xi Jinping with David Cameron made national news as they bonded over a pint of IPA. It left an impression, as Chinese investors bought the pub a few months later. It has become a popular spot for busloads of tourists seeking a traditional pub 'experience' of a ploughman's lunch and an Instagram photo or two. Excellent for the owners; terrible for the locals.

The reason for its political popularity becomes evident. A mile further on you skirt the boundaries of Chequers and enter a land of CCTV surveillance. The prime minister's country retreat has not yet been acquired by Chinese investors, though the Chancellor of the Exchequer might consider selling it if the country's financial position falters. Perhaps they could share the chancellor's country house, nearby at Dorneywood. They could even share a taxi from Downing Street on Friday afternoon, after a busy week in Parliament. Somehow, I suspect this would be at the bottom of a list of assets for sale. What politician gives up any status symbol of office?

The next section is a delight as you approach Wendover via the Coombe Hill monument, erected in 1904 in memory of 148 men from Buckinghamshire who fought in the Boer War. It is one of the first to commemorate loss rather than victory. It stands 260 metres above the surrounding landscape, overlooking the land where many of the men lived.

Grim's Ditch continues (it is quite a long ditch!) from Wendover towards Tring, where you cross the Grand Union Canal. Here, I catch up with an elderly disabled woman and her daughter, the first people I meet who are walking the whole of the Ridgeway.

The daughter explains their journey. 'We're walking in memory of my father; we started two weeks ago in Avebury,' she says. 'He died two months ago, and it was his dream to walk the path.'

They are both grieving, easing their loss each day, as if on a pilgrimage. They are determined to finish. I am not sure I have their levels of endurance and resilience. I will complete the journey shortly, but they have two days to go. For a few hours afterwards, I reflect on their single-minded determination and the daughter's unfailing patience – patience I do not have. I can walk the Ridgeway in five days, but I am not sure I could walk it in two weeks. I might have the physical endurance, but would I have the mental fortitude?

'Good luck,' I shout back as I walk ahead.

They smile and wave, stoically plodding ahead.

The final stretch towards Ivinghoe Beacon follows beautiful chalk ridges and dry valleys. This open landscape was once a Second World War army training ground, and unexploded ordnance occasionally surfaces. 'Where there is beauty there is danger', as the saying goes, so I keep to the path, unlike a dog walker's boisterous cocker spaniel.

'Have you read the warning sign?'

'Oh! Don't worry about Benji, he knows his way around,' the owner replies. I visualise a 1970s Pythonesque sketch involving a special effects smoke explosion and a stuffed dog flying through the air.

The Ridgeway terminates at Ivinghoe Beacon. Radio-controlled gliders fill the air, swooping and looping in the updraft – a fitting metaphor for the happiness I feel after a great day's walking. I linger for too long, gazing at gliders and the Icknield Way to the north-west, wondering if I should continue to Hunstanton. The Ridgeway might end here, but the geology does not. Another time perhaps. Hunger wakes me. I drop off the hill into Ivinghoe to catch transport home. The only village shop open is a local hairdresser. They overcome their suspicion of a man with a number one haircut and fill my water bottle before I wait to board the bus to Aylesbury and a train home.

Now it is time for that pint.

3

SOUTH WEST COAST PATH

Distance: 630 miles
Days to complete: 37 days
Mileage so far: 272 miles

COASTAL CHALLENGE

A journey of a thousand miles begins with a single step.
— Lao Tzu

I was getting restless in my full-time job, working on projects which I knew would be reassigned or cancelled. I started to day-dream about walking the South West Coast Path, staring at an inbox full of unread emails. The courage to quit and start a freelance career came one afternoon as a beam of spring sunshine fell on my desk. Impulsively I handed my notice in.

'Got a new job?' my boss asked me.

'No. I'm off on a long walk and will worry about that when I get home. I fancy starting a new career as an interim manager.'

'Er … OK. Can you finish your project first?' He looked concerned for the project delivery – or was it my sanity?

We worked up a plan to hand over my work and set a departure date, but my heart was in planning a 630-mile, two-month journey around the coasts of Devon, Cornwall and Dorset. I'd found the time, but had yet to tell my wife – a more significant challenge than the walk.

'Get it out of your system – you've been restless for months, and it'll do you good,' she announced, after we'd shared a bottle of wine. Then she delivered the punchline: 'Now can we talk about the decorating you promised to do?'

I knew there would be a cost, but a few weeks with a paintbrush in the summer seemed a fair exchange, while I started my new business venture and found a client.

PART 1 – MINEHEAD TO PADSTOW

The South West Coast Path (SWCP) is unique on planet Earth and perhaps taken for granted by the inhabitants of the British Isles. Follow fifty degrees latitude on a globe, and you will not encounter another peninsula blessed with a temperate climate. Only Ireland could compete, but it does not have the legacy of a coastguard footpath and passionate organisations to promote its use. The South West Coast Path Association publishes an excellent no-nonsense guide that lists accommodation and route information. It can't be that hard: just keep the sea on the right, I think.

Only one thing remains before departure: choosing organisations to raise money for, as I want to give something back to the local community. They have to have a connection to the area or the coast in some way, which leads to selecting the Marine Conservation Society, Children's Hospice South West and Seafarers UK. I contact each one to register and ask for advice; this is the first time I've ever raised money for any charity. I have no particular target and will collect cash as I walk or point people in the direction of *justgiving.com*, a new website that is just gaining traction collecting charitable donations for a reasonable fee.

I book a one-way train ticket to Taunton, committing to start the journey instead of fretting over the weather forecast. I set off a week later, swapping a modern InterCity 125 for a steam train on the West Somerset Railway, the longest independent standard-gauge heritage railway in Britain.

'Single to Minehead, please.'

'You must be off for a walk,' the ticket clerk says. 'We don't get many requests for a single.'

'Yes, I'm starting the South West Coast Path, and this seems like the perfect way to get to Minehead.'

He punches out a second-class cardboard oblong ticket and deals it to me as if I was at a card table. A few moments later the engine chuffs its way through the countryside; a buzzard flies carefree alongside for half a mile, matching my new emotion of freedom; my anxiety and fears slowly fade now the journey has started.

I can't think of a more elegant way to start a walk than to arrive at Minehead station, a Victorian summer seaside terminus, by steam train. It is a short walk to the start, marked with a sculpture designed by Sarah Ward, who won a competition in 1999 as a teenager. A pair of galvanised steel hands hold an open Ordnance Survey map; a different sculpture marks the other end of the path at South Point Haven in Dorset. A big white arrow points in the direction I should walk, steeply into woodland above the town. This start is no gentle introduction, as the path brutally introduces me to the geology of Exmoor. My reward a mile later is stunning views north across the Bristol Channel from Selworthy Beacon, at 308 metres. This landscape is 'Exmoor-by-Sea': dramatic sandstone cliffs marking the northern boundary to the National Park. Exmoor ponies amble around, keeping the grass trimmed and fertilised.

The moors fracture at Porlock, the location of the steepest A road in Britain. A gradient of twenty-five per cent marked the end of the world in the eighteenth century, when the village was captured in a poem by Robert Southey. Not much has changed:

Porlock, thy verdant vale so fair to sight,
Thy lofty hills which fern and furze embrown,
Thy waters that roll musically down
Thy woody glens, the traveller with delight
Recalls to memory, and the channel grey
Circling its surges in thy level bay.
Porlock, I also shall forget thee not,
Here by the unwelcome summer rain confined;

But often shall hereafter call to mind
How here, a patient prisoner, 'twas my lot
To wear the lonely, lingering close of day,
Making my Sonnet by the alehouse fire,
Whilst Idleness and Solitude inspire
Dull rhymes to pass the duller hours away.
– Robert Southey, 'Porlock' (1799)

I shed 250 metres in height within as many metres laterally, to cross a footbridge into the village. The B&B is ridiculously cosy and near to an unpretentious restaurant that serves a five-star roast dinner and cherry pie. If this is the standard I am to expect, I will be gaining weight on this walk.

It is with some relief that I find I do not have to climb out of Porlock, as the path veers around the cliffside woodland at Porlock Weir. Gentle tracks meander around combe and hill to maintain a constant elevation. The oak woodland is tranquil and meditative, cocooning you in a secret world. I startle red deer and wary buzzards, who both remain motionless until you enter their personal space. St Beuno's Church nestles in the neck of Culbone Combe, probably the smallest parish in England, completing a picture of pixie-like paradise. It must be quite pleasant to wander here in the late evening or early morning: the longest stretch of coastal woodland in the England and Wales, sheltered from the southwesterly winds, retaining an unspoilt ancient ecology.

I stop for a rest and meet a man plodding up the path with an enormous backpack.

'Hiya. Walking the coast path?' he asks.

We walk together. His name is Stuart and he has ten days off work to walk as far as he can along the SWCP.

'Where are you camping tonight?' I ask, assuming he's carrying a tent.

'I'll find a decent pub mid-afternoon and settle in.' His strategy is cunning: he sinks a few pints, has a meal and then asks the landlord if he can pitch in the garden. 'Works nine times out of ten. Saves money on accommodation that I can spend on beer.' He smiles cheekily.

We exchange life stories as we enter Devon. Stuart peels off, sensing a pub in range, while I continue to Lynmouth, descending steeply into another fracture in the Exmoor sandstone. I cross the footbridge across the confluence of the East and West Lyn rivers, which flooded catastrophically in 1952 after an intense storm on the moorland above. The boulder-loaded torrent destroyed much of the village, killing thirty-four people. Old pictures show a scene of devastation. A cafe provides refreshment while I wait for the youth hostel to open. I meet the wardens – a lovely young couple – an hour later, and they show me to a cosy dorm. They cook a splendid meal, made with organic garden vegetables and local produce. We fall easily into a pleasant conversation about folk music and the eco-friendly ethos they follow. It is such a pity that this youth hostel is to close, as they later announce, part of a cull by the Youth Hostels Association (YHA) in order to reinvest in its remaining properties. They have one last summer to enjoy. It seems the criteria for closure are financial, without thought to the value and pleasure the accommodation provides.

The weather is holding up (it is my third day in shorts), even though it is early April. I welcome the extra ventilation as this is a hard day, with over 2,000 metres of ascent (and subsequent descent) over twenty miles into Ilfracombe. Now the SWCP shows its true colours as a rugged path, cutting across the grain of the landscape where rivers and streams carve their way to the sea. The day starts through the Valley of Rocks, an improbably dry valley surrounded by crazy rock formations. Wildflowers are beginning to bloom, and yellow gorse will soon run riot. An endless succession of muscular hills runs west, rudely interrupted by unannounced descents to sea level, just as you get into your stride. I might as well get used to this, for the pattern will repeat for the next few days. This coastal path is far more challenging than I expected; it is like the Pembrokeshire Coast Path on steroids.

It seems inexcusable not to rest at Great Hangman, the highest point on the SWCP, at 318 metres. You can almost touch Wales, some twenty miles across the Bristol Channel. Lundy is just visible through the haze. The cairn gives some protection from a northeasterly wind, but insufficient for me to linger. I have crossed Heddon's Mouth, but have one more calf-burning ascent through Combe Martin to Ilfracombe. I visit the harbour to put up a charity poster for Seafarers UK at the harbourmaster's office. The ex-naval commander is smartly dressed and sitting with a cup of tea. He gives me a fiver and makes space on the noticeboard, handing me a drawing pin.

'Good luck with your walk and thank you for supporting people who earn their living at sea,' he says. 'Your B&B's just down the road there. Take a shortcut past the tourist information office.'

> Let me speak, in truth, of my life,
> tell of toilsome days of travel,
> days suffering hardship,
> bitterness of heart:
> how I endured sorrowful times on ships,
> on dreadful rolling seas.
> Hard night's watch at the ship's prow
> was my frequent task,
> the ship often tossed along towering cliffs,
> afflicted with cold feet, numbed by frost, chill bonds.
> My sorrows burned in my heart,
> I sighed forth hunger that rent my mind,
> I, the sea-weary man.
>
> – from *The Seafarer*, an Old English poem

Seafarers UK helps the maritime community in times of difficulty, both commercial and military. They support families, promote safety and develop self-supporting communities. The charity started in 1917, to help vast numbers of seafarers who were maimed in the Great War. The impact on families was so significant that King George V gave his name to the charity: King George's Fund for Sailors. It seems an appropriate charity to support on the SWCP, as it passes through major fishing and naval ports.

It is a relief to be greeted by the landlady, accustomed to exhausted walkers. She has the routine of a tea and cake offering down to a fine art, managing the transition from exhaustion to relaxation.

It is time to post home a map or two I no longer need. Every little gram of weight loss is going to help in these conditions, so a pair of gloves and spare socks go in the plastic envelope too. It is 2007, too early for the full gamut of social media options; Facebook is yet to get moving, and the smartphone is a few years away. I'm carrying a simple candy bar phone, which takes good pictures which I can email to Flickr. I also write a daily diary on a postcard to send home. My wife collects them together for my return. This trick solves three problems: a journal that stays dry, letting everyone at home know how I am doing and saving weight.

It is easy to note the numerous named references to smuggling as the path unfolds: the coastguard track walks past Brandy Cove, Briery Cave, Wild Pear Beach and Hangman Point. How they managed to offload their illicit goods is a mystery; even in calm daylight conditions, the treacherous cliffs are ominous. My legs are waking up to the routine now, as I join the Tarka Trail for a few miles before turning south for the first time. The views from Morte Point are worth a few moments; it is a place to sit and observe, listening for seals and watching the seabirds circle overhead, before walking into Woolacombe and mixing with the tourist crowds. The tide is out. I remove my boots and tie the laces together, slinging them over my shoulder. It is a two-mile walk along the beach in bare feet – a delicious, refreshing luxury.

I wait for the sand to dry before putting on socks and relacing my boots for a short climb to Baggy Point. I'm far too early to arrive at the B&B on a warm day. My footwear comes off again after I find a natural armchair on the headland. I lie back, drifting off, unintentionally, into a pleasant afternoon nap to a chorus of seabirds and gently rolling surf crashing against the rocks below. The sand-walking foot massage has tickled soporific nerves in my feet – nature's mild acupuncture therapy. I'm chilling out big time, along with a colony of surfers waiting for their perfect wave in Croyde Bay, looking like seals in their black wetsuits. It is a popular spot.

I'm met by the landlady, Rose, who is relaxing in the garden with a friend. 'You're not too early. Join us for tea.' I sit down with her neighbour, goggling at the huge fruitcake on the table. 'Have a big slice,' she says, reading my thoughts.

'Oh, thank you. You don't know how much I love homemade cake.'

A few hours roll by, in tune with the surf and pleasant conversation. Her husband passed away recently, and she is keen to maintain social contact. The garden is a ragtag collection of flotsam and jetsam collected over many years, mostly fishing floats, but with an occasional rarity from across the Atlantic Ocean, marked with American or Canadian port names. She offers a beer as the sun sets. The 'seals' are still falling off their boards in the bay, but are in no way discouraged. The sun sinks lower, projecting a hazy orange glow from behind layers of cloud to the horizon.

I take the shortcut across Croyde Bay in the morning after a precision-cooked breakfast and a mug of coffee. The surfers are waking from their tents and waiting for the swell to build. Hopping back on a B road I get a loud toot from a car. Rose has driven to find me.

'You forgot your sun cream; you'll need that today,' she shouts.

'Oh, thank you so much, and thanks again for such a wonderful stay.'

'Take care. Bye now.'

Somehow I missed my daily routine this morning, and now apply the cream to the tops of my ears, nose and cheekbones; a tan is developing nicely on my arms and legs, but it takes a mirror to see red and peeling exposed areas of my face.

Saunton Sands Hotel overlooks an enormous expanse of dune and beach, running almost four miles to the south. It would be lovely to walk along the shoreline, but the path moves through the dunes to avoid the military training areas. It is challenging to navigate through, but as I set off into the labyrinth, Stuart appears.

'Hey, Stuart!' I shout. 'Where did you camp last night?'

'With the surfers on the beach,' he says. 'Nice pub in town, very lively.'

'Shall we walk together through the dunes?'

'OK.'

We value each other's company, as the signposting is non-existent and there is no frame of reference to follow other than the sun. We climb and descend endless dunes, rarely reaching a summit for an overview of our surroundings. We are locked in a nature reserve and the most substantial extent of dunes in Britain, home to a lost community of rare flora and fauna and an occasional abandoned army vehicle, stuck in the sand. It takes a good hour and a half to reach the seawall overlooking the River Taw estuary. I can see Instow and Appledore. They are so tantalisingly close, I consider swimming at low tide, but the safer option is to stay on the cycle track via Barnstaple and Bideford. I wish I had a kayak as the thought of pounding the pavement for the rest of the day is horrible.

'Come on, let's go,' says Stuart. 'You'd be daft to swim with that current.'

He's right, of course, so we walk along the seawall to Braunton to pick up the Tarka Trail and head east. Stuart stops at another pub that has just opened for lunch.

'I'm just popping in for a few pints … Catch you up later.' We both know the routine now. I plod on, walking to the side of the path to allow cyclists to pass, into Barnstaple for lunch.

Henry Williamson, the creator of *Tarka the Otter*, lived in this area when he wrote his famous novel, published in 1927. It is an unsentimental tale of the life and death of an otter, born on the banks of the River Torridge. This animal is now a tourist superstar, promoting a fantastic cycle track that runs deep into the Devon hills along former railway lines. It is one of the longest continuous off-road stretches of cycle path in the country, more than enough to keep the most energetic child happy.

My dreams of paddling a kayak morph into dreams of riding a bicycle; I wonder if a one-way hire might work, but resign myself to the endless hard pavement to Instow. The surface doesn't bother the Royal Marines; they march in columns of two, to a rhythm of 'I don't know what you've been told … A frogman's money is

33

good as gold ... ' They will not move out of the way for anyone, and it is impossible to keep pace with them. I make up my own version.

'I don't know why I'm here ... one, two, three, four ... better in the pub and drinking beer ... one, two, three, four ... keep your hat on, you are bald ... one, two, three, four ... plenty of sunscreen on your nose.'

I double back along the road to Yelland for a welcome B&B. It is run by a couple who knew my father, a coincidence that I unearth as I study photographs on their mantlepiece.

'That's 46 Squadron, Thorney Island?' I say.

'How do you know?'

'I used to live there in the 1970s; my father was a warrant officer,' I say. 'Chichester Harbour was a beautiful place to live. I went to school in Southbourne for four or five years.'

More photo albums appear. We cannot find pictures of my father, but they stir memories of a carefree childhood, spent sailing and mucking about in the estuaries. It is where my sense of adventure was born, in the style of a *Swallows and Amazons* storyline by Arthur Ransome. My mother would kick me out of the house on Saturday morning with a pack of sandwiches and would not expect to see me until Sunday lunch. An old white canvas pup tent and army sleeping bag were all my friend and I needed, plus a good penknife (every boy's prized possession). We would tickle mullet in the creeks and build fires from driftwood.

At breakfast, I study my map. I must circumnavigate another estuary inlet tomorrow. Tedious.

'The ferry hasn't run since 2007,' my host declares, 'so you have no option but to walk into Bideford and cross the bridge. It's a nice walk, but a long way around.'

One foot has picked up a blister, which I cover in tape before setting off – a result of hard-pavement walking. I can see Stuart ahead, walking wearily along the path. He has passed me again, but I am catching him up.

'What time did you set off?' I ask, concerned about his slow pace.

'About 5 a.m.,' he whispers wearily. 'Couldn't sleep, woke up to pee and thought I might as well get started.'

We reach the bridge together to cross the river, saying our good-byes as I head north again to the working shipyard at Appledore. Worn-out shipping vessels are moored to the dockside, their future uncertain, full of rust-riven, lethal-looking fixtures covered in bulbous layers of paint, applied over decades.

The quayside is busy, so I walk on to Northam Burrows, the continuation of the strand running from the Saunton Sands Hotel, which stands sentinel over the bay to the north. Its helio-graph windows wink the southern sunlight at me, beaconing me to wade the inlet. I can wiggle my backside into the pebbles for a relaxing lunch and contemplate the power of the channel as the tides reach peak ebb.

Huge pebbles line Westward Ho! beach. This famous seaside resort has the only place name in Britain with an exclamation mark – a derring-do type of name, from an 1855 novel by Charles Kingsley which recounts the adventures of an Elizabethan corsair on the high seas. I have to weave my way through aimless crowds focused on their melting ice creams. I'm a bowling ball in a skittle alley and have to adjust my speed before I take out a child. I'm not the only hazard: fearless herring gulls sit menacingly on the lampposts, waiting to strike the unwary. Some statistics say that eighty per cent of walkers will not venture more than 400 yards from their cars, and this proves to be the case. Within a few minutes, I am walking alone along a pleasant grassy path just a few metres above sea level. I have covered eighteen miles, and it is time to find a meal and my accommodation – a farmhouse B&B. A riot of animals greet me: chickens, dogs, cats and horses, all interested in a new guest who might be a soft touch for food and petting duties.

The sun is beginning to set, backlighting Lundy Island, a lump of granite in the middle of the Bristol Channel worthy of its ship-ping forecast name: Trafalgar, Fitzroy, Sole, Lundy, Fastnet, Irish Sea, Shannon. It is time to tune in to BBC Radio 4 long wave at 17.54. Better to trust this forecast than any given for landlubbers. A coastal walker has one leg in the sea after all.

'Lundy: northeasterly, becoming easterly 2 or 3, smooth becoming slight, fair'; this is what I want to hear. It is going to be another good day tomorrow. I notice a poster in the bedroom giving an alternative version for someone in a midlife crisis:

Forties; restless: three or four.
Marriage: stale; becoming suffocating.
Sportscar, jeans and T-shirt; westerly, five.
Waitress; blonde; 19 or 20.
Converse All-Stars; haircut; earring; children;
becoming embarrassed.
Tail between legs; atmosphere frosty;
Spare room: five or six.

– Dan Maier (2008)[2]

I can't say I recognise or relate to this ditty. I have thought about a tattoo after completing all the National Trails: a nice acorn on my calf muscle to satisfy my mid-life angst.

The *Shipping Forecast* is a much-loved British institution. After a storm claimed over 800 lives in 1859, Admiral Robert Fitzroy, a pioneering meteorologist, developed forecasts (a term he introduced to the world of weather). These were transmitted by telegraph to the fishing ports and evolved into the scripted *Shipping Forecast* we know today, broadcast on Radio 4 LW (long wave) and FM (frequency modulation) at 00.48, 05.20, 12.01 (LW only) and 17.54 (LW only except weekends). The coded, scripted and melodic 380 words describe the sea conditions for thirty-one areas around the coasts of Great Britain and Ireland, starting with Viking, then North and South Utsire, Forties, Cromarty, and ending with Bailey, Fair Isle, Faroes and South-East Iceland. Each word carries precise meaning: 'veering' means the wind is changing clockwise, 'imminent' means within six hours, and 'phenomenal' (my favourite) means wave heights exceeding fourteen metres. It is a daily, prayer-like ritual for any seagoing captain. On 10 January 1993, it issued one of the worst-ever forecasts: 'Rockall, Malin, Hebrides, Bailey. South-west hurricane force 12 or more.' This was the Braer Storm, the lowest-pressure depression ever recorded in the Atlantic (914 millibars). Many forecasters wait a decade to issue a force 11 (violent storm) or even rarer 12 (hurricane force) warning. While the *Shipping Forecast* is useful to seafarers, a coastal walker should use the inshore forecasts from the Met Office, far more accurate than the national reports on TV or radio.

I am served eggs for breakfast, laid that morning by the chickens pecking away in the yard. The deep yellow yolks mix well with homemade bread and butter – delicious, I want for nothing more. The day's schedule is now a routine: I am replacing a commute, coffee, log-in, meetings, lunch, more meetings and conference calls with a day-long walk through stunning coastal scenery. I open conversation if I need to, or lock myself away in my thoughts. This morning I am chatty, and enjoy the company of a day walker for a few hours.

'I'd love to walk the whole path,' he says.

'Getting my wife's permission was the hardest part,' I reply, ' … and finding the time.'

'How many days do you expect it to take?' A standard question.

'Forty maybe, with a couple of breaks to attend a wedding and meet work commitments.'

'What's your favourite bit so far?'

This question is not easy to answer. It depends on several factors: the company I keep, the weather, the terrain, and how I am feeling at the time; every day is different.

'All of it,' I reply, flippantly. 'The fact that I'm walking the whole path, the whole journey, not a snippet, but also the week-after-week endurance and sense of achievement.' I am more serious now, having given it further thought.

We carry on in good conversation into Clovelly, along Hobby Drive – a relaxing woodland walk. Some god has nailed and glued this picture-postcard fishing port to a ravine cut into the cliffside. Charles Dickens wrote about the village in a short story, *A Message From the Sea*, in 1892:

> *Captain Jorgan had to look high to look at it, for the village was built sheer up the face of a steep and lofty cliff. There was no road in it, there was no wheeled vehicle in it, there was not a level yard in it. From the sea-beach to the cliff-top two irregular rows of white houses, placed opposite to one another, and twisting here and there, and there and here, rose, like the sides of a long succession of stages of crooked ladders, and you climbed up the village or climbed down the village by the staves between, some six feet wide or so, and made of sharp irregular stones.*

Nothing has changed; he would have eaten at the Red Lion pub, overlooking the harbour, where it seems appropriate to order a mackerel pie. Anything more substantial would hamper the climb afterwards to the car park and busy visitor centre. I have another five miles to reach Hartland Point. I sit on a wall, eating a pasty for energy. A lycra-clad young German woman comes bounding up the hill like a gazelle.

'Hi, lovely day.' The usual Englishman's opening line.

'*Ach ja, ein schöner Tag,*' she replies. '*Wie weit zu Bude?*'

She is walking the coast path to Bude, and it is 4 p.m., I think she says; my German is rusty.

'That is a long way, over some very tough terrain,' I answer (in reality, it's some eighteen miles away).

'*Kein Problem,*' she says, smiling, and bounds off carrying a small bottle of water, as if on a short run. She is wearing a 1970s outfit: simple trainers, bright lycra jumpsuit and little else; no backpack, no walking poles, nothing. I think I have just seen an elf-being, on her way home to J.R.R. Tolkien's Rivendell. Is she some fictional character, able to cover greater distances than mere mortals? Perhaps she has Lembas bread in her pocket.

I bivouac for the first time behind a clump of bracken overlooking the sea – a secret place away from the path. I have tea in a flask and a chocolate bar to finish the day. The sun sets gracefully, and the stars and planets emerge in the evening sky. Sleep overtakes my desire to see another shooting star. The brightness of the satellites fades as the sun moves further behind our planet –

astronomical twilight replaced by the core night darkness.

Cloudless skies mean a cold night and I wake shivering; it is time to pack and get walking at dawn. The early eastern light illuminates the fields and rugged cliff folds that enter the sea around Hartland. The massive zigzag sandstone and shale strata have been contorted and eroded by timeless, elemental forces. The low golden-hour light brings texture to the landscape and geology. The view compensates for the effort of reaching each summit; the excess intake of oxygen fuels my euphoria and joy on such a beautiful morning. I will take a rest day today at Elmscott youth hostel, where the warden is happy for me to relax in the garden before it is formally open. I need to catch up on washing both body and clothing. Factoring in a half-day rest seems sensible, to counter a competitive streak that could result in injury.

The next section of the SWCP is the toughest, a monster wash-board of hill and combe for fifteen miles. I keep climbing to 150 metres over endless false summits and dropping into blind descents and sea level, all crafted to dishearten you. It has to be done, so no use complaining; I could be sitting in a traffic jam on the M25 with only a clutch pedal for exercise. It is a remote section, difficult to reach by car, isolated and facing the raw Atlantic swell. Over a hundred shipwrecks lie offshore, the victims of the first rocks encountered by a stricken vessel approaching Britain. A calm and pleasant sea can turn into a raging cauldron in moments. This naked exposure to the elements has inspired writers and poets for centuries, so it is no surprise to stumble upon a writer's hut or two.

The first is Ronald Duncan's shack, a legacy of the famous playwright, journalist and author who retired here to write undisturbed. The family maintain the hut for all to enjoy. A much older shelter can be found a few miles further south, near Morwenstow. Hawker's Hut is a former coastal observation shelter, constructed from driftwood by an eccentric clergyman in 1844. The Reverend Robert Stephen Hawker would retire here with his literary friends Tennyson and Dickens, perhaps indulging in an opium pipe or two, like errant teenagers smoking a joint.

The hut has developed a patina of weathered timber and dateless graffiti; it is the smallest property under the protection of the National Trust. Yomping onwards, my lungs are flushed with sea air. The secret GCHQ radio station comes into view, with its satellite dishes pointing every which way, snooping on international communications. One last major climb at Combe and I can relax the pace into 'budeiful' Bude. The tidal pool looks inviting, but I need calories, found quickly in the town between the surf and beachwear shops. The meal is a proper pasty now I am in Cornwall, washed down with a pint-sized mug of tea.

'Walked far today?' asks the owner.

'From Elmscott. I left at 9 a.m.'

'That's good going,' he says, cutting me an extra-large slice of fruitcake – a favourite of mine.

I can relax a while overlooking the harbour. Closer inspection reveals tidal locks and canals, and perhaps an old railway line and the breakwater protecting the beach. The sun is out, and everyone is happy; there is no reason to complain. A delightful local family runs the B&B, and they fuss over me. Boots tidied, another cup of tea and cake from the landlady and then an unusual offer.

'You can use the hot tub if you like,' she says.

Luckily I have swimming trunks; my legs are itching for me to jump in. The sensation is exquisite: tired legs turn into jelly, aches and pains float out of my bones and muscles, water jets massage a back accustomed to carrying heavy loads. Relaxed, I sleep a deep sleep, unable to complete the usual daily postcard before succumbing to the night.

It is with some shock that I learn that the landlady has cancer. Her beautiful family is giving her full support with dignity and grace; they only found out last week. I feel like an intruder, but they are keen to hear about my adventures. I would lose both my parents and younger brother to the same disease over the next decade. Recalling this encounter helped me cope with the pain and loss. I am in reflective mode as I stride into another glorious day, vowing never to take my health for granted. This lesson is one subconscious factor that has driven me to complete my journey, and worry less about status and money. I like to live in the moment, count my blessings and strive for a regret-free existence.

It is a gentler walk along the cliff edge, a continually changing boundary of coastal erosion. The low tide reveals layer upon layer of shale, combed by a geological hairdresser, leaving tidy striations and neat gulleys in the sandstone. Crackington Haven is an excellent place to stop for lunch. The Cabin cafe is staffed by cheery girls, enthusiastically serving appreciative customers. I am happy to sit inside, out of the weather. I can indulge in home-cooked wonders, each crafted with passion in a family-run business.

I have booked into the youth hostel at Boscastle, rebuilt after catastrophic floods in 2004. An intense micro-storm inundated the moors above the port, sending a torrent down the rivers. In scenes reminiscent of the Lynmouth flood disaster fifty-two years earlier, almost to the day, rescue helicopters plucked frightened residents from the roofs of their homes as cars were swept out of the car parks into the sea. The hostel has just reopened after a full restoration. The pictures show water pouring through the building, undermining the foundations. The building was lucky to survive. It is ironic that this port with such strong sea defences could be so cruelly flooded from the land.

It is tough going into Tintagel, a tourist hotspot trading off dubious legends of Merlin and King Arthur. The medieval castle undoubtedly played a role in securing trade routes in the Bristol Channel, taking advantage of its island location's natural defences. I am happy to continue, bypassing this visitor attraction, and move on to Trebarwith with its isolated beach. The Port William pub looks tempting; I half expect to see Stuart, but he must be on his way home by now. Fulmars are squabbling and soaring on the cliffs, settling into their breeding season. I can see the occasional seal in the water, but nothing more exotic offshore. Lambs are mischievously gambolling around in the fields, exercising new limbs in a new world. Their joy will soon diminish as they become organic lawnmowers – dull and monotonous masticators, keeping the grass trimmed and weed-free.

Port Isaac is a pretty Cornish fishing cove, with narrow streets and alleyways, fighting to maintain its heritage and retain a viable local fishing industry. My B&B has every conceivable decorative cliché: lighthouses, mermaids, seashells and ships in bottles. Somehow, they give me a sea view room and I can relax, gazing over to the horizon, thinking about the route ahead.

I need to return home tomorrow for work – one final project handover. My manager has agreed to match my salary in charity donations for three days' work – a condition I extracted to compensate for the interruption. So, I'm up early, walking in a sea mist that will soon burn off. I have a train to catch. I have barely walked a mile when I come across the uncommon sight of a grown man studying an IT service management reference book (a subject I know well) – not exactly holiday reading at six in the morning in thick mist. It is time to play a trick.

'Er ... best to study the section on configuration management,' I say, opening the conversation. 'Always comes up in the exams, usually one hard question about federated databases and CI granularity,' I continue.

'Er ... er ... yes, you're right. Er ... thanks.'

'Have a good day,' I reply.

He looks quizzical, but I don't linger, attempting to amplify the surreal encounter in the sea mist. I've seen Galadriel from Rivendell and a beer-powered Bristolian (Stuart); now it's my turn to freak someone out. Unfortunately, the joke backfires, as it reminds me of work.

It is a short walk to Pentire Point to reach Padstow Bay. Climbing over herringbone-patterned stone walls, with the delightful local name of 'curzyways', I come across a rare public drinking water tap at Port Quin. These are always a joy to find on a walk rather than a refrigerated cabinet full of the sugary drinks that seem to plague shops nowadays. Hayle Bay is teaming with surfers on one of the best beaches in the area. My mind is elsewhere, focused on catching the ferry to Padstow in time for the bus to Bodmin. The captain, I assume, knows of the dangers of Doom Bar, the treacherous shifting sandbank in the channel:

Sunset and evening star,
And one clear call for me!
And may there be no moaning of the bar,
When I put out to sea,

But such a tide as moving seems asleep,
Too full for sound and foam,
When that which drew from out the boundless deep
Turns again home.

Twilight and evening bell,
And after that the dark!
And may there be no sadness of farewell,
When I embark.

For tho' from out our bourne of Time and Place
The flood may bear me far,
I hope to see my Pilot face to face
When I have cross'd the bar.

– Alfred, Lord Tennyson, 'Crossing the Bar' (1889)

Pasty in hand, I board a train home with an expensive ticket bought on the day. At least it's a return. I'll be back in a few days to continue the walk.

PART 2 – PADSTOW TO LOOE

My workmates are generous, bringing the donations total to £1,800.

'You're looking tanned and relaxed; you'll never get a job like that,' they jest.

'I thought you were walking in Cornwall, not Greece,' another says.

I am thankful for their contributions, which, together with small token collections on the path and generous mates down the pub, are adding up nicely. Children's Hospice South West will be pleased. They work tirelessly to enrich the lives of children with life-threatening conditions, making the most of their short and precious time. It was an easy decision to select this organisation when I searched for local charities before the walk. Working your notice is one of the most unpleasant experiences, running down the clock until the final day. Some colleagues ignore you, not wanting to invest their time in friendship for someone they might not see again; others, I will miss dearly. A growing sense of loss develops; change is never easy, and I start to doubt my future as an independent consultant. Too late now. They give me a proper send-off – down the pub for a few pints and an evening of banter.

I can't wait to get back to Cornwall; the long-range forecast is good. My body has adapted to fifteen- to twenty-mile days, and I can lighten my backpack, discarding items I haven't used. I am back on the train, crossing the Royal Albert Bridge into Cornwall, courtesy of Isambard Kingdom Brunel's engineering skills – it's a stunning 1850s structure. A poor bus connection means I have to wait until late afternoon to set out north to Stepper Point at the mouth of the River Camel. I'm hoping to stay at the youth hostel in Treyarnon. It is warm enough to sleep on the beach if they are full; I can relax into a leisurely pace into Trevone.

In the mid-1970s, my parents nearly decided to run a pub in this village. My life could have been very different, compared to my upbringing in a rural pub in Berkshire. My mind imagines a life surfing and fishing in between lucrative work as a plumber or builder, refurbishing cottages for second homes. Somehow I fell into information technology after walking into a job centre in Maidenhead. My first day of work was spent preparing Apple II Plus computers for sale, by rewiring the American power cord with a UK thirteen-amp plug.

I would undoubtedly have enjoyed the stunning Harlyn Bay, and Mother Ivey's Bay, with that unique quality of light peculiar to north-facing beaches. The early evening surf sparkles and glistens as it washes and drains gently on the golden sands; quite different from the west-facing Booby's Bay, reached after turning south at Trevose Head, its shores exposed to the Atlantic swell. The cliff slopes are a riot of spring flowers as I descend the coastal grasslands to Treyarnon youth hostel.

'Any vacancies for tonight?' I ask.

'We are pretty full – surfers are on a course for the week – but let me see what we can do ... Yes, we have one bunk free if you don't mind sleeping in a dorm with a few Scotsmen.'

A dozen lads have strewn their gear around the room, but they welcome a new face. There is a strong odour of pubescence mixed with stale sweat from youngsters yet to discover deodorant. I can't complain – I'm only carrying a toothbrush and tend to avoid soap unless it's on offer.

'Top bunk's free,' one says.

'You're a long way from home.'

'Aye. We're studying for our life-saving exams in warmer waters.'

They're a lively bunch of lads, living frugally and following their passion for watersports. We talk at length about the north-west Highlands of Scotland and the glorious Sandwood Bay, somewhat wilder, colder and more remote than the busy north Cornish coast. This week is a summer holiday for them. Their passion for Scotland is evident in their enthusiastic description of the coastline.

'You've been to Arisaig? That's gorrrrgeous,' they declare, rolling their r's. 'You should go kayaking around the inner islands: you'll see minke, dolphins, seals, otters. If the weather's set fair, there's nowhere like it!' It's a small conditional sentence, with the significant word 'if'.

I have casually knocked off twelve miles from Padstow, but need to up the pace to pass Newquay, as I don't want to stay in the town. I leave the common room to the students, deep in their studies; it's not all practical work, and they have difficult health and safety exams at the end of the week. Within moments I have the cliff path to myself, passing cove after sandy cove and glorious beach inlets flushed clean twice a day by the tide. Bedruthan Steps, a sequence of orphaned cliffs, stand defiantly in the bay ahead – mythical giant stepping stones. The beaches compete in length and dramatic scale until I declare a winner: Watergate Bay, a two-mile stretch of sand that ends at Newquay. While the bay is unchanged, I am shocked at the scale of development over twenty years: blocks of flats are breeding towards the airport, like an out-of-control game of Minecraft. I daren't think about stopping for lunch; the hotel and restaurant prices are eye-watering. It is a pity a commercial approach has replaced the relaxed surfer vibe, destroying the atmosphere businesses seek to emulate. Brand names hijack the very essence of what is free, for profit.

I pick up a hot pasty in the town and walk through the busy streets to Fistral Bay, past a motley collection of surf shops and amusement arcades. I find a memorial bench to sit on for lunch, this one dedicated to a British surfing champion, Randall Hayes Davies, who lost his life at twenty-four. I'm not a fan of memorial benches, having passed a hundred or more on the path, sometimes so dense it feels as if you are walking through a cemetery, but this one seems justified, overlooking one of the prime surfing beaches in the UK. I walk through Pentire, in search of Penpol Bridge, a low-tide shortcut across the Gannel estuary, a deep sandy inlet that marks the southern border of the town. I stop to ask for directions from a man tending his garden.

'Do you know how to get to the footbridge?' I ask.

'I'm sorry, I'm not sure what you mean.'

'I'm walking the coastal path, and there's no ferry.'

'Sorry, I can't help.' He continues to cut his lawn.

A few yards later a sign points to the bridge, a slatted wooden structure that gets covered at high tide. So much for local knowledge, or perhaps he is sick of the question. I reach Crantock beach, and the crowds have vanished; only one lone dog walker is flinging a tennis ball with an arm extender. Porth Joke (known as Polly Joke locally) is empty, as is Holywell Bay further on – both gorgeous, quiet beaches. I wonder, could I pitch a bivvy? I decide to carry on to Perran Bay, another two-mile remote wild beach. It is time to remove my boots again and enjoy a sand foot massage into Perranporth, arriving at a pub built on the beach. I physically cannot pass the door without ordering a lager shandy and fish and chips, resting before I reach a B&B after a twenty-five-mile day.

Climbing the hill, I find out why the youth hostel is full: it has been block-booked by a stag party! Fluorescent wetsuited young men are descending in flippers, with diving belts loaded with beer cans. The groom is being fed foaming lager down his snorkel; others peer through masks half full of a similar liquid. They are off for a swim, the start of a secret schedule, known only to the best man, that will probably end with duct tape and a lamppost. It is a pity the YHA allows such bookings, but unusually, the B&B is cheaper, more comfortable, and without the threat of a 3 a.m. fire alarm.

The breakfast tables are occupied by surfers building lunch-time sausage sandwiches out of the remains of their full English breakfast – not a bad idea, which I copy. We depart together, in very different outfits: one ideal for the sea, another for the land. The coastal landscape changes: disused mineshafts, pumping sheds, demolished buildings, slag heaps and tailings – a rich industrial heritage. Air shafts are protected by cone cages, to prevent walkers from falling in, yet allow bats to enter and exit. Their rest in darkness will end later that evening, but for now, kittiwakes dominate the sky around St Agnes Head. Wheal Coates tin mine comes into view, announced by the iconic Towanroath Shaft pumping house – a photogenic Cornish scene. The juxtaposition of nature and industry against a seascape is poignant; the organic materials compete with rock and human-made structures. Underneath our feet lie deeper scars: mineshafts and tunnels that extend like veins under the sea, flooded and lost to the world.

I enter Portreath, but something is not quite right: the streets are empty, and the shops closed. The village is dominated by holiday homes, each marked with telltale door key boxes. This village will soon explode with holidaymakers, but for most of the year it is a ghost town, the local population unable to compete with money from the cities to the east. It will awaken for Easter, but now it is lifeless. The mobile cafe is a disappointment, and is serving only dog walkers. A photographer is taking pictures of a couple in their wedding gear. They pose, shivering in the wind for the sake of a memorable picture before their formal ceremony.

They wait for a dog owner to bag up a mess, as the excited mutt circles and barks, threatening to tug at the bride's dress. The sadness of the scene makes me grumpy as I settle in for a bivouac on the cliffs. I pull the bag over me as the sun sets on a clear night. It is going to be cold. I peer out at the shimmering sea, lit by a crescent moon. Rabbits retire to their burrows after bouncing around the grass clumps, nibbling fresh buds for their evening meal.

Something is refreshing about a raw, cold, early morning awakening – an adrenaline survival surge that makes you feel alive. I yomp to Godrevy Point to keep warm. I can hear loud grunts from the coves below, full of grey seals, the bulls guarding their harems at breeding time. Seabirds cackle around me, popping up unannounced from the cliff face. It is a lovely place to stop, breathe deeply and let nature wake up in front of you before you meet any human form. You are alone with nature and feel a part of the day-to-day life in coastal Cornwall.

A wooden shack, Godrevy Cafe, has just opened. It is a gem. I devour a huge breakfast marketed as the 'full Cornish' with a large coffee made with barista precision, filling my stove-stomach with fuel and stimulants for the day. The staff are delightful and wish me well as I depart, pinning the sponsorship note I left them to their noticeboard. My feet rejoice at the sensation of another barefooted beach walk into Hayle. The pleasure ends there, with the sight of another irritating estuary walk. I could throw a stick to the opposite bank at low tide, but wisely take the dull road to Lelant. At least I pass the 'oldest Cornish pasty maker in the world', although the baker looks quite young to me. Shall I buy lunch or wait until I reach the famous seaside town ahead? I walk into St Ives, where I just can't help recalling the well-known, but anonymous children's rhyme:

As I was going to St. Ives,
I met a man with seven wives,
Each wife had seven sacks,
Each sack had seven cats,

Each cat had seven kits:
Kits, cats, sacks, and wives,
How many were there going to St. Ives?

– Anonymous, c.1730

I'm sure everyone who walks this path does the same. The town is bustling with tourists having their ice creams and pasties knocked out of their hands by aggressive herring gulls. The council has hired a Harris hawk to discourage them; the handler wisely wears a wide-brimmed hat, as the gulls deposit guano bomblets in retaliation. It is a harsh environment on the quayside, so I find a safe place near St Nicholas Chapel on The Island (a headland that protects the bay) to eat my pasty. There is no doubt that St Ives is a beautiful place, but I can't help feeling that the balance has tipped in favour of the requirements of grockles, emmets and in-comers (Cornish slang for tourists). The town is losing the charm that makes it so attractive, becoming a Disney pastiche of glorious former days as a fishing port and Victorian retreat.

The geology now changes noticeably as the path becomes rugged underfoot. A granite igneous intrusion has nailed the Cornish peninsula to the Earth's crust. Bold rocks and boggy ground make this an awkward section, akin to a mountaintop walk in Scotland. You have to reset your pace and rhythm, placing your feet carefully to avoid a fall. I rest, exhausted, at a trig pillar to take a photograph. To the west, the sun lights the coves and cliffs in green and turquoise. To the east, the cliffs are grey and the sea colourless in the backlight of a west-setting sun. I scan the sea for dolphins, without luck. It is getting dark, so I pick my way carefully through the paths towards Zennor. Instead of camping, I walk inland, in the hope of a bed at the Tinners Arms.

'Er ... by chance, um ... I haven't booked ... but ... er, do you have a vacancy?' My expectations are low.

The landlord knows this but teases me by looking at the diary, thumbing through the pages. He has an answer on his lips but is sizing me up.

'Let me see.' Another page turns. 'I think we can fit you in.

Will you have dinner this evening too?' A silly question really, as I can see an excellent menu above the bar and the next pub is miles away.

The room is modern. I can wash the weariness and mud away in a hot shower, before returning to the bar. The food is excellent, the beer great and, even better, a fellow SWCP walker joins me. We instinctively recognise the tanned windswept face and worn outdoor clothing of a long-distance walker.

'Hi, I'm John. Walking the South West Coast Path?'

'Yes. From Minehead to Bournemouth. This is day sixteen, I think.'

We are a similar age, but John is running sections and is far fitter than I, hoping to cover the distance in fewer than thirty days. He has an ultra-light pack and is not camping. He is wearing battered, mud-encrusted trail-running shoes.

'Wow, that is fast. How did you cope with the terrain from St Ives?'

We drop into pleasant conversation, recalling events since Minehead and working through the challenges ahead. Each of us now has an intimate knowledge of the path. We continue to chat.

'Any idea how to cross the rivers after Plymouth?' he asks. It is a well-known challenge we will both face.

'I'm going to work that out when I get to Wembury. It all depends on tides. Ferry timings must be a real risk to your schedule,' I reply.

We order another pint to contemplate the permutations, maps spread out over the table. John's calculating arrival times and consulting tide tables; the conclusion is an early start for him. The forecast is dreary for tomorrow; any departure will do. He will leave before breakfast and pays the landlord that evening. I will go later, togged up in full rain gear, leaving the comfort of a pleasant stay for the wild Cornish coastline. The Tinners Arms gets my vote: great hosts, excellent company and superb food. Worth every penny.

I regain the coastal path and set a sympathetic pace for the conditions. There is little to report scenery-wise, as the sea mist cocoons me in a dream-like world. My focus adjusts to near distance, to study a beautiful and ancient stone bridge with a white keystone holding the structure in compression, as it has probably done for hundreds of years. Cattle appear out of nowhere, perplexed to see a coastal walker. After a glance they resume their grazing; they have a lot of grass to eat today.

Geevor mine emerges through the drizzle – a spooky sight made all the more dramatic with a soundtrack of crashing waves in the zawn below (*zawn* is Cornish for 'sea chasm' – a useful word to remember for Scrabble). It is a rough, unforgiving landscape, known to be the most dangerous coastline in Britain, the first abrupt landfall after an Atlantic crossing. Add to that the hard working conditions of the mines, tunnelling miles out to sea; this environment must have claimed many lives. The weather is a fitting backdrop, hiding the landscape of grief and tragedy from the world.

I can just glimpse Cape Cornwall, purchased for the nation by the Heinz Corporation in 1987 to mark its centenary year. It is the only cape in Britain, a location where two bodies of water meet, once considered to be the most westerly point in England until Land's End took that title. Some pedantic surveyor measured a few extra feet, I assume. I sneak away into a field to bivouac, its unmanaged grassland a comfortable spot for the night now the rain has stopped – what a contrast to last night's accommodation. Like the wet owl, hunkering on a branch nearby, I go without a meal. He is unable to hunt in these conditions. I have eaten all my food, having forgotten to resupply on the route.

The next day I meet Andrew on the path as we approach Sennen Cove. He talks non-stop about early retirement: painting, walking and the joys of good coffee. He invites me to join him at a cafe overlooking the crashing waves – an easy decision, although I want to press on.

'A good breakfast is what you need,' he says sympathetically.

'And I could do with a large cappuccino.'

Another walker pops in and joins us; it is like a rambling club of retirees, meeting before setting out for a day's walk.

'Hi, I'm Roy,' a newcomer announces.

'Tim. Nice to meet you.' Another joins us.

I let Andrew, Roy and Tim chat as I devour bacon, eggs, beans, tomatoes, sausages and toast. The meal and warm cafe revive me completely. I am in danger of falling asleep; my legs shut down to donate energy to my stomach to digest the meal. There is no chance of rest, however, as they all get to their feet and put on their rain jackets.

We walk together to Land's End and mingle with the daytrippers just arriving by the coachload. I have an obligatory photo taken at the signpost to add to the Land's End to John o'Groats (LEJOG) photos I am collecting from previous cycling and walking trips. I get chatting to the photographer.

'Can you take my picture?'

'Of course. What's your adventure?' he asks.

'I'm walking the coast path to Bournemouth.' He takes one shot, knowing he has captured the right smile on film. I walk back to his hut to pay.

'It's weird. The same company runs the signpost business in John o'Groats too,' I say.

'Yes, that's right,' he replies. 'We've been going for many years.' I hand him a tenner.

'Have a look inside my hut – we get all sorts here, including the famous naked rambling couple.'

The pair are standing completely naked, only wearing boots and their backpacks (containing clothes? I wonder). They have been walking for years and are frequently arrested, once spending time in jail for refusing to cover up.

'Saves weight and skin's waterproof, but they must get brass-monkey cold at times,' I jest. 'His balls must hide in his stomach most of the time.'

The photographic collection covers the inside of the hut, hidden from view. It can only be seen by those who pay. It is an impressive record of the hopes, dreams and eccentricities of all LEJOGers (or JOGLERs, depending on the direction).

'You should publish a book – they are such wonderful pictures.'

'One day, one day.'

Many grumble at having to pay to pose for a photo at the signpost. On a later visit to Scotland, I see that the popularity of the North West 500 tours has overwhelmed the business; people are ignoring the fact that the signpost is private. The photographer's abandoned hut stands in a field, a company for sale that no one wants in an Instagram world. Local commercial interests acquired the land and a substitute post was put in place, now covered in gaudy stickers.

Now to turn *the* big corner and head east, a significant milestone on the journey. A 'RED ROUTE – ABLE-BODIED ONLY' sign warns the non-able-bodied who have made it this far. The sun can now tan my right-hand side to balance the asymmetric colouring developed over the last few weeks. The wind direction is new too. It takes a few moments to adjust to new sensations and reset my body compass. The swell is crashing on to the cliffs and rocks below, thumping great sprays of water into the air. I now see more gannets; their pure-white wings stand out clearly against the dark blue sea as they glide and twist. At Minack, a magnificent open-air theatre nestles in the cliffs; the rolling sea provides a backdrop for the stage. Shakespeare's *The Tempest* could have no better setting.

The gannets are plunging into the sea just offshore, but no one notices, being too preoccupied in the cafe, eating pasties. Porthcurno has no vacancies, and the prices are too high anyway. Instead, I walk on to the beach and sit above the transcontinental communications cables that lie under the sand. Looking at the map, I contemplate a night under the stars, or perhaps I will walk further to the next village. I decide on the latter. Penberth is probably the most picturesque of all Cornish fishing coves, with cobbled streets and a small fleet of traditional crabbers hauled to shore with a windlass operated by hand. I walk inland, past stone cottages and into the silence of a sheltered combe to Treen. After two B&B rejections, I walk beyond the Logan Rock pub. One more door to try.

'Hi, I know I haven't booked, but do you have a vacancy?'

'Ohh ... come in, you look cold,' she says. 'The boiler's just come on so the water should be hot. I can dry any wet clothes near our Aga.'

I shower and change into new clothes and put on my boots to walk to the pub I have just passed.

'Pint of Tribute, please.' I order the local beer from St Austell, 'and steak and chips, with all the trimmings.' No need to dwell on what to eat; I'm starving.

I sit by a roaring log fire, loosening my laces, and stare at my pint, ready to drain it in one go. The pub cat curls up next to me, thinking I have ordered fish and chips.

'Switch on the telly, George,' the landlord shouts, 'Champions League semi's on now.'

George reaches for the power switch and adjusts the station. It is Liverpool away to Chelsea; kick-off is in five minutes. A monstrous steak arrives which the plate can barely contain. I have died and gone to walker heaven.

The next morning I idle along the cove road. Subtropical plants thrive in the sheltered conditions, fed by the warm air of the Gulf Stream. Lilies and orchids join fields of bluebells, coating the cliff fields with colour. Huge rhubarb-like plants hang over the roadside stream, a species from another continent. The horticulture tour continues on the coast path; gardens propagate beyond their boundaries, seeking freedom beyond the control of man. I'm back in shorts, striding along the trail, fully refreshed, into Lamorna, whistling:

So now I'll sing to you, about a maiden fair,
I met the other evening at the corner of the square.
She had a dark and roving eye, she was a charming rover,
And we rode all night, through the pale moonlight
away down to Lamorna.

Chorus:
Twas down in Albert square
I never shall forget,
Her eyes they shone like diamonds

and the evening it was wet, wet, wet.
Her hair hung down in curls,
she was a charming rover,
And we rode all night,
through the pale moonlight,
away down to Lamorna.

As we got in the cab, I asked her for her name,
And when she gave it me, well, mine it was the same,
So I lifted up her veil, for her face was covered over,
And to my surprise, it was my wife,
I took down to Lamorna.

Chorus

She said, I know you now, I knew you all along,
I knew you in the dark, but I did it for a lark,
And for that lark you'll pay, for the taking of the donah:
You'll pay the fare, for I declare,
away down to Lamorna.

– Cornish folk song

I know the tune, but if only I could remember all the lyrics. I remember the message for sure, and thoughts turn to my wife at home. Did she have such a lovely evening too? I am turning native, a transformation brought on by excess local beer and sunlight. I have discovered Stuart's secret: pop into the pubs and take it easy.

Mousehole (pronounced 'Mowzel') is a labyrinth of tiny streets and fishermen's cottages, entirely unsuitable for modern traffic, but somehow a bus squeezes through; I have to dive into a shop doorway to allow it to pass. This manoeuvre reminds me to stock up on postcards and write home; the shop sells stamps too. To the north of the village lies a memorial to the Penlee lifeboat disaster on 19 December 1981. The eight names of the crew of the RNLB *Solomon Browne* are etched on a granite plaque underneath, accompanied by the words 'Service not Self'. It commemorates their heroic efforts to save the crew of the MV *Union Star* as it crashed against the rocks at Boscawen. I have just walked past that cove, a scene of tranquillity, in sharp contrast to the hurricane conditions on the night of the rescue. I walk into the Royal National Mission for Deep Sea Fishermen at Newlyn to place a Seafarers UK sponsorship poster on their noticeboard. They offer me a cup of tea. The modern Penlee lifeboat, the Severn Class RNLB *Ivan Ellen*, lies moored in the harbour, ready to launch at a moment's notice if the red maroon flare fires. Both of these institutions support and protect a sizeable community of seafarers at this vital fishing port.

The huge hostel at Penzance has more than enough room for an out-of-season walker. I sleep in an empty dorm and rise early to pick my way through the streets to the port in the morning. Jubilee Pool, a celebrated Art Deco seawater lido, would be in any top-ten outdoor swimming lists. It is very tempting but has yet to open. The path joins a cycle track around Mount's Bay towards St Michael's Mount, the long-lost Cornish sister to Mont Saint-Michel in Normandy, France. Each is crowned with a stone chocolate-flake monastery on an ice cream cone of rock, adrift in a tidal bay.

I see a kestrel perched on a lichen-covered post ahead, staring at me intently. I creep slowly towards it until I am within a few metres. It twists its head to study me closer with each eye until it lifts gracefully into the air. By chance an RSPB warden is scanning the cliff face a few metres further on.

'Did you see the kestrel?' I say excitedly.

'No, but they are quite common here, mind you. I'm watching the choughs,' he says.

Sure enough, a pair are putting on an acrobatic display on the cliff face.

'Look like crows to me,' I say in ignorance.

'Look carefully ... see the red beak and red legs? They're quite different and full of character. Watch out for them along the path, you can't miss their aerobatics, especially when it's windy.'

'Oh yes, I see.'

'Hear them call too. It's a very distinctive cheooawh ... cheooawh,' he mimics.

These black birds are returning to Cornwall, much to the delight of the locals – a natural repopulation, possibly from Ireland and not from Pembrokeshire in Wales as you might expect, considering the distances.

'It's the symbolic bird of Cornwall. You can see it on the coat of arms, standing between a fisherman and a miner,' he adds.

My interest grows.

'They're returning after thirty years. Look out for them on the Lizard peninsula. There are a few breeding pairs there.'

I meet Roy again at Praa Sands, sipping a cappuccino and forking cake into his mouth. It is lovely that a 630-mile path can host a small community of walkers, continually meeting and drifting apart, each at their own pace. I have to join him.

'Seen Andrew or John?'

'Yes, John passed me a day or so ago, moving at some pace. I have yet to meet anyone walking the SWCP clockwise, have you?'

'Only a man with seven wives, stealing forty-nine cats,' I suggest, knowing it is the wrong answer.

'No, no, it is only the one walker is going to St Ives.'

'Yes, I know, I'm joking. I just did the maths in case the man turned around.'

I must have a slice of cake before we depart together for Porth-leven; Roy carries on, but I have plans to meet friends in Helston.

Steve meets me at the Blue Anchor after work. We get stuck into a few pints of Spingo, brewed behind the pub. We start with 'Middle' beer at 5% ABV, but I'm sure it is stronger; next I try a pint of Bragget, which is a robust 6%. A hen party walks in the door, on a pub crawl; this looks like their final stop, judging by their inability to stand upright.

'This is going to get messy,' I say to Steve, who is fond of a few pints.

'Here, try this,' he says, holding a foaming dark ale in my face. Now we are on to the 'Special' at 7%, it seems; who cares. My legs are feeling wobbly, full only with beer and no food. The hen party has broken into song, but we are saved by Steve's wife, Tina, popping her head around the door.

'Come on, luv!' No other words are necessary, everything that needs to be said clearly written in her eyes. We are grateful for a car ride home and a lovely meal.

We spend a pleasant evening catching up. Tina gives me a lift to Porthleven in the morning. My legs just about carry me across Loe Bar, a sand barrier that separates a freshwater lake from the sea. It would seem credible that Helston was once a port. No records exist to support any claim, but plans exist to create one by removing the bar. My mind cannot contemplate such engineering; I have a hangover to nurse. A nap on the cliffs after a salty pasty revives me.

I recognise the choughs now, adding to a list I like to recite of black-coloured birds: crows, ravens, jackdaws, rooks and now choughs, not forgetting blackbirds, of course. Someone told me that the subtle differences in bird species are what stimulate the obsession of birdwatching, a desire to complete a taxonomy, recognising subtle patterns: once seen, you have to complete the puzzle.

Waking, I put on pace through a sizeable rambling group, believing they might overrun the cafe ahead at Kynance Cove.

'He's not one of us, Peter, is he?' one woman remarks, as I stride through the group.

'Save us a slice,' one shouts out after I mention the cafe ahead.

The cafe is initially quiet, but a moment later it is packed, so I can sit rather smugly on the prime chair outside, drinking tea and breaking chunks of fruitcake into my mouth. They are a social group, with many completing the SWCP in stages over many years.

I can relax now into Lizard, stopping at Britain's most southerly tip. The youth hostel, built right next to the lighthouse, is a real gem: cosy, clean and full of information and reading materials, which I am beginning to miss dearly. I have the sweet pleasure of another dorm to myself. As night falls, I enter REM sleep, to be rudely awoken by a beam of light flashing every three seconds. The lighthouse must do its thing. I wrap a buff neck tube around my eyes to solve that, but I have no earplugs for the foghorn that starts moments later.

I need a lie-in anyway, for Ann's Famous Pasty Shop doesn't open until 10.30 a.m. I order two, made traditionally, with the skirt of beef, turnip (swede), onion and potato.

'I see that you post them too!' I read their pamphlet while I wait. 'Could you make one to this recipe and post it to my wife at work?'

'Of course. It'll be a few days, but it will keep nicely,' Ann says.

My backpack has doubled its weight as I haul it on to my shoulders and head towards Cadgwith, stopping at the National Coastwatch Institute lookout station. The gorgeous smell of warm pasty leaks through the fabric; I just can't resist an early lunch. It is delicious, the gravy gathering in the crimp as I munch it north to south. I pop the last corner into my mouth and dust the pastry from my hands.

If you are a coastal walker, you will have seen a National Coastwatch Institution (NCI) lookout station. There are fifty-six in England. Volunteers assist in the protection of life at sea and along the coastline, working closely with the Maritime Coastguard Agency (MCA). The NCI keeps a visual watch and monitors radio channels to support the more sophisticated radar, satellite and telecommunications systems. This back-to-basics organisation was formed after the loss of two fishermen in 1994, off Bass Point nearby. When you pass one of the huts, you might think of cups of tea and big binoculars, yet they provide a valuable service, particularly for the public during the holiday season. Casualty incident logs record person walking a dog, person camping, and person walking or running. This service may one day be vital for me. I always pop a few coins into their donation boxes.

As I get up, my eye catches something in the water: a basking shark, lolloping around with its distinctive dorsal fin and trailing tail, waving at me. Its sizeable white mouth is hoovering up plankton, circling back for seconds. It is a joyful sight; I cannot bring myself to leave.

The Lizard lifeboat sits quietly, a chain pin away from descending the slipway with its twin 1,000-horsepower engines running. It must be a magnificent sight when it is launched, but for now, it lies idle. I keep going, through the pretty thatched cottages at Cadgwith, to Coverack, and another excellent hostel. Once again, I have a dorm to myself, with a large bay window and stunning views across the sea. I can relax in an armchair and plan my week before a healthy evening meal, with all my gear spread out around the room, either drying or ready for inspection, as if a sergeant major might knock on the door at any moment. My fellow guests are all in their fifties, with shared interests and experiences that keep the conversation going for hours.

'Do you know you can get a discount on a senior railcard with your youth hostel membership?' someone says. We all have to laugh at that.

I am almost run over by a builder's lorry the next morning. I gird myself for a few sharp words, but Steve leans out the window.

'Fancy a walk?'

He parks up, and we spend a day walking to Helford River. He talks more openly about his memories of a previous job. Before becoming a builder, he worked in the mines; the last one closed in 1998.

'We didn't call it tin, we called it sten,' he says.

'Interesting. Why is that?' I ask.

'Comes from the Latin name *stannum*. We used to mine all sorts of minerals and metals: silver, copper, zinc and even arsenic. The rivers around here are still poisonous – don't drink the water,' he says. 'It was the end of an era, and we had to find something else to do. Renovating cottages has kept me busy for years and pays well.'

He opens up about his life in Cornwall and his hopes and fears for his children. The walk is therapy for both of us.

'I'm not sure what I'll do when I go home, I'm fed up with corporate life.'

'Well, it's a nice day, so let's not worry about that,' he replies. 'It's my day off.'

'Mine too.' Saying so makes me realise how lucky I am to be here at this moment.

We meet Tina at Helford and settle into the Shipwright Arms. Steve has passed quite a few cottages he has restored, and he recalls the difficulties of each job. He has pointed them out all day, together with the rock geology familiar to any miner, along with a few tales of shipwrecks. I miss their company within minutes of crossing the river on the local ferry. My mother has a friend in Helford Passage with a spare room. Even though he is away, I can pick up the key at the pub, busy with an evening crowd enjoying the last rays of sunshine, sipping cocktails and drinking beer.

Deep rivers and estuary incisions penetrate Cornwall's southern underbelly. To walk around them would add weeks to the walk if there were no passenger ferries in operation. Helford was the first, and tomorrow I have to cross Falmouth Bay to the Roseland Peninsula using two services.

A good night's rest promotes an eager pace to Pendennis Castle to view the Carrick Roads estuary to Zone Point. Falmouth, once one of England's busiest ports, is full of maritime heritage, taking advantage of the deep natural harbour. I can stop for breakfast before catching the ferry to St Mawes to hop on another boat to Place Creek, which the ferryman assured me was running. I suspect otherwise, as I can see the ferry covered with a tarp, moored in the harbour. I ask around to confirm.

'Is the ferry running today?'

'No, mate. He's taken a sickie,' comes a reply with an unusual Antipodean accent – an Australian lad on his way to work at a local cafe.

I have no choice but to catch the bus to Gerrans to avoid a dangerous road walk, and then walk to St Anthony and the ferry pier on the opposite bank, which I can see clearly. I rejoin the path to round the headland and follow the coast back to Portscatho to check in to a horrible last-minute B&B. I was hoping to stay at Portloe tonight, but my feet would complain about another five miles into a strong easterly wind.

The path is quiet in the early morning and definitely off the beaten tourist track. The beautiful fishing village of Portloe appears out of nowhere, hidden in a notch in the cliffs, geologically protected from the worst the Atlantic can throw at it. Over the centuries, the locals have developed all possibilities to access the sea. These ports punctuate the coast every few miles, leaving a pleasing cadence of path and village and path, ideal for exercise and rest.

The gannets are feeding out at sea, folding into steep dives, their take-offs delayed as they upend a catch down their gullet. I could watch them for hours at Dodman Point by the trig pillar, but continue to Gorran Haven. The beautiful Vault Beach, unspoilt and deserted, is lit by the southern sun bringing a vivid glow to the golden sands and azure waters.

'What a beautiful beach,' I declare to a dog walker, who has stopped to admire the same sight.

'Wasn't there last year,' he says. 'It can completely disappear, washed away, and then reappear again overnight after a storm.'

'It does look brand new, probably the best remote beach I've seen for a few weeks.'

Gorran Haven is in full swing. It will be May bank holiday next week, and some families have made a start. The beach is busy with children swimming in the harbour, braving the cold water and jumping off the pier. Everyone seems happy in the sunshine. It is a good time to lie in a natural rock armchair before I walk into Mevagissey to enjoy a few more moments of tranquillity. The white cottages of Chapel Point seem idyllic and provide a foreground for a ribbon of headlands to the east. They look so distant, and yet you reach them more quickly than you would expect, as the day progresses.

Before entering busy Mevagissey, I have to run the gauntlet of Portmellon. The easterlies and spring tides have brought the waves to the lip of the road. They crash periodically into the sea wall, sending a plume of seawater into the sky. I have no easy way around and need to time a run correctly. I have an audience of jolly customers at the Rising Sun pub, who cheer me on as I make my dash, applauding my dry passage and raising their glasses to toast my victory over the crashing waves. To my delight, there is a Marine Conservation Society stall on the port side, handing out leaflets.

'Hi there, I am doing a sponsored walk for you guys.'

'Oh wow. That's cool,' the young girl says. 'Had much response?'

'Not on the path, but I think I've raised about £3,000 now for three charities. Tell me more about what you do.'

The Marine Conservation Society tries to manage what goes into the sea and what comes out of it, protecting what most people cannot see beneath the waves. The health of our seas and oceans is fundamental to the survival of all species, humans too. They campaign on many fronts to keep the waters free from pollution, and to maintain sustainable fish stocks. Today they are fighting to keep the local beaches clean, and display a selection of unwelcome jetsam and flotsam on their tables. I take a few leaflets to read.

The adrenaline drains from my legs as I search for my B&B; it has been a tiring day. The local pub is showing the second leg of the Champions League semi-final between Liverpool and Chelsea. The home team win on penalties; the crowd erupt in tears. Liverpool are going to the final (which they later lose 2–1 to AC Milan, who exact revenge from their loss the previous year, in Istanbul). I'm timing my accommodation perfectly.

Smoked haddock and poached eggs are a welcome change for breakfast – deep yellow yolks lying on a fluorescent smoked fillet. The sun is out, and the winds have eased. It is going to be a hot day over a strenuous section of coastline, so I down a good litre of water before leaving. I walk into Charlestown harbour, near St Austell, and immediately recognise the film-set location often used for TV. Today, three tall ships are in the dock, and a small city has sprung up to service the filming of a period drama. I walk past actors and extras dressed in their Victorian finery (yet smoking their Marlboro Lights), ready for filming to start. I'm only going to be a nuisance if I hang around, but I can't help squinting my eyes for a moment and imagining what the real scene might have looked like a hundred years ago.

The paths are busy with dog walkers enjoying the glorious weather. Soon the real industry of the area makes itself known as I walk past the china clay works covered in the white dust of kaolin. Inland the Cornish Alps (mounds of the spoils of the clay pits) loom into the sky as if covered in snow. The unseen Eden Project is a few miles inland; massive biomes have blistered in former clay pits, protecting artificial ecosystems which are hugely popular with tourists.

I am happy to walk on to Gribbin Head and admire the striking red and white daymark, a twenty-six-metre tower that has guided seafarers into Fowey since 1832. My remaining few miles are hampered by over-friendly bullocks wanting to make a nuisance, but they keep a respectful distance from my upturned walking poles. My heart rate only settles as I walk into the village and search out another delightful B&B. I can open the bedroom windows to views across the rooftops of Fowey. A deep bath is blissful, followed by steak and chips in another superb local. How am I going to explain this luxury to my wife when I get home in a few days for the second break of the walk? Sending her a cold pasty is not going to cut it (her workmates, initially excited at the sight of a large parcel, scolded me for years afterwards, when they discovered the contents).

It is only twelve miles into Looe, along a rugged and glorious section of path. It is like the first summer's day that triggers well-being in everyone. The ferry to Polruan carries happy walkers to the opposite bank and into one of the most beautiful sections of the path since Land's End. The seas are shimmering in the early morning light, and the skies are clear and deep blue. It is an exhilarating yomp up hill and down combe to Polperro, another impossibly quaint Cornish fishing port, a worthy subject for any postcard photographer. The Blue Peter pub is a tempting stop for lunch, but I have a train to catch and snack briefly at Talland, a secret bay that would be a challenge to find by road.

My arrival into Looe is signalled first by St George's Island and confirmed when I see Banjo Pier. I grab a pasty and board the branch line to Liskeard to be whisked away east by an InterCity 125 to Plymouth, Exeter and London. I have a family wedding to attend.

PART 3 - LOOE TO SANDY HAVEN

A four-day break is welcome: no walking, plenty of good food and enough conversation for me to lose my voice.

'Blimey, you look toned and tanned – been on a long holiday?' says a friend.

'Can I talk to you about the decorating?' asks my wife.

'Isn't it time you got a job?!' adds my brother.

I detect a hint of envy, but it is great to see the family again, gathered together in one place for a wedding. My mind is elsewhere: the hiatus is too short to switch out of a walking routine; my life is on the coastal path, and I cannot wait to return.

It is drizzling and overcast as I arrive in Looe, and the streets are quiet now the bank holiday is over. It has a very different atmosphere to the joyful buckets and spades of a week ago. I slot quickly back into pounding the paths, with legs and feet refreshed and a backpack full of clean clothes and food. Seaton and Downderry add to the gloom; there are no pretty coves on this stretch of coast. I spend the night in Portwrinkle before walking through the Tregantle ranges, which are open to the public. This military facility reminds me that I need to time my arrival at Lulworth Cove precisely; there is no point arriving early.

Unusually for me, I sketch out an itinerary for the next ten days. I usually prefer a three-day loose schedule, sufficient to consider any accommodation that I might need to book (such as youth hostels). I only have a simple mobile phone, so research is challenging. I have to rely on a map and conversations with people I meet. Arrival times for ferries in Devon are critical, and I am unsure of their schedules. I can wade across other estuaries at low tide using a timetable written by science and nature – accurate and unchanging (available at most newsagents for £1.50).

Rame Head and Penlee Point mean that I have arrived at the entrance to Plymouth harbour. St Michael's Chapel overlooks the seaward approaches from its promontory cliff mound, forlorn yet resolute. It is too early for lunch, and I would like to get through the city without delay, so I march on around Cawsand Bay into Mount Edgcumbe country park. I see, then hear, a cuckoo – the first of the year – sitting on a branch. Its striped white chest and grey throat bellow as it sings, a call without an answer, the silences heavy with expectation. The number of repeats you hear supposedly indicates your longevity; I strain on every note. The green clock at Cremyll Ferry shows 1.22 p.m. I'm in good time. A few choice words circle the clock face.

> *DOST THOU LOVE LIFE – THEN DO NOT SQUANDER TIME*
> *TIME AND TIDE TARRY FOR NONE*

Remarkably poignant: you cannot pause time, so you had better get on with it! The ferryman's mate agrees and calls to us.

'All aboard. We leave in five minutes,' he shouts, holding the bowline looped around a bollard, ready to depart.

Plymouth is naval, its fortifications, warships, barracks and architecture overwhelmingly pragmatic and purposeful. I wiggle around the austere streets to the Hoe – a promenade that commands extensive views across Plymouth Sound. Rich military heritage, from Sir Francis Drake's game of bowls to modern-day memorials, marks moments from seafaring generations. The views from here at the peak of the British Empire must have been a wonder to behold, the Sound full of brooding First World War battleships and cruisers and their tenders.

Tinside Lido is another glorious open-air swimming pool, similar to the Art Deco structure at Penzance. It's tempting to stop, but I am more interested in taking another ferry to Mount Batten to continue along the path rather than explore the River Plym in detail. Plymouth Breakwater lies offshore, providing a level of protection from the Atlantic swell that is the very foundation of the city. Structural work started in 1811 and was officially completed in 1841. It is still maintained today, to hold back the swell that would otherwise batter the city.

> *I reach the marble-streeted town,*
> *Whose 'Sound' outbreathes its air*
> *Of sharp sea-salts;*

I see the movement up and down
As when she was there.
Ships of all countries come and go,
The bandsmen boom in the sun
A throbbing waltz;
The schoolgirls laugh along the Hoe
As when she was one.
I move away as the music rolls:
The place seems not to mind
That she – of old
The brightest of its native souls –
Left it behind!
Over this green aforedays she
On light treads went and came,
Yea, times untold;
Yet none here knows her history –
Has heard her name.

– Thomas Hardy,
'The Marble-Streeted Town', Plymouth (*c*.1914)

I leave the cityscape over a steel plate, which amusingly reads (upside down), 'WELCOME TO PLYMOUTH – PLEASE WIPE YOUR FEET'. I happily remove my boots before entering a delightful B&B in Wembury. Another couple are staying, walking the Devon Coast-to-Coast route around Dartmoor (a well-known cycle route too). We enjoy a good meal at the local pub together, chatting away about our adventures and offering advice about the ferries. The landlord chips in.

'I think you may need a taxi around the River Erme, it's high tide at eleven and the ferry isn't running at the moment.'

I wonder how I will cross the Yealm, Erme and Avon tomorrow. My brain is unable to process the permutations, so I will just have to see what happens.

After breakfast, the first ferry is on time – a good start. I can now march on through a dreary day to Erme Mouth. The path is quiet and remote, isolated by the inlets. The National Trust seems to own everything, and the bright purple marker-pen boundary lines on the Ordnance Survey maps are distinctly annoying, over-writing the very path detail I'd like to see. I hate the homogenous NT branding on signs and information boards. The whole of Britain's distinctive heritage is becoming a bland theme park, overpainted in standard corporate colours. It would be much better to retain local and regional diversity; I want to experience what is different and learn from it.

I round the headland. It is high tide, and there is no ferry. I can wait at Schoolhouse cafe, a cosy and friendly place, for a taxi. Ten pounds seems fair to me, considering the value of a pleasant chat with the driver; he knows the area well. The ride saves me a six-mile walk around the estuary. The Erme can only be crossed an hour either side of low tide in calm conditions, as long as you are prepared to wade up to your knees to the eastern bank.

I now press on to Bigbury-on-Sea and run to the last ferry. If I don't make it, I will drown my sorrows at the Pilchard Inn on Burgh Island. I can see the ferryman across the river, rowing home. I frantically wave my walking poles in the air, with an occasional loud whistle to attract his attention. He sees me and turns around.

'Glad I caught sight of you, that's my last crossing for the day. Are you walking the coast path?'

'Oh, yes [puff … puff], all the way around [puff]. Thank you so much for turning around.'

He is a retired city executive, happy to provide a valuable service to walkers and tourists. I am eternally grateful, even more so when he recommends a good pub in Hope Cove – a more than suitable alternative to the Pilchard Inn.

The Hope & Anchor is expensive, but worth the stay, for the excellent food and beer. A gale blows in. I sleep fitfully – as if sleeping in a tent – but I can console myself with a day gained (and accommodation cost saved) crossing the three rivers. It is a straight run now to Salcombe and Dartmouth. The weather remains nondescript, a canvas of colour-leaching grey. I don't mind the cold, or being wet, but a combination is uncomfortable and sometimes dangerous. I keep warm maintaining an eager pace across a rugged and beautiful section of the path, cocooned in a soggy waterproof. The rough seas and dramatic skies are at their most visceral, the raw elements at their most energetic, bringing some texture (at least) to the sea and skyscapes. I'm eager to see more after crossing Salcombe harbour.

The place names reflect the drama of the day: the Bull, Raven's Cove, Shag Rock, Ballsaddle and Gorah Rocks. Gammon Head defiantly stands against the full force of the sea. The sky turns black, and the sea is white, inverting imprinted images on my retina that have set firm after four weeks on the coast path. I'm quite out of breath until I turn north at Start Point to join a relaxing track that needs no effort to navigate. I can take in the new coastal vista of Start Bay. I run for the shelter of a fish and chip shop at Torcross, bumping into another drenched walker, Andy.

'What a day,' we declare. 'But an awesome walk.'

Andy and I demolish our meals and order more tea as we slowly dry out and regain our energy. A deep satisfaction replaces our excitement as our legs absorb fuel and we steam up the cafe windows. Andy catches a bus into Dartmouth; I walk into the village of Slapton and find the Tower Inn for a few pints before retiring to a lovely B&B run by a slightly batty yet captivating landlady – a Miriam Margolyes character, full of life and energy.

The beach is peaceful and quiet in the early morning light. Waves lap gently against the pebble shore now the storm has blown through. It was on this beach that a tragic D-Day landing rehearsal (Exercise Tiger) unfolded on 28 April 1944. Over 700 American servicemen lost their lives that day when four German E-boats fired their torpedoes at the landing craft. The local population knew nothing, having been evacuated from the area in 1943. It was not until 1984, when Ken Small recovered a Sherman tank from the seabed, that the tragedy became more widely known. Many lessons learnt on that day were implemented during the actual D-Day landings just a few weeks later, saving many lives. One of the Second World War's greatest tragedies remained secret for decades, an embarrassing moment covered up to maintain morale.

I wander north, past Blackpool Sands, quite different from its northern namesake, with a broad golden beach and light crowds, enjoying an ice cream or two. I grab a light lunch in Dartmouth. Not wishing to linger, I board the ferry to Kingswear and arrive early in Brixham to relax at Berry Head, cuddling up next to the stubby lighthouse that does not need to be taller than the fifty-eight-metre cliff it stands on. None of the fast-food restaurants in the town appeals to me, so I consume the remains of my food bag and let my stomach rumble until breakfast. The forecast is grim.

After scoffing every available calorie at breakfast, I get into full waterproofs. The rain is set for the day, as there is little wind to move it on. The conditions turn to my advantage by clearing the path on the seafront – no ambling tourists today. Dog walkers linger only to gather up their dogs' doings before returning to the car – quick toilet stops only, no chasing tennis balls along the beach. Every beach hut is locked tight, greased polythene bags wrapped around padlocks to protect them against the salt air. Residents peer through the net curtains to check the skies. Those who spend a lot of time outdoors know the weather is always better outside than in, but not this morning: the English Riviera is closed – but not for me.

Turning north around Hope's Nose, I can leave the last of Tor Bay's wet holiday scenery. On a day with excellent visibility, the coast will reveal itself. Even without that visual clue, I can sense that the journey is coming to an end as I approach Dorset. It is a tedious few miles to Shaldon, where I meet Rebecca. She is carrying a huge backpack and smoking.

'You're the first walker I've met today. Are you walking the SWCP?'

No reply.

'Everything OK? It's not far from the ferry to Teignmouth.'

She is tearful; I daren't ask why.

'Would you like to walk together for a while?'

She stubs out the cigarette and begins to open up.

'I have bad blisters,' she cries.

My wife would not classify compassion and empathy as my

strong points, but I do my best to encourage Rebecca to the ferry terminal. She says her goodbyes and I leave her to find accommodation. I jump aboard the black and white Teign ferry and stay at a B&B full of character, run by a Danish Morris dancer, who has moved to England to follow his passion. This Anglophile keeps me amused for hours, talking intimately about the local culture with a Danish accent he could never erase. You can't help but warm to his enthusiasm.

The Great Western Railway now hugs the coastline, finding the easy route around Dartmoor to the south-west. The tracks are dangerously exposed to the ravages of the sea, tunnelling where possible through cliffs I must ascend. At Starcross, in 1848, Isambard Kingdom Brunel created the Atmospheric Railway, a system which propelled the carriages by a difference in air pressure, created by steam engines in the pumping house, which is still standing now. Unfortunately, rats found the leather sealing flaps rather tasty and the venture failed, even though it was surprisingly efficient.

The Starcross ferry shuttles me across the River Exe to Exmouth with its beautiful holiday beach. I climb up to Orcombe Point and hopscotch along a sequence of stones to the Geoneedle sculpture. Each stone represents a section of the Jurassic Coast, and I have just danced through 185 million years of geology. The needle represents the start of ninety-six miles of this World Heritage Site, which finishes at Old Harry Rocks. I will now journey through the Triassic, Cretaceous and Jurassic landscape to the end of the walk. Any geologist might spend a lifetime of study here; if they married a palaeontologist, they could unpick Earth's ancient past, both mineral and biological, together.

The nature of the walk has changed. The coastline is like a broken Crunchie bar, revealing a golden inner core, nibbled by the sea over millennia. There is evidence of coastal erosion at every headland. Landslides and rockfalls are frequent, some of a considerable scale. I'm in shorts again and can sunbathe at a cafe in Budleigh Salterton before crossing Otter Mouth to resume an easy walk into Sidmouth for the night. A curry feast does wonders for my energy, topped with another full English for breakfast – an intake that would be unsustainable as an office worker. I am marching along at an impressive pace, now fully conditioned to coastal walking. My body has adapted to repeated twenty-mile days, and I am covering greater distances each week. Maybe I am spurred on by homesickness too.

The MSC *Napoli* lies semi-submerged a mile off the coast, having shed several containers loaded with goods. The merchant vessel got into difficulties during a storm and was towed into Lyme Bay. Twenty-foot containers washed up on the beach. The local population revived smuggling skills, written in their DNA, to strip the contents. Young men rode brand new BMW motorcycles away, fuelled and with keys in their locks. They were claiming salvaging rights, later reported to the Receiver of Wreck, and kept their booty.

I can see the Isle of Portland to the east on reaching Beer Head. To the west, Hooken Cliffs have been ripped apart and are tumbling into the sea. A row of stone-faced cottages, all identical, lead the eye into Beer village for a lunchtime nap. I am going to need the rest because ahead lies the Undercliff: a three-hour journey into an underworld along ankle-twisting muddy paths that pick their way over roots and vegetation for five miles. The entire route weaves through landslides and rockfalls that have crumbled seawards and remain unstable. The microclimate and ecology envelop you, quite different from the cliff coast path. It is like entering a *Lord of the Rings* woodland, so oppressive that it infringes every thought, the deeper you go. I half expect the trees to start talking to me.

It is with some relief that I exit on to hills that overlook Lyme Regis. I meet a weary couple, hobbling into town.

'That's a tough walk,' I say.

'No kidding! It's taken us all day to get from Axmouth.'

'I'm never doing that again,' his wife agrees.

'It wasn't that bad,' I suggest, promptly tripping over my pole as I turn to walk away – the first fall in five weeks. The Undercliff has exacted karma, my levels of concentration and energy depleted to far lower than expected.

The B&Bs are getting more expensive as I travel eastwards. Second homes plague the town, as the landlady confirms.

'This place is like a ghost town in winter. None of the locals has a chance to buy a home. It's criminal that these properties remain empty for six months of the year. It's quiet now after May Day, the newly-wed and nearly-dead season. Fully booked for summer, you can't get a bed anywhere.' She barely pauses for breath. 'Another cup of coffee, dear?'

The hosts are a downshifting couple, yet to adjust to a slower pace of life in Dorset, away from London. I am grateful for their incomer enthusiasm and perspective, however long that may last. The community will soon assimilate their city ways, like antibodies destroying a foreign virus.

> Calm, azure, marble sea,
> As a fair palace pavement largely spread,
> Where the gray bastions of the eternal hills
> Lean over languidly,
> Bosom'd with leafy trees, and garlanded!
>
> Peace is on all I view;
> Sunshine and peace; earth clear as heaven one hour;
> Save where the sailing cloud its dusky line
> Ruffles along the blue,
> Brush'd by the soft wing of the silent shower.
> In no profounder calm
> Did the great Spirit over ocean brood,
> Ere the first hill his yet unclouded crest
> Reared, or the first fair palm
> Doubled her maiden beauty in the flood.
>
> – Francis Turner Palgrave, 'At Lyme Regis' (1870)

I walk down to the beach and sneak around Church Cliffs at low tide, avoiding a high-level route into Charmouth. Fossil hunters are out early, fossicking along the cliff edge, drawn to recent rockfalls in the hope of finding a prize in the clay. Patience will result in a modest specimen, a personal memento exceeding the value of any item purchased in town. Anyone, at any time, could uncover an ichthyosaur or plesiosaurus, as Mary Anning did in the early 1800s, much to the dismay of Victorian creationists who refuted this emerging evolutionary evidence.

The coastline beyond Charmouth is familiar to me – a regular camping destination for over thirty years. I demolish the hills without effort, something that would be daunting from my usual comfort of a deckchair. Lethargy breeds idleness; exercise awakens energy. Golden Cap is the highest point on the south coast of Britain at 191 metres, with stunning views east and west. I can now see Portland, some twenty miles away, connected by the thin pebble cord of Chesil Beach. I roll down and up the hills like a marble, maintaining momentum into West Bay for a superb seafood lunch at one of the food shacks in the harbour. You could walk the entire length of Chesil Beach if not for the military firing range in the middle. It makes more sense to ascend the cliffs and avoid the many rockfalls on a high-tide shoreline, although this means missing the views of the million-layer-cake cliff face of West Bay and East Cliff.

Turning inland to Abbotsbury I meet Terry, quite obviously adorned in the gear of a long-distance walker.

'You look like you're on a long walk.'

'The entire coast of Britain,' Terry replies.

'That's quite a load you're carrying. Where did you start?'

'Five days ago in Bournemouth. I'm camping every day.'

He is carrying an at least eighty-litre backpack and a front pack too. I don't believe he will last long, carrying that weight; he'll learn soon enough. All his gear is new and shiny and yet to acquire the patina of use.

'Good luck, take it easy.'

He plods off, and I walk to the pub in the town, to sink a few pints of Guinness before the B&B opens. It is the cheapest I have stayed in for a while, the landlady somehow locked in a time warp. She is either in denial of the market price or oblivious to the nature of inflation. I tuck two £20 notes in the visitors' book – double her proposed fee.

The inland route is a pleasant change from the cliff-edge path, with views over the East and West Fleet hosting a swannery of mute swans once bred for lavish Dorset banquets; the 'BABY SWANS' road sign in the village is written to attract the attention of bored children and force parents to the popular tourist attraction in exchange for a £25 entrance fee (or more). If the sign had read 'CYGNETS', the business income would fall forty per cent, I am sure.

The Fleet (an inland lake) was the testing location of Barnes Wallis's bouncing bomb, repeatedly dropped from a Wellington aircraft until they found the perfect speed and height for it to skip along the water; the application of spin was critical, like throwing skipping stones across a smooth lake, but this time perpendicular to the surface of the water. On reaching the quarries on Portland, I can see the full length of Chesil Beach. It is a magnificent sight, a geological marvel created by wave motion. Fishermen can tell where they are in a fog by the size of the pebbles, sorted by size over millennia.

The island will take the remaining day to circumnavigate, but I can relax my pace, knowing I have a hostel to look forward to at the end. I was not expecting much of Portland, but it is a beautiful day walk, full of heritage and dramatic sea views, particularly if the ebbing tide opposes a strong southwesterly, throwing up destructive standing waves at Portland Bill. The 1844 TH obelisk stands proudly at the tip. I initially thought it meant Thomas Hardy, but it is an abbreviation for Trinity House, although the former would be more appropriate; this landscape is Hardy country after all.

The path weaves through quarries and dismantled industrial heritage to a viewpoint at the battery just behind the prison, built initially to house convict labour for the construction of Portland harbour and its breakwaters. The views of the Royal Navy Fleet would have been spectacular in the 1900s, perhaps more so than at Plymouth. The hostel is cosy, but full of tourists waiting to catch the cross-channel ferry in the morning. I sit with a Brummie couple for breakfast. The wife has a peculiar habit of repeating everything her husband says.

'We're catching the ferry at 10.30,' he says.

'Catch the ferry at half past ten,' his wife confirms.

'I've got my tablets for seasickness.'

'Tablets for seasickness.' She checks her handbag.

'A good breakfast inside you is what you need.'

'Eggs and bacon, a good breakfast,' she continues.

The parrot-like behaviour continues until she inexplicably starts a conversation.

'Where's your passport, George?' she shouts; the contents of her handbag are now on the table. Fortunately, his documents are found a moment later in George's suitcase; the comedy sketch concludes as they depart.

'I'll drive, dear.'

'You drive, yes, that's best. I hate boarding ferries,' she mutters.

'Where's my keys?'

A smaller 50p ferry carries me across the River Wey into the town of Weymouth and the long sandy beach, quiet on a Friday morning. Windsurfers are enjoying a reasonable force 5 breeze in the bay. I watch in awe as they gybe moments before crashing into the shoreline. I'm in no hurry to reach West Lulworth, enjoying the last days of the Jurassic coastline. Durdle Door is almost an anticlimax to a mind used to dramatic coastal scenery for six weeks. Well-worn paths are now durable stone steps, an indicator of how busy this area can get. I sit and relax, beginning to contemplate the end of my journey. The youth hostel is cosy and does a good meal. I'm settling into an empty dorm when several gentlemen arrive and dump their gear on the bunks.

'Hi, I'm Martyn.' They return with their names one by one: Peter, Mike, David and others I cannot recall.

'Look like you've been on a long walk.'

'Yes, this is day thirty-five of the South West Coast Path. What are you guys up to?'

'We're the Hart Road Runners, we spend a week away every year together, on a challenging walk. Tomorrow we're walking across the Purbeck Hills.'

'Is the firing range closed?' I am referring to the Lulworth range, which has yet to open for the season.

'Think so; check with the warden.'

A pleasant evening is spent in the common room, recalling tales of walks around Britain. It is lovely to see a group of life-long friends with such a passion for walking outdoors. The warden pops his head around the door.

'Everything OK? I checked the Lulworth Camp hotline. The range opens tomorrow at ten.'

I wake early, apologising for the noise to my dorm mates, but I want to be at the gate when the range opens. I'm just in time. I can see the red flag being lowered and the army Land Rover departing along the track. I am the first walker to enter for several months, on to a dramatic unspoilt chalk downland, a full grade 5 (super scary) rollercoaster ride to Chapman's Pool. The climbs and descents are exhilarating. My new, six-week, fully conditioned body has wolf-like levels of endurance. It is surreal to feel how quickly I progress. I have lost weight, and my pack is light. My leg muscles are toned, used to the stresses and strains of a challenging path. This landscape is a firing range. Amongst the carcasses of blown-up tanks, deer are grazing in an environment that is, perversely, a haven for wildlife. The abandoned village of Tyneham lies inland, requisitioned by the army in 1943. The villagers left a poignant message on the church door, in the hope of one day returning:

Please treat the church and houses with care; we have given up our homes where many of us lived for generations to help win the war to keep men free. We shall return one day and thank you for treating the village kindly.

I can rest at St Aldhelm's Chapel by the National Coastwatch Institute hut. I don't want the walk to end. It is tempting to walk to Worth Matravers and the famous Square & Compass pub for a celebratory pint, but it seems premature with another ten miles to go. I dawdle into Swanage, having walked twenty-two miles in seven hours, to find my B&B, with a convenient curry house opposite. The hosts have seen the satisfying glow of an SWCP completer before and know the genuine article by the gnarly windswept tan lines and toned body. I have comical white-skin socks when I pop downstairs for a pot of tea, barefoot.

In the morning, I have plenty of time to walk the remaining few miles. I get a lump in the throat as I turn to pass Old Harry's Rocks into Studland; deeper emotions are surfacing. Is it joy or something more? My thoughts will have to wait, as I meet the Hart Road Runners again. They walk with me along the beach through the naturists to South Haven Point. I've finished. They each shake my hand and are genuinely pleased for me. There is no doubt I have a long-distance walking bug now. The SWCP is a significant milestone in what will become an obsession to walk all nineteen trails.

I count up the money I have collected and check the *justgiving. com* website when I get home. Over £5,000! I write letters to each charity, enclosing a cheque with the proceeds and receive lovely thank-you notes a week later.

4

THE THAMES PATH

Distance: 184 miles
Days to complete: 7 days
Mileage so far: 902 miles

MARATHON MAN

I know the joy of fishes in the river through my own joy,
as I go walking along the same river.

– Zhuangzi

The Thames Path is on my doorstep. I have often walked sections between Windsor and Reading; but now is the time to walk the entire path, from the Thames Barrier in Woolwich to the source near Cirencester. It is 184 miles long, exactly seven marathons, so I hatch a plan to complete it in seven sprints over the winter of 2011–2012, sneaking days off from work.

You may ask, why winter? The simple answer is that I am slightly mad. It is going to be wet, muddy, cold, flooded and dark at times. On the bright side, the path will be quiet and free of holiday river traffic. I am itching to get some walking done rather than sulk at home in front of the TV. Accommodation will be easy enough to find, but expensive, and camping is for the brave in winter. After a little thought and planning, I realise that I can use public transport and a car to walk each section. I set a target to walk a marathon a week leading up to Christmas, where I can spend my newly earned health credits without guilt – a New Year resolution paid in advance.

I decide to walk out of London, away from city life and into the countryside. This direction is against the flow of the river, going backwards in time to the place of its birth. There may be some deeper meaning in that but, to be honest, transport connections are more manageable this way around. It is not as if I am paddling upstream, but I will experience an illusion of walking at a slower pace, like watching a train leave the station while yours remains stationary.

I wake very early to catch the 5.40 a.m. into London, full of the usual pinstriped city workers who start the day ahead of the markets. Everyone is reading the *Financial Times* or emails on their BlackBerry. I follow their clacking brogues on to the Jubilee line: they alight at Canary Wharf, I catch a bus from North Greenwich to Woolwich and walk to the start of the Thames Path. The sodium street lamps extinguish one by one, to announce a new day.

Someone has built a nondescript sculpture from driftwood near the Thames Barrier control room. It is a flimsy structure in contrast to the brooding authority and permanence of an engineering marvel that will one day save London from catastrophic flooding. It looks like a sequence of seashell pillars, housing powerful rams that rotate the floodgates to vertical. Since 1984, those gates have protected London from minor flood events, but they stand ready for the day when spring high tides, a storm surge (low pressure) and wind combine to threaten the capital. The devastating North Sea floods of 1953 resulted in the loss of over 2,000 lives in Europe, the most terrible disaster since the war. The floods will come again, a statistical certainty when probabilities coincide.

The scene is sombre for the next few miles as I navigate through the chain-link-fenced industrial landscape. The clouds are low, and there is little colour to please the eye until I reach the Millennium Dome (opened on 31 December 1999). The O2, as it is now known, is a vast branded spaceship, blaring out neon sponsorship advertising from large plasma screens, in sharp contrast to the dull, drizzly overcast sky. The Thames Path crosses the meridian and heads west into maritime history at Greenwich. I could spend at least a day exploring the museums and the famous *Cutty Sark*, but I head for another dome which marks the entrance to a foot tunnel under the river. I descend, then ascend the spiral staircase on to the Isle of Dogs, a dockland area redeveloped beyond recognition. Private apartment blocks have spread like ivy along the north bank, and I have to keep a sharp eye to follow the acorn direction signs into Wapping. It is still early, and the capital has yet to wake.

> *Ne'er saw I, never felt, a calm so deep!*
> *The river glideth at his own sweet will:*
> *Dear God! The very houses seem asleep;*
> *And all that mighty heart is lying still!*
>
> – William Wordsworth,
> from 'Composed upon Westminster Bridge' (1802)

Tower Bridge comes into view, the first of many bridges I will see today; I'll count them as I go. Old Thames barges rest, unable to proceed further under sail. The Shard pierces the clouds in the background. I have a choice of north or south bank according to the guide. Choosing the latter, I enter the hurly-burly of London and walk past endless tourist attractions and commercial interests. Keeping up a good pace, I struggle to avoid collisions with smartphone zombies.

The city is in full swing now as I cross Westminster Bridge (the tenth in the list) and pass the Houses of Parliament – not your usual National Trail vista, but exhilarating architecture. Less so the bland property developments built purely for investment returns and positive yields. They have a displeasing aesthetic, adding little to London's heritage. Chelsea is another world altogether, a J.G. Ballard bubble-land of wealth dystopia (read *High-Rise*, published in 1975). I am pleased to reach Putney Bridge; the rowing club marks the start of the towpath and a return to normality. Someone has turned the volume down as I pass empty sports grounds and playing fields. Hammersmith Bridge, the twenty-first I have walked past today, wins my bridge-of-the-day award. It is beautiful, serene and timeless, spanning a slow-moving muddy Thames, flowing with hidden force downstream. The powerful movement of the water overwhelms the senses; you feel like a helpless animal on a floating log, vulnerable to capsize at any time.

> *Twenty bridges from Tower to Kew*
> *Wanted to know what the River knew,*
> *For they were young and the Thames was old,*
> *And this is the tale that the River told ...*
> — Rudyard Kipling, from 'The River's Tale' (1911)

I begin to tire. The relentless pavement wears you down. I find it easier to traverse a moorland than city streets. I reach Kew Bridge as the light begins to fade and make a decision to push on to Richmond, past Kew Gardens. I tap the Thames Path signpost after the railway bridge and head in the direction of the underground. I flop on to the train exhausted and can barely move when I get to Edgware Road. Just about everyone overtakes me as I walk to Marylebone, but I am not complaining; that was a thirty-mile day in eight and a half hours. I'm ahead on my marathon-a-day plan.

* * *

One week later I drive to Windsor to park my car and return by train to Richmond. I kiss my forefinger to touch the same post as if clocking in for work and turn towards Teddington. The lock marks the tidal limit of the river, now flowing downstream only, instead of breathing slowly, in and out, twice each day as the planet rotates. Many imposing eighteenth-century houses are competing with each other as fashionable country dwellings. They are all eclipsed by Henry VIII's opulent Hampton Court, a few miles upstream. One has to keep up with the Tudors, you know.

Victorian reservoirs and waterworks are evident as I approach Weybridge. I have to cross to the north bank to stay with the river.

I am grateful a ferry is running; the alternative route would have been a nuisance. I ring the bell on the quarter-hour to call the ferryman, as instructed by the arrival sign.

'How many walkers do you get at this time of year?' I ask.

'You're the first today, but it does get busy at weekends.'

'Is there any flooding ahead? I heard Ham Island can be a problem.'

'You should be OK into Windsor.'

This area suffered severe flooding in 2014; walking the path would have been impossible. A network of gravel pits, flood relief schemes and lakes provide a buffer to prevent London flooding, much to the dismay of the residents who pay the price to protect the city.

As I walk along the towpath, a cacophony of squawking ring-necked parakeets make themselves known. A non-native tropical species, there are many theories about their introduction: an escape from Shepperton Studios when John Huston was filming *The African Queen*; or perhaps the blame lies with Jimi Hendrix, who released a pair in the 1960s. In all probability, people have set free pet birds over decades, realising how cantankerous they can be. Now at pest levels, roosts can number in the thousands. Sunbury rugby club is one epicentre, but they spread along waterways, roosting and arguing in the willow trees. I wonder how far upstream they have migrated.

I cross under the M3 motorway and then the M25 after Staines, a sure sign that I am leaving Greater London for the countryside. I pass Runnymede and Magna Carta Island before approaching Old Windsor, a village that had its name downgraded when 'New' Windsor assumed the title after the construction of Windsor Castle in the eleventh century. Old Windsor served as a crossing point to the hunting forests many generations before the signing of that famous document in 1215.

The ducks are roosting in the fields as I finally approach the town. It is getting dark, and they do not appreciate a walker disturbing their bedtime. I take a shortcut to the car park, admiring the imposing walls of the castle above the fields. It has been a long, quiet day; I have only spoken with the ferryman. It dawns on me that he is the first person I have talked to on the Thames Path since I said goodbye to the bus driver at Woolwich, despite London's population of nine million people. Day two completed, I sit exhausted in the car before turning the key to start the engine for the drive home.

* * *

Ignoring the weather forecast, I drive to Shiplake station for the third section. Heavy sleet batters the platform shelter. I catch the train to Windsor Central via Twyford and Slough. I realise I have to double back a mile to touch the same signpost I left last week – not a good start. The purist in me is at odds with an eagerness to get up to walking temperature. It is a cold morning, and a mist lies low over the river, chilling the air. The towpath leading to Dorney is closed. A construction team are preparing for the 2012 Olympics. I divert inland via the redundant St Mary Magdalene Church at Boveney, now in the care of the Friends of Friendless Churches. It is a lonely, ancient, abandoned building – long past its prime, but beautifully set in peaceful surroundings that reson-ate with a religious purpose. Expensive riverside properties line the opposite bank at Bray. I reach Maidenhead to walk under the famous railway bridge built by Isambard Kingdom Brunel (he fea-tures a great deal in my walks). The sounding arch is the flattest, most extensive brick-built span in the world. I whistle loudly to hear the echo and get spooked as a train passes overhead, answer-ing my call unexpectedly with a loud toot. The M4 motorway bridge earlier was a different experience – a mono-tune chorus that assaults your ears.

I meet my wife unexpectedly at Bourne End, walking with a friend and her Labrador.

'Hello, dear, are you coming home for dinner?' she asks sarcastically.

'That's the plan. Not sure when.'

'Could you just … pop into the supermarket on the way home?'

'I'll try, I'm not sure how long I'll be.'

I quicken my pace, not wanting further instructions. Her friend's dog follows me, sensing a long walk is on offer. Why they have chosen this section for a walk and talk is a mystery. The wet, muddy clay is a nightmare to walk on. I have to adopt a cross-country skiing technique to make progress into Marlow using my walking poles for balance. The conditions get worse as I leave the town, where it would be inconsiderate to stop at a cafe in my muddy state. Some sections are almost impassable until I reach Temple Lock. I cross the wooden bridge, which pays tribute to Brunel's brick-built wonder. It is the longest hardwood span in Britain and beautifully constructed in teak.

The Flower Pot public house at Aston is a tempting stop. I can smell the wood-fire smoke, drifting in the still, cold air as I approach. It takes supreme willpower to carry on into Henley. If I stop now, the shops might close, and I'll be later for dinner. I understand the consequences of delay, so carry on past the rowing clubs into Henley and cross the bridge into the town, busy with smart shoppers and tourists. Shiplake is a few miles further south. This area is wealthy: one private house is so large it has a miniature railway in the garden. The day's walking is complete: twenty-six miles; three marathons in three weeks.

* * *

It is snowing a week later as I park my car again at Shiplake to walk to Shillingford. It soon clears, and the parakeets come out in force to rejoice. The business park at Reading is busy. I can see one bored worker staring idly out of the office window, perhaps following my progress and dreaming of freedom. The river and I sneak through the city together, oblivious to its commerce and industry, seeking the quieter countryside towards the Goring Gap. The path remains muddy and slippery; it is not a day to tiptoe around puddles, you can only battle through without concern for dirty trousers or boots. Road and rail links funnel up the river valley towards the ancient Ridgeway ferry crossings – the first at Whitchurch, over a bridge established in 1792. At that time, I would have paid half a penny ($\frac{1}{2}$d) to cross. The tariff board lists the options: horse, mare, gelding (laden or otherwise) – 2d; bull, ox, cow, steer – 2d; pig, sow, boar, sheep or lamb – ½d; and finally 2d per wheel for any carriage, not forgetting 2d for each horse drawing the vehicle. Pre-decimal (there were 240 pennies to a pound) a flock of fifty sheep would cost you 10p in new money. Thames Path walkers are free, but cars 50p; that's a ten-bob note (thank heavens for decimalisation in 1971).

I walk across the bridge at Goring, crossing the Ridgeway National Trail (stopping at the same shop for lunch) and following the east bank to Wallingford, one of the most besieged towns in England in the Middle Ages, whose fortifications protected a strategic ford across the river. I wish the ford still existed as the lock ahead is undergoing repairs and the path is closed. I have to take an unwelcome road diversion to Benson. It is a lonely, quiet section of river to Shillingford as darkness falls; the evening chill envelops me as a mist forms on the river surface. The trees lose shape and structure as the light fades. A bus takes me back to Henley, where a Christmas fayre has taken over the town. I walk through crowds and swarms of wide-eyed children to the station to catch a train back to Shiplake. Another tiring twenty-nine-mile day.

* * *

I am not sure walking in winter is such a good idea; the water level runs close to the path at times. Conditions are awkward, sapping energy from your legs where your feet cannot secure good grip. The weather is cold and usually wet, with an occasional wind to add to the misery. Yet the path is quiet, except for brave dog walkers with a garden hose at home. You can lose yourself in thoughts. If you find a harmonious pace, you can meditate. I believe memories of your journey persist more effectively when walking; any faster and your circuits are overloaded. I have noticed my ability to recall intricate details about my adventures, years after the walk; yet I can barely remember a motoring holiday a few years ago. It seems that our brains have evolved to operate at this speed, to navigate, to map, and to explore. Many therapists suggest you live in the present, but time cannot pass without the context of the past and anticipation of the future. It is like judging a symphony by a single note. Walking has the perfect tempo to absorb memories, as easy as remembering a tune – one that will become your story of the walk.

I have one free day before Christmas, so I return to Shillingford by car and set out north to Oxford. It is not the mud or the weather, but the solitude that is wearing me down. I have yet to meet a Thames Path walker to talk to, and only pass occasional dog walkers near car parks and villages. The river is getting narrow, but no less at risk of flooding. I walk past the iconic Wittenham Clumps, a prominent hillfort, topped by beech trees. This enigmatic landmark is a far more delightful sight than the Didcot power station cooling towers nearby.

> As up the hill with labr'ing steps we tread
> Where the twin Clumps their sheltering branches spread
> The summit gain'd, at ease reclining lay
> And all around the wide spread scene survey
> Point out each object and instructive tell
> The various changes that the land befell.
>
> – Joseph Tubb[3]

I pass Abingdon, another strategic crossing point, to reach Oxford. The river path ignores the city centre to reach Port Meadow, an old, unploughed grazing pasture. It is on this stretch of river that Lewis Carroll first imagined *Alice's Adventures in Wonderland*. I am wary of the rabbit holes, but by coincidence, a surreal situation follows: a German family have hired bicycles for the day and stop me to ask a question.

'Can we cycle to the source of the River Thames?' the father asks, holding a road map towards me as if I am a guide. I don't know where to start.

'Er, that is probably eighty kilometres away.' I translate from miles to metric. 'The paths will be very muddy, and the light will fade soon.'

'Oh. *Kein Problem*, we have bicycles,' he reassures me, '*mit* lights.'

I get out my map and trace the route for him, telling him what he might expect. I'm not going to judge their abilities.

'*Danke schön*.' He thanks me and leads his smartly dressed family northwards. They are up for an adventure. I make a bet that I will see them again soon.

An hour later, they pass me on their way back to Oxford. The father has a stoic expression, unlike his wife, who throws a knowing smile in my direction. I turn to see them ride away, each of them covered with the telltale strip of mud on their back and mudguards full of glutinous clay. I can imagine the conversation with the hire-shop manager – positively not printable here. Sure enough, the path conditions deteriorate as I reach Swinford Bridge, its isolation a delight, orphaned from modern transport infrastructure, but once a strategic crossing. The toll is ruinously expensive compared to Whitchurch: car – 5p; bus (sixteen or more seats) – 12p; lorry – 10p per axle. The bus to Shillingford costs £6.90, via Oxford city centre, without a bridge toll surcharge.

* * *

Thoughts of the path recede over Christmas and New Year. I lazily check the flood maps to realise that any plans to continue walking this winter are pointless. The river has burst its banks. So I put my energy into work until I stop to think about how to spend a few days the following summer to complete my ambition. Nothing stops a walk as effectively as a flood; it is hazardous to try to wade through when potholes and sunken branches lie unseen under the murky surface.

This time, train and car logistics defeat me, so I rummage around in the loft to get my backpacking kit together. The plan is to walk from Swinford Bridge to the source in two days. Two trains and one bus later I am rereading the toll bridge tariff – no increase this year, but drivers must wonder why they even bother to collect such small change. Inflation has long since overtaken the pricing covenant established decades ago. I expected the river to be busier

in summer, but now I am walking the outer reaches into Oxford-
shire. At Pinkhill Lock, I meet three men in a boat.

'Morning. Where's your dog?' I ask, referencing Jerome K.
Jerome's famous travelogue and the fourth member of their crew
– the fictitious Montmorency.

'We left him at home,' they reply, obviously having read *Three
Men in a Boat*.

'Are you camping?'

'Where we can. The landlords at the local pubs are very accommodating.'

It all looks very civilised. I can see crates of beer acting as ballast.
I wonder, have they considered impending disaster as they get
slowly drunk and their ballast gets lighter, something that could
precipitate a fall, as one of them stands to pee over the gunnels?
They have not rowed a boat before, but jolly good show for their
imagination and companionship.

> *Sweet Thames, run softly, till I end my song.*
> *The river bears no empty bottles, sandwich papers,*
> *Silk handkerchiefs, cardboard boxes, cigarette ends*
> *Or other testimony of summer nights.*
> — T.S. Eliot, from 'The Waste Land Part III –
> the Fire Sermon' (1922)[4]

The bridges are getting smaller and the paths more relaxed as I
dawdle into Lechlade. Rafaelle Monti's *Old Father Thames* sculpture rests at St John's Lock; he holds a spade looking over his
creation as if he dug the river personally. This monument was
once located at the source but was moved to avoid vandalism.
I cross the ha'penny bridge into town (once a toll bridge too) in
search of fish and chips. The campsite is nearby. I settle down to
rest a pair of legs unaccustomed to walking since winter, scoffing
my supper from a cardboard box.

Conscious of a long day ahead and the journey home, I depart
early. The path deviates from the river; the towpath is of little use
at the limit of navigation. Cricklade is an opportunity to stop for

lunch before the last section of the walk – a pretty village with an excellent bakery. My onward journey is thwarted by flooding as I approach Cotswold Water Park. I cross a flooded stile determined to walk through what seems like shallow water, but it soon becomes apparent that the ground is heavily waterlogged and riven with deep channels. I do not linger, extracting myself back to dry land to meet a farmer.

'Morning. How bad is the flooding?' I ask. 'Can I get through to the Thames Path?'

'No, mate. Your best bet is to take a taxi from Cricklade to Ewen. The area's been in flood all year. It's perilous to enter, there are ditches and channels you can't see.'

Someone who works the land ought to know, so I follow the disused railway line to a leisure centre, where I remove my mud-soaked boots, before walking into the reception.

'Do you have a taxi number I can call to get to Ewen, please?'

'I'll phone one for you,' the helpful young girl replies as tidily dressed fitness enthusiasts walk to the gym, glaring at the odd sight of a mud-soaked rambler.

Soon I am dropped off in a small village about five miles north-west. The taxi driver doesn't mind my dishevelled state and muddy boots that I tried to clean before he arrived. Embarking, I can see the shimmer of flooded lakes behind me. It is a disappointment to have taken a necessary shortcut, but I vow to return to tidy up loose ends one day.

The river is now a gentle chalk stream, with rushes and weed wafting gently in the crystal clear currents and disappearing into the trees until it opens up again into a delightful valley leading to Thames Head. I cross the Fosse Way, a Roman road, traversing cattle fields until I reach the end of the walk, marked by a coin-covered stone and fingerpost where *Old Father Thames* once rested. The spring is dry, having not flowed for decades (it does so again in the extreme floods of 2015). The sign reads, 'Thames Barrier – London – 184 miles'.

Seven marathons in seven days. I have half a mind to walk it again in the other direction – it is downhill, after all. Somehow that direction seems wrong: who would want to walk back to the city and get swept out to sea? I make my way to a deserted Kemble station and jump aboard to buy a ticket to London.

'Single to Slough, please.'

I am home in seventy minutes.

5

OFFA'S DYKE PATH

Distance: 177 miles
Days to complete: 10 days
Mileage so far: 1,086 miles

MARCHING IN THE WELSH MARCHES

It's a dangerous business, Frodo, going out your door.
You step onto the road, and if you don't keep your feet,
there's no knowing where you might be swept off to.
– Bilbo Baggins,
The Fellowship of the Ring, J.R.R. Tolkien

The plan is to walk both Offa's Dyke and Glyndŵr's Way in one continuous journey, backpacking with my indestructible and heavy gear that serves me well for short trips. I will camp as much as I can to keep costs down, so my pack weighs more than usual. The entire route is over 300 miles.

Before I have time to doubt my sanity, a series of perfectly connecting trains leave me standing on the platform at Chepstow, wondering what on earth I am doing. Have I taken a reckless first step only to pay the consequences later? I dawdle to the start of Offa's Dyke at Sedbury and gaze over the Bristol Channel to the Severn Bridge, contemplating the journey ahead. A sign congratulates me on completing the walk, somewhat prematurely. I hope to find a similar sign 177 miles further north at Prestatyn (plus another 132-mile loop around Glyndŵr's Way).

A quiet but straightforward campsite is an ideal starting point. A field of rabbits keep me company as I cook, keeping the grass cut short, but hopefully they will not nibble my guy ropes when I am not looking. Waking early, a pair of black spaniel puppies join me for breakfast. They have escaped from the farmhouse and scare the rabbits into their burrows. These bundles of joy come into my tent, sniffing for food and wanting to play with a new camper in their garden. It is a challenge to eat breakfast and pack up as they compete for my attention; they are sniffing every possession I own.

'Luuuucie! Saaaally!' comes a loud call.

In a flash, they run to the farmhouse door. I follow to pay my fees and meet the farmer's wife.

'It's my first day on Offa's Dyke. These two characters want to come along, I think.'

'Lovely, aren't they? In a few months, they could join you, after their jabs. They seem to like you, and they'll need exercise.'

'Me too, how much for the pitch?' I ask.

'Five quid OK?'

A pair of mad spaniels would be more than I could cope with, but the thought of having companions appeals to me; it can get lonely on the trail. I head without them into the woods towards Tintern Abbey, their collars held as I turn the corner. Spaniels must cover three times the distance of a walker following a straight line – a breed that will search every corner and crevice. A 1,000-mile walk would be an epic adventure for a four-footed friend.

The views from Wintour's Leap are stunning; this vast meander in the River Wye is still tidal at this point, strangely moving upstream against the downstream flow, seawater mixing with fresh. The deciduous trees cling to the sheer cliff faces, growing from any crevice. In a month they will change into a stunning palette of red, brown and gold, as autumn arrives. Offa did not need to build a defensive barrier here, but the traces of the ramparts are discernible in the woodland ahead, hinting at the scale of the structures required.

The Devil's Pulpit reveals the full beauty of the Wye Valley, a stunning viewpoint overlooking Tintern Abbey: the first Cistercian abbey in Wales, which survived for some 400 years before the dissolution in 1536.

> Five years have past; five summers, with the length
> Of five long winters! and again I hear
> These waters, rolling from their mountain-springs
> With a soft inland murmur. – Once again
> Do I behold these steep and lofty cliffs,
> That on a wild secluded scene impress
> Thoughts of more deep seclusion; and connect
> The landscape with the quiet of the sky.
> The day is come when I again repose
> Here, under this dark sycamore, and view
> These plots of cottage-ground, these orchard-tufts,
> Which at this season, with their unripe fruits,
> Are clad in one green hue, and lose themselves
> 'Mid groves and copses. Once again I see
> These hedge-rows, hardly hedge-rows, little lines
> Of sportive wood run wild: these pastoral farms,
> Green to the very door; and wreaths of smoke
> Sent up, in silence, from among the trees!
> With some uncertain notice, as might seem
> Of vagrant dwellers in the houseless woods,
> Or of some Hermit's cave, where by his fire
> The Hermit sits alone.

> – William Wordsworth,
> from 'Lines Composed a Few Miles above Tintern Abbey,
> On Revisiting the Banks of the Wye during a Tour' (1798)

Tintern Abbey is a glorious ruin, sitting peacefully at rest on the east bank, seemingly undisturbed by the tourists. On the descent into Brockweir, I meet a walker, Jonathan, who is about to complete the trail. He is ecstatic, knowing he will finish shortly.

'Not far now,' I say. 'Just a few miles.'

'Phew, yes. I'll be glad to get home. The weather's been good, but the trail's much harder than I expected,' Jonathan puffs, resting on his walking poles.

'You look a bit muddy too.'

'There are a few sections of slippery mud, but passable. Then wait until you get to the Clwydians – they're hard going when the wind's up,' he adds.

His boots, trousers and backpack have an artistic pattern of mud in the style of a Jackson Pollock painting. Deep blacks fade to grey splashes from foot to shoulder, a record of the soil type along the border path. He is smiling and practically running for his train home.

The descent into Brockweir reminds me of an epic finesse my wife-to-be played on me midway through a Wye Valley backpacking trip in the late 1980s. After loosening my resolve with a few pints in the local pub, she befriended a taxi driver while I popped to the loo. Before I knew it, they had loaded both packs into the boot, and my wife sat on the rear seat, demanding, 'Are you coming or not? I'll feed you to my relatives if you don't.'

I had no choice (she has an extensive Welsh family originating from Newport) – the consequences were clear; they are very protective of their flock. We married a few years later, and I came to appreciate her style and crazy family – a counterbalance to my task-oriented disposition and introvert nature.

The walking would have been easy for her today, as I hug the west bank of the River Wye for a few miles. I am straining my neck upwards to study the village of Llandogo, nestled in the woodland. It is very picturesque, a community untroubled by time, living in a literal and social microclimate. I reach Bigweir and ascend the ridgeline again through pleasant and contemplative woodland, picking my way through the trees into Lower Redbrook. The woman at the village store heats a pie for lunch, an alternative to visiting the Boat Inn opposite, somewhere I have been before. I know if I set foot inside my afternoon will pass by, and another 200-metre ascent to the Kymin monument will extract a heavy price from non-compliant legs and a weak resolve. It is the right choice:

the views over Monmouth and into the Black Mountains are superb. Besides, I might find one of my wife's cousins at the bar.

I'm in the heart of the Welsh Marches now, the area of land that separates England from Wales, once guarded by the Marcher lords of England. Monmouth is a busy town, sat on a peninsula between the Monnow and Wye rivers, connected by ancient bridges. The campsite is cosy, with a popular onsite cafe serving fish and chips.

I depart early into a heavy mist lying low on the landscape. The path heads west, deeper into the unspoilt Welsh country-side alongside the River Trothy, punctuated with picturesque villages with long names: Llanfihangel Ystum Llewern, Llantilio Crossenny and Llanvetherine. The sleepy lanes and paths lead to the strategically placed Norman stronghold, White Castle, built almost 1,000 years ago to protect trading routes to Hereford. It is a massive structure, an architecture that a schoolchild would recognise on a beach, complete with moats and drawbridge. It is an excellent place to stop and admire the deep green rolling farm-land, before descending to Llangattock Lingoed and into Pandy on the A465.

The campsite is busy at the weekend. It is like Moonbase Alpha: enormous tents with extensions and interconnecting tunnels; windscreen enclosures surrounding barbecues; tennis swing balls standing idle, yet ringing unused space – all meant to establish territorial boundaries. The occupants have been drinking all day and are holding an *X Factor*/karaoke-style singing competition (for the best song or worst song, I cannot tell). I avoid the campsite pub – it is a scene of devastation, with kids running amok. I walk to the Skirrid Mountain Inn instead, reputed to be the oldest inn in Wales (a mere 900 years). It claims to be a rallying point for Owain Glyndŵr's men, and a courtroom with adjoining execution hall where they hanged 180 criminals. It has a justifiable reputation for ghosts and hauntings – all good for business.

The campsite is snoring harmoniously at 7 a.m., but I am keen to climb on to Hatterrall Ridge, having seen the heavy rain forecast for late afternoon. Touching the first trig pillar, I have a further ten miles to Hay Bluff along an exposed ridgeline that marks the boundary between England and the Brecon Beacons National Park in Wales. It is windy, cold but bright, with extensive views. I wrap up warm and relax into a pace which will maximise the enjoyment of the scene to the left and right of me. I'm low-level flying at 500 metres above the Golden Valley and a labyrinth of English countryside lanes and villages. Underfoot, flagstones have been placed to counter erosion, and provide useful navigational aids, gently leading me to a high point of 700 metres, not marked by any cairn. My head is just touching the cloud base. Another fifty metres higher, and I would not see a thing. I meet a very young lad on a small motocross bike, his helmet too large to fit him. It is a surreal sight – the first person I have met in three hours. I try to ask him if he is OK, but he is too absorbed in riding through the rocks to notice me. Moments later, two adults appear on trail bikes, and I wave to them to explain what I have seen.

'Are you looking for a young lad on a red bike?' I ask.

'Thanks, yes. Archie's tough to catch nowadays, just loves it up here. He ran out of petrol last time, so we put in just enough fuel to stop him going too far.'

There is no doubting Archie's sense of adventure.

On reaching Hay Bluff, the view opens out northward. I can see the border town of Hay-on-Wye below. I dive off the bluff and bounce down sheep-nibbled spongy grass into the township. This is a haven for second-hand book lovers, so I ask to leave my backpack in a cafe while I browse the bookshelves to use up time before walking out to a campsite across the bridge. The site is tents only, with quite a few Duke of Edinburgh Award campers and some guy in a bivvy bag who looks a bit exposed, like a caterpillar cocoon on the roadside.

Offa's border-control path follows the River Wye for a few miles before heading inland to Newchurch, never moving far from the boundary between Wales and England. There is not much evidence of the dyke as I traverse a series of hillocks and vales through a network of farms and fields that would take a lifetime to learn. Ascending Hergest Ridge, I meet a middle-aged man at a gate.

'Afternoon, how's it going?' I ask.

'Not too well. I've had enough of walking; I want to go home,' he declares, almost in tears. 'I fancy a pint and I want to sit in front of the TV and watch football.'

'Gosh.'

I'm taken aback by the outburst of emotion; he probably hasn't seen anyone for a while. He has been walking for ten days along Offa's Dyke, and loneliness has overtaken him. We chat for a while about his homesickness – something that gets to me after a few weeks. But not this bad.

'It's hard to get a phone signal in the evenings, and I'm bored of walking in these muddy fields,' he adds.

I try to persuade him to finish the path, but he is adamant that he will look for public transport in Hay-on-Wye and find the shortest way home.

'I'm sure there'll be a bus to Hereford, then you can pick up a train from there,' I suggest. 'Why not just take it day by day and see how far you get?'

He seems better after a chat, but I am quite shocked that his condition has resulted in him deciding to finish the walk early. I wonder what my limit would be. When would I throw in the towel and find the quickest route home? Here is evidence that long-distance walking is a mental challenge, not just a physical one.

Mike Oldfield (of *Tubular Bells* fame) wrote his second album, *Hergest Ridge*, nearby and named it after the gentle ridge leading me into the village of Kington. It was once a Victorian racecourse, commanding superb views over Radnorshire. The campsite in town is part of the sports complex next to the football ground and bus station. It has the rare marvel of a centrifugal drying machine, so I spend the next hour washing clothes and spinning them dry. A woman in a caravan kindly makes me a cup of tea as I hang my base layers to dry.

The town is busy, with barely a national-brand chain shop evident. Butchers, bakers and grocers are competing on the high street in a scene that has long since disappeared elsewhere with the arrival of supermarkets. It is nice to be able to buy what I need without swearing at multipacks of apples at the Co-op. Kington is proudly English and a 'centre for walkers', with an organised walking festival in April. One walk piques my interest: the 'eight pubs challenge' over twenty-six miles in one day. The taxis must be busy for those who get waylaid, as my wife would know.

Offa's Dyke becomes more evident after I pass Burfa Camp, an Iron Age hillfort that has been consumed by woodland. The path diverges from the modern border and follows the earth embankment for several miles, but it is hard to walk along, with frequent rabbit and badger holes – mostly hidden. Even though I am careful, my leg disappears down one. I arrest my fall instinctively with my walking poles and avert any severe damage. These marvels have been with me for a few years now, and I have developed a natural walking rhythm with them. My knee is sore, but I can walk.

The dyke must have taken considerable effort to build: it is up to eight feet tall with a similar-depth ditch facing west. It is post-Roman, assumed to have been made in the eighth century to defend the kingdom of Mercia from Powys and named after Offa, the Anglo-Saxon king. The sections around Knighton are impressive, giving you a real sense of scale for Europe's most significant defensive earthwork. I descend into Knighton, which lies alongside the River Teme and is home to the Offa's Dyke Association.

The ranger is very helpful. I now have to make a decision to turn west on to Glyndŵr's Way or stay on Offa's Dyke walking north. I want to do both paths in one continuous journey, and a study of train timetables suggests I walk to Welshpool (via Glyndŵr's) and catch a train back to Knighton. Accommodation and campsites are a rarity if I turn into the interior of Wales. Still, he has a list of every option on a photocopied sheet of A4 for me. I make my mind up: go west.

I wander about town before walking to the campsite and come across manna from heaven, in the form of a simple restaurant serving a fixed three-course meal for £8.50. It is almost French in concept: a set menu, friendly matron front of house, husband in the kitchen cooking everything from scratch. It is delicious. Suitably refreshed, I search for provisions for several nights' camping. A local directs me to the petrol station. On entering, I pass through a simple door with low expectations but then walk into Tuffins supermarket, an Aladdin's cave of wonder that sells just about everything in the style of a Welsh Marches IKEA and Aldi/Lidl store combined in one.

The campsite is quiet until a group of young university students turn up, walking Offa's Dyke north to south. They have scraped together whatever gear they could find and are having a good time. It is not often you see such a young independent group. We chat for a while, and I let them know where I have camped over the past week. It is a cold night: an overnight frost has frozen my tent solid; it remains erect after I take out all the pegs. I carry it into the barn to defrost, like an umbrella, holding the central pole. After a concurrent breakfast and packing session, I leave Offa's Dyke and head out on to Glyndŵr's Way (see Chapter 6).

* * *

I return to Knighton the following spring, arriving via Shrewsbury on the mainline train; from there I join the Heart of Wales railway line, connecting Shropshire to South Wales – a single-carriage service. It takes a full two minutes to announce all the stations to Swansea (first in Welsh, then in English) and hours to reach Knighton. I'm not bothered: the gossip and chatter onboard are so noisy I can't hear the carriage rattling along; everyone has so much to catch up on. It is a lovely community; everyone knows each other. I am drawn into the conversation.

'Where are you going, then, with all that gear?' A good icebreaker.

'Oooh, it's lovely walking there, especially at this time of year.' Others chip in, and so the talking flows until they have my life story.

'Your wife is from Caerleon? Oooh, my sister lives there. Do you know her?'

'Er, no.'

'Never mind, you can meet her in the pub most nights.'

'Ah yes. That's a lovely pub, all posh nowadays, lovely landlady, but getting pricey.'

'You mean the Walnut Tree? Had a lovely meal there once,' says her friend.

'Oooh no, that's in Abergavenny.'

It is a small world, getting smaller by the minute.

The chatter dies down, and we enjoy the views of the countryside. It is a lovely train service full of beautiful people, open and approachable, in such sharp contrast to a soulless London commuter train.

'Don't forget to stop at Pantyffynnon, will you?' one woman asks (it is a request stop).

'No problem, Wendy,' notes the guard.

Quite a few passengers are using the service to link up linear walks in the Shropshire and Powys hills. I alight at Knighton in good time to walk to Newcastle, eight miles away. Touching the clock tower in the town square, I walk north, up into the Shropshire Hills and along a very well-preserved section of the dyke. Newborn lambs are bouncing around, finding their feet. It is such a pleasure to see them as North Wales suffered severe winter snowstorms in March, arriving just after peak lambing time. Many mothers did not survive, buried in the deep snow. Carcasses still lie in pockets of snowfall, behind walls where they tried to shelter – life and death side by side, separated by just a few weeks.

I spend a few minutes at the trig pillar which marks the highest elevation on the walk, drinking in the views over the Teme Valley, which weaves its way through the rolling green hills, marking the border. I break my descent to a B road to phone the White Horse Inn at Clun; they said they could pick me up, but I struggle to get a mobile signal in the valley. I manage a garbled message; a few moments later, a battered Volvo arrives driven by a ruddy-faced landlord. He is not fussed about my muddy boots, he is used to tired walkers. 'Are you Martyn? Hop in.'

The bar is full of life, a real buzzy atmosphere: not so loud you can't hear, not so quiet as to be boring – just right. It is St George's Day and the Clun community (being in England) are celebrating with a special steak pie menu, washed down with foaming pints of real ale. A rocket scientist (seriously) brews beer behind the pub, having found his calling. A couple of pints of Citadel (5.9% ABV) is more than enough to promote a deep sleep in my room above the bar, the conversation still humming below. I grew up in a public house, my bedroom also above the public bar. The familiar sounds of punters talking are comforting and homely, in a way that would annoy almost anyone else.

I get a lift after breakfast, a combined school run/walker drop-off, into Newcastle. The bill for the night: £44 for accommodation, meal, beer and transport – not bad at all. Crossing the River Clun, I'm back on the distinctive Offa's Dyke again, weaving its way around the hills and the occasional village. Signs of a bygone era are evident: an old petrol pump lies abandoned outside the Blue Bell Hotel – 74p a gallon!

It is tough going until I reach Montgomery Vale, lying beneath the town of the same name, perched on a crag with an imposing castle. The structure is an example of a defensive network built by the Marcher lords to protect the historic county of Montgomery-shire, overlooking the mighty River Severn. I meet the trail officer as I enter woodland above Forden. He says he is married to the Glyndŵr's Way warden. We chat for ages about the path. Today he is dealing with a complaint.

'Someone's putting up unauthorised signposts along the trail. One says, "Please minimise use of the public path"; another says, "Do not enter the woods".'

The suspicion falls on the Leighton Estate, seeking to divert (or scare) walkers away from the shooting grounds.

'The path is a legal right of way, and someone's unhappy that it runs through their land,' he says. 'Let me know if you have any trouble ahead.' He hands me his phone number.

The woods are full of tame pheasants, so docile you could pick them up. Bred to be shot, it can hardly be a sport when they chirp up to your feet, seeking food. In the woods, an abandoned hydro-electric dam has seen better days, an early nineteenth-century experiment in eco-friendly energy, designed to power farm mach-inery, but now a murky duck pond. The estate appears to be for commercial interest now, and the signs I had been warned about discourage my progress, but I know my rights and the route ahead. I head up towards Beacon Ring, an early Iron Age ring fort, preserved and unexcavated, dominating the Long Mountain ridgeline above Welshpool. It is a beautiful place to survey the landscape before descending into the border town. The spot is ideal for mobile communications masts, but they are ugly and spoil the skyline.

At the last farm, a sign of a different kind warns me about the local sheepdog. 'Tell her to get off home,' it says. 'If you allow her to follow, she will do so all the way to Buttington.' The dog likes a long walk, it seems. I meet the owner a few yards further on, who tells me it is common to get phone calls to collect her, the phone number etched on her dog tag. My experience of sheepdogs over the years tells me this intelligent animal has the better of its owner and knows the boundaries of passive-aggressive behaviour.

The farmhouse B&B in Welshpool is a delight. A deep iron bath occupies the middle of a huge bathroom. I have to climb up into the bed, the mattress is so thick. The breakfast room is a traditional Welsh dining room, complete with a period oak dresser, Spode plates and jugs. Photos record several generations of farmers; a clear resemblance to the present owner is unmistakable. The hosts are friendly, their dog is happy, but the cat ignores me, preferring to chase the sparrows in the hedgerow outside.

In the morning, I catch a train to Machynlleth to complete Glyndŵr's Way and do not return to Offa's Dyke for another month (for reasons that will be clear in the next chapter). I have a wallet full of train tickets now, accumulated when I realise a return ticket is usually only £1 more than a single.

* * *

After another long train journey, I'm back in Welshpool. It is lunchtime as I head north once again, alongside the serene Montgomery canal, patiently restored by a local trust. The counterbalance bridges, signposts, locks and road bridges evoke another age. It is gentle walking until the path diverts to the River Severn along the floodplain. Flood banks stand defiantly, but are no defence against severe flood events; this route would be quite impossible at such times. The cattle have churned up the mud, making progress difficult. The tidemark of broken trees and rubbish indicates how high the river level can reach: several metres above where I am walking now. I feel more comfortable to be back alongside the canal, which runs above the river level, crossing the River Vyrnwy later, on a stone-built aqueduct, before entering the border town of Llanymynech.

The Bradford Arms is comfortable and full of character. I decided not to bring a tent this time, travelling much lighter than before. I couldn't see many campsites in the second half of the walk and didn't want to wild camp. I value the company and interaction with the local hosts, who offer a more in-depth insight into the landscape. As a single walker, I am more approachable and find it very easy to strike up a conversation, particularly in Wales.

The cafe at the crossroads is open for business at 8 a.m. The young girl builds a monster baguette for me that I have to strap to my backpack; it won't fit inside.

'Kids all off to school, I see.' The roads outside have two groups of kids, dressed in different school uniforms.

'Yes, some are off to Oswestry [England] and the others are off to Welshpool [Wales]. The English kids have to pay for their bus service; the Welsh don't,' she says.

It is a multicultural town, where the border runs right down The Street, as the main road is known. One pub claims the border runs right through the bar, handy when the old licensing laws meant the pubs in Wales had to close early on a Sunday. Everyone would lift their seats and shuffle along for another pint in England.

Offa's Dyke would have run through the town, running up to the ridgeline in the hills to the north. I ascend to a quarry, passing a sign that declares a connection with Charles Darwin: he measured the angle of my path accurately while building a map for his geological studies in the area. This accurate calculation led to him securing passage on HMS *Beagle* in 1831 – the start of many epic journeys. The quarry was also the scene of an explosion in 1868 when a rather enthusiastic Thomas Savin used too much dynamite to loosen rock. The tremendous blast showered the surrounding area with large boulders, causing much damage. Residents in Welshpool, ten miles away, wondered what had happened.

I leave the history lesson behind me to follow the escarpment into the Welsh landscape. After endless hillocks, the ground flattens out; I have reached the Victorian racecourse above Oswestry, long since abandoned, but with commanding views. Descending, I'm lost in a maze of pastoral fields and villages along the borderlands until I arrive in Pentre, too early to check in to the B&B. I have enough time to follow a canal into Froncysyllte, stopping to eat the other half of my baguette and to study the stunning Cefn Mawr viaduct and Pontcysyllte aqueduct that span the River Dee. Car traffic must descend to the valley floor around hairpin bends, and give primacy to rail and canal traffic, which bridges a gap some forty metres above the valley. The aqueduct is an impressive feat of engineering, completed by Thomas Telford in 1805; it took ten years to build the eighteen-arched stone and cast iron structure. It is the longest aqueduct in Britain and the highest canal aqueduct in the world. What I find incredible is the laser-sharp accuracy of the alignment of the stone, still faithful after 200 years. It cost £47,000 to build.

You need a head for heights to walk along the towpath and adjust your understanding to see boats gliding gently along the narrow canal, as if suspended in the air. It is a wholly unforgettable walking experience. I visit the museum for coffee and cake, before traversing the aqueduct for a second time to my B&B for the evening. My host is terrific; she shares a home-cooked evening meal, and we chat for a while. Now in the later stages of her life, she was, and still is, a beautiful woman, whose sideboard photographs tell of a glamorous life as a model and Cordon Bleu chef. She is my Lady of Llangollen (the legendary Ladies of Llangollen were two well-to-do Irish women, who enjoyed each other's company and settled in the area in the late eighteenth century).

A stream, to mingle with your favourite Dee,
Along the Vale of Meditation flows;

So styled by those fierce Britons, pleased to see
In Nature's face the expression of repose;
Or haply there some pious hermit chose
To live and die, the peace of Heaven his aim;
To whom the wild sequestered region owes
At this late day, its sanctifying name.
Glyn Cafaillgaroch, in the Cambrian tongue,
In ours, the Vale of Friendship, let this spot
Be named; where, faithful to a low-roofed cot,
On Deva's banks, ye have abode so long;
Sisters in love – a love allowed to climb,
Even on this earth, above the reach of Time!

– William Wordsworth,
'To the Lady E.B. and the Hon. Miss P.' (1824)

I take the lower river crossing to see the full beauty of the aqueduct, and rejoin Offa's Dyke to skirt beneath Eglwyseg Mountain. The views down the valley to Llangollen are stupendous, framing Castell Dinas Brân, sitting derelict on a natural promontory above the River Dee. It ceased to function as a castle in 1277. A lonely manor house nestles below World's End, a final secluded valley before open moorland. The path turns west towards Llandegla, through forests in a state of harvest. The tracks are ideal for mountain-bike recreation; I have to stand to one side to see lines of bikes curving around berms, steeply descending to the road below. It looks like a lot of fun.

I wait outside the post office for it to open after lunch until a passer-by tells me it is closed all day Wednesday. So I rummage through my pack and devour anything of calorific value to power my ascent into the Clwydian Range, to summit at Moel y Plâs. The views are excellent, but I have passed my accommodation in the excitement of entering the mountains, so I double back. A vast Airbus Super Guppy climbs into the sky from the airport manufacturing site in Broughton, North Wales, delivering wings to the factory in Toulouse.

I'm staying at a centre for fishing and horse riding, with a room available for hire. I can buy a simple microwave frozen meal and make myself comfortable in a self-contained cottage with TV and kitchen; it is the only option in the area. The host makes sure I am warm and fed, with a practical service attitude, ideal for managing horses. It is an unfussy approach, which I like; no airs and graces here. The forecast tomorrow confirms a strengthening north-westerly wind and heavy rain, so an early night seems sensible rather than a late-night film on TV.

I wrap up with just about all my clothing to face rain that has turned to sleet and hail at this elevation. It is a full-body shot blast, cleaning any trace of dirt from my clothing and boots. The hail-stones reach pea-sized dimensions, and hurt like hell when delivered at fifty miles per hour – horizontally. A pair of ski goggles would help, but a buff pulled tight to meet my hat suffices. I peer out through a slit in the fabric, the cap of my peak dipped low to catch the worst of it. Fortunately, the conditions ease as I reach the A494, to meet a group of walkers sat in their cars, wondering if they should even start the day. One of them winds down the window for a weather report.

'Southwesterly 7, veering northwesterly, decreasing 6 at times,' I jest. The mountain forecast for Snowdonia would be more ac-curate, but we can all see the weather is terrible.

'It's not too bad,' I add, with typical English understatement. 'It appears to be easing, and I haven't had hail for an hour.'

The conditions do improve, and I have first-hand sight of any incoming squall as I lean into the headwind. The sun briefly pokes through, shining a torch beam on the land below, lighting it up in vivid electric green. The sunbeams race across the ground as the clouds move. Another appears briefly and then is gone, as if in a time-lapse video. It is an exhilarating experience summiting a sequence of peaks and hillforts until I reach the pinnacle at Moel Famau, crowned with a Jubilee tower built to commemorate the golden jubilee of George III in 1810. 'Georgia III Brittaniarum Regi, Pio Justo Patri Patrio Comitatus, Denbigh et Flint, Jubilantus Posuere, 25 Octobris, Anno Domino 1809', it reads. Work has started to restore the base, which is collapsing into a heap of rubble –

hardly surprising given the weather conditions it has to endure.

Looking north, I can see a vast array of wind turbines earnestly doing their job. A clear path descends to Moel Arthur, and one more fort at Penycloddiau before the final farm track runs into Bodfari and the A541. A South African Boer goat herd run towards me and poke their heads through a fence. They like the taste of my bootlaces. I'm used to sheep getting out of the way, but these goats are inquisitive. They are boisterous and would happily eat my clothing and gear given half a chance. I search for food in the village, but there is nothing. I rest in the church lychgate, absorbing a rare spell of sunshine. A van turns up full of flowers; there is to be a wedding tomorrow, and it is time to decorate, so I get out of the way and climb a steep hill to my B&B, which turns out to be a cosy static caravan in the driveway.

'Anywhere to eat around here?'

'The Downing Arms down the hill does a good steak,' she says, knowing I have just climbed the hill.

My legs are sore after a tough day, but I must eat. The food is excellent and the hosts welcoming. It is a busy place on a Thursday night; I'm lucky to get a table. I drink one more pint than usual; the climb home hurts like hell on a full stomach, in a tired body, somehow supported by uncooperative stiff leg muscles.

It is my last day, and I'm up early to time my departure to a train that will connect at Chester without a long delay. The mountains are behind me as the landscape turns to the usual pastoral scenery. I'm marching along, wanting to reach Prestatyn quickly, crossing busy roads connecting North Wales to England. It is a pleasant relief to walk along the final escarpment with views out to the Irish Sea and the town below.

I can see my final destination, arrow-straight through the town. Golden National Trail acorns adorn each lamppost as if to celebrate a final last mile. I can see *Dechrau a Diwedd* – a sculpture that represents the 'beginning and end'. A stylised representation of the sun sits atop three curved pillars, signifying the sunset of the journey if you look west. I should dip my boots into the sea at this point, but it is still blowing a strong onshore force 7, and I would get soaked. A sign points to Chepstow, 177 miles south, but there is no congratulation notice I can see.

That same wind pushes me to the station, only for me to read that they have cancelled my train. I can see a fire to the east, and also notice subsequent train cancellations appearing on the board. The ticket desk knows nothing, but I conclude that this will take a few hours to resolve. To save costs, I ask if anyone wants to share a taxi ride to Chester. No one dares to share with a bedraggled, soaked, muddy walker (or maybe the smell put them off), so I make the call to take it.

It is not as expensive as I thought, and later announcements at Chester station confirm I made the right decision. Buses are non-existent, unable to compete with rail, and I did not fancy a night looking for accommodation in Prestatyn at a late hour.

6

GLYNDŴR'S WAY

Distance: 132 miles
Days to complete: 7 days
Mileage so far: 1,263 miles

TIME WARP

I haven't got any special religion this morning.
My God is the God of Walkers. If you walk hard enough,
you probably don't need any other God.

— Bruce Chatwin

I walk around my tent, removing every peg, but the tent remains erect. The dew has frozen it to a dome; I dare not fold it flat in case I break the fabric. After a few moments in a nearby barn, it collapses as it warms in the morning sun and I make breakfast. Camping near a river in a steep-sided valley is not always a good idea as the temperature is a few degrees lower. You have to wait for the early morning sun to crest the eastern hills for the warmth to return.

I have just completed Offa's Dyke from Chepstow to Knighton, and it is time to head into deepest Wales and Glyndŵr's Way. The university students on the campsite are sleeping in, a teenage two hours out of phase with my body clock. They will walk later into the afternoon, but I prefer the early morning light of a new day. I touch Knighton clock tower to symbolically mark the start of the walk at the exact moment it chimes 8 a.m. It has marked the hours every day since 1872, a model of reliability. Now I am heading due west to the Irish Sea and Machynlleth on the Dyfi estuary.

Immediately the landscape feels different. It is similar to Offa's Dyke and yet I sense I have been transported back in time, 100 or 200 years – all modern visual cues filtered out. The buildings are older and unrestored, the shape of the fields and the woodland is unchanged by commercial interests, and industrial and mechanical noise has gone. A new illusion appears as a rainbow forms. Now sun and showers float across a *Teletubbies* landscape of rolling hills and smiling-baby sunshine bathed in a vivid palette of green, blue and yellow. This day is not a day to rush, but to walk in a dream-like state, with no urgency, destination, goal or plan.

On the subject of surreal worlds, I recall that after 7.5 million years, the supercomputer Deep Thought in *The Hitchhiker's Guide to the Galaxy* calculates the answer to the meaning of life: 'forty-two'. Douglas Adams then describes how the Earth (an even bigger organic computer) goes on to calculate the long-forgotten question, revealed in Arthur Dent's subconscious mind, 'What do you get if you multiply six by nine?', to which he comments, 'I always thought there was something fundamentally wrong with the universe' (although six times nine in base thirteen is correct). Yet, what I did not realise is that forty-two degrees is the angle that reflects sunlight from a water droplet to form a rainbow on a showery day. Such beauty in mathematics, I thought, until I later read that forty-two is considered the zenith of a mid-life crisis. At least that is behind me. The things that can occupy your mind as you walk; I check in to ensure I have not developed a Tinky Winky persona.

The signposts gently remind me of the direction I should take. Not only have I subtracted a hundred years from time, but time is running more slowly too. Nothing seems rushed; even the birds are relaxed. A buzzard stares me down before gently lifting into the air from its perch; it is as close an encounter as I have ex-perienced recently, always magical.

After reaching sleepy Llangunllo, I cross both river and rail to ascend into a sequence of hills with unbroken views across this new landscape. I am now drawn deeper into Mid Wales and yet remain close to the English border, which intrudes, uninvited, into a land of Welsh place names. I reach Felindre and my camp-site for the night: an open paddock attached to a multifunctional holiday farm that caters for riders, cyclists and walkers. The owner brings me a tray of tea and cake as I pitch my tent and asks what I plan to eat tonight.

'I have another guest staying in our B&B. I was going to offer him a lift to the local pub at seven,' he says. 'Do you want to join him?'

How can I refuse? After a wash and gear check, I put on what glad rags I can find and meet Kevin, a GP from Burnley, also walking Glyndŵr's Way. The Radnorshire Arms, just a few miles east, is a welcoming local community pub, serving real ale and homemade food. It is an opportunity to address a calorie deficit, so I do not hold back: lamb shanks and pavlova.

Kevin is delightful company, and it is great to get my vocal cords working again; walking long distances can be lonely.

'I didn't expect to meet anyone walking Glyndŵr's Way at all,' I say.

'I don't have your free time to walk the entire way, just a decent section in a week.'

'Why Glyndŵr's?' I ask. 'It isn't the most popular National Trail.'

'I'm trying to get as far away as I can from my stressful work, somewhere with no chance of meeting anyone I might know.'

Walking is the tonic he needs. He is envious of the free time I have to attempt my odyssey in Wales. I'm proud of the decision I made a few years ago to quit full-time work. He has considered locum work too, but has too much at stake in a practice partnership. A succession of pints leads to more philosophical dialogue about work–life balance until our host arrives to give us a lift back to the farm.

Too much drinking means getting up in the night for a pee, standing naked in sockless boots, shivering and stargazing. The owls hoot in protest, unable to comprehend this strange naked creature in their midst. Returning to the warm sleeping bag,

I curse myself for forgetting my brother's fiftieth birthday; I'll call him when I get a mobile signal, which might be a few days in this part of the world. No wonder the local phone boxes still have phones in them in each village, yet to be converted into love shacks and book exchange libraries as they have been elsewhere.

The morning is wet, misty and deeply overcast, in a manner that leaves no doubt that this state will remain for the day. I hunker down and plod along the paths and tracks that lead to remote hills and farms, now unquestionably Welsh in character. A community shop in Llanbadarn Fynydd is a welcome sight and vastly improves my lunch options. I ascend again into misty hills and promptly get lost, climbing an unnecessary hill. I can see a walker a few hundred metres below me; this must be the path I need. I descend grumpily to the corner of the field to join Kevin, who set out from Felindre after a full Welsh breakfast.

'Where are you off to?' he asks with a cheeky grin.

'Er ... I got lost. Daydreaming again.'

'Where's your finish point today?'

'Abbeycwmhir. I guess we're about halfway there. Shall we walk together and finish last night's conversation?'

'Talk to me about your other walks. I'd like to do the Pennine Way one day.'

'I'll probably do that next year, so I don't know it at all, yet.'

We set off together, Kevin at a faster pace than my heavy pack allows. The rough, sloping ground doesn't help either, but we soon synchronise our tempo and natter away contentedly. My perception of time shifts again as we find ourselves resting against the church lychgate of St Mary the Virgin. Where did those eight miles go? We seem to have walked them in two hours. Kevin's taxi turns up a few minutes later, which explains his pace and timing precision. He has accommodation in Llandrindod Wells, a few miles away. I plan to camp in the grounds of the abbey.

'See you tomorrow, maybe. Safe travels. Have some biscuits. It doesn't look as if the shop will open for a while.'

He hands me a half-eaten tube of Jaffa cakes. As his taxi pulls away, I question the nature of such a package: Jaffa cake boxes are either full or empty, never half-full.

I shiver and wait around the entrance to the post office opposite. It is unclear if it will open, but I spy a tin of sausage and beans through the window, with my name on it. The Jaffa cakes vanish, and my backpack is empty of food. The landlord pops out of the Happy Union Inn.

'My wife will be along in a minute,' he says.

Sure enough, she unlocks the shop door, and I collect together a meal of sorts – a tin of this and a packet of that, hopefully not hot-dry or cold-wet in texture (poor combinations for a back-packer).

'Can I camp in the grounds of the abbey?'

'Sure. You can use the pub toilets. We leave them unlocked. The pub opens at sixish.'

I wind my way through the farmyard to reach the grounds of what was once a Cistercian monastery, built in 1143. Little evidence remains of a more permanent stone structure built to replace wooden buildings, which once had the ambition to compete with the scale of Winchester, Durham or York. Now, its carved-stone arched nave has been plundered for materials for Llanidloes church, ten miles away.

What remains is a grave containing the body of Llywelyn ap Gruffudd, the last native Prince of Wales, 'Llywelyn the Last' – his head severed and sent to London. He will be my companion for the night. I do not anticipate seeing any headless ghosts wandering in the nave later, but at least I'll recognise him should he appear.

The Happy Union Inn, a pub name that has to rank with the best, opens to serve me a pint. What follows is a strange ritual to produce a Guinness. The landlord gleefully explains.

'First take a cold can of special Surger Guinness.' He collects a can from the fridge.

'Open it ... Pour it into a clean pint glass.'

I'm intrigued; it pours flat.

'Place it on the special ultrasound bowl, filled with a little water.

'Press this button and be amazed,' he concludes with a proud smile as if he invented the process.

The flat black Guinness liquid now transforms into a cloud of bubbles and foam that settles into a perfect pint. I am sceptical until a sip confirms nigh-on ideal nectar, indistinguishable from a standard pint of Guinness served in Dublin.

'We just don't have the throughput to justify a keg, but this is good stuff.' He has poured a pint for himself. 'I love gadgets.'

'Can I get something to eat?'

'Sorry, just crisps, peanuts and chocolate.'

'Two packets of cheese and onion and a bar of Dairy Milk, please.'

The latter complements the pint, which is a meal in itself, and soon I am the other side of the bar, pressing the magic button for a second, staring intently at this unique beer technology. The pub is full of glorious pictures of famous moments in Welsh rugby. The sport is the religion in the area. The landlord is a third-generation school-bus driver, postman, sheep farmer and expert Guinness server. You have to be resourceful in this remote part of Wales. I retire contentedly to sleep alongside the Prince of Wales.

'No ghosts,' he confirms. 'At least, not that I have seen,' implying others have.

Owain Glyndŵr fought for the title of Prince of Wales title 130 years later, but lies buried elsewhere, at a location known only to his men.

Three swordsmen they were, out of Harry's wars …

But they sang no longer of Agincourt,
When they came to a grave; for there lay Glyndŵr.

Said the one: 'My sword, th'art rust, my dear:
I but brought thee home to break thee here!'

And the second: 'Ay, here is the narrow home,
To which our tired hearts are come!'

Said the third: 'We are all that's left, Glyndŵr,
To guard thee now on Gamélyn moor!'

Straightway I saw the dead forth-stand,
His good sword bright in his right hand …

And still it shines, – a silver flame,
Across the dark night of the Norman shame.

Oh, bright it shines, and shall brighter gleam,
For all that believe in the Cymraec dream.
– Ernest Rhys, from 'The Ballad of the Buried Sword' (1895)

The home/farm dog will not tolerate a lie-in. There is someone new in the field who needs checking out. I poke my head out: an insistent bark and phlegm-covered tennis ball greet me. Sensibly, I know not to throw the ball a few yards, for it will return in a moment. I meet the landlord again after packing in twenty minutes. Waving goodbye, I ascend again into the ancient hills, throttling back into a relaxed pace adjusted to Powys spacetime.

After a few miles, I meet another farmer, inspecting his sheep on the usual red Honda quad bike, with sheepdog alongside. He switches off the engine, signalling a desire to talk. I start the conversation.

'Lovely day.' He opens up the conversation. 'Where are you going?'

'I've walked from Chepstow, now heading for Machynlleth and then Welshpool and Prestatyn.'

'Lovely to see people walking this path, it's not that popular. We could do with more like you. Do you like it?'

'Yes, the pace of life gets slower the deeper I move into Wales.' I start to explain my experience of switching direction deeper into central Wales and how pleasant it is to walk through the landscape, untouched by time.

'Aye. But we'll have to adapt to modern ways. It's a challenge to make a living around here. As the economy falters, the money runs to the border, see. Prosperity breathes in, and out. We need more tourism, but the campsite floods in Aberystwyth a few years back have scared people away,' he goes on.

'That's a pity,' I say. I probably won't speak to anyone else today in this lonely landscape. I treasure these interactions: they shake me out of the bubble-land of London life and teach me more about the British Isles.

My pronunciation of Machynlleth is improving: 'Ma-kunth-leth'. I practise as I walk the path alone, learning to breathe the consonants correctly in the opposite direction, I'm told. Turning a corner, a large wind farm appears; west-facing blades are turning eagerly. My dream state collapses; I am reminded again of the modern world and its challenges. I enter Llanidloes, with a stunning timber-framed market hall at its centre. Built *c*.1600, it is one of the last surviving examples in Wales. The town straddles the River Severn, building strength towards the sea – the origin of my walk. I find an eco-cafe serving an excellent range of home-cooked wonders. It is time for an early dinner of soup, quiche and cake, washed down with mugs of tea. I browse through the pamphlets and ask about a campsite, just a few miles away. An older woman asks if I am walking Glyndŵr's Way; she too has hiked it a few times and plans to walk the Wales Coast Path later this year. We talk in the language of the long-distance walker, without having to explain why we do such things – a fellow wanderlust sufferer.

The campsite is comfortable, and I can pitch near the river and light a fire using driftwood from the shingle river beach. The showers are warm, but I should have taken a cold dip in the river too, for the thrill of it. I wash and wax my boots, using a small packet of Nikwax that has lived at the bottom of my pack for two weeks. It is better spread on my boots than remaining in its little container.

The sound of a flowing river lulls me to sleep. Just as a pleasant dream kicks in, I am startled by an announcement:

'LADIES AND GENTLEMEN, PLEASE GIVE IT UP FOOOORRR … LAAAAAADEEEEEY … GAGA!'

A Lady Gaga tribute band has just opened with 'Poker Face' at full volume. I had not clocked the wedding party gathering at the rugby club across the river. The singer is outstandingly good; it might even be her! Asking them to turn it down seems unwise, so I dig into my kit to find earplugs (an essential, as any tent camper knows) and wrap my head in fleece sleeves and a hat to deaden the sound. The tunes peek through, and I find my feet twitching uncontrollably to the beat. I get up and throw a few more logs on the fire; I have no choice but to enjoy the show. I'll lie in tomorrow. I wish I had a few marshmallows to heat in the embers. I am missing friendship and company, but remain comfortable with my thoughts of the journey ahead.

In the morning, a heavy mist has flooded the valley. The fire is dead and it's time to pack up quickly and depart. I'll take breakfast later. In a few miles, I reach the head of Llyn Clywedog, a vast reservoir. I walk through the former Bryntail lead mine buildings, a relic of an intensive industrial age. At one time this region produced more lead ore than the rest of the world put together. Small boats would transport it to the coast down the River Severn. It closed in 1844. A few roofless buildings remain, others long since cannibalised for stone.

The dam is huge. I climb to the water level to gain a new perspective on this vital water resource (lead-free, I hope). A sailing club is an excellent place to stop for breakfast. The buoys mark out a course designed to give locals a distinct advantage. The wind could come from any direction on a given day, changing 180 degrees as it rushes down the valleys and curves around the headlands. I walk alongside the southern banks and rest a while, looking at a pair of fishermen sitting patiently in their boat a hundred yards from the shore, facing west, resigned to a fruitless day.

Without warning an osprey appears overhead from behind me. It descends, glides and strikes, lifting a trout out of the water. The fish furiously convulses to seek purchase in the new medium of air and effect an escape, but the talons are in deep. The raptor settles on the shoreline, ripping sushi with its hooked beak. Both fishermen are blissfully unaware of the commotion behind them. The hairs on the back of my neck are goose-pimple stiff; I can barely breathe with excitement.

Walking back to the road, I meet a ranger in his Toyota pickup.

'Did you see that!' he shouts out of the window.

'Unbelievable,' I respond. 'Definitely an osprey, you could see the highway robber eye mask. The fishermen didn't see a thing – a moment impossible to catch on camera.'

We both laugh heartily together and reflect on our luck. These birds occasionally use the Llyn on their migration route but are rarely seen. It is a comedic memory that will stay with me for a long while – a raptor showing fishermen with expensive gear how to fish.

I enter the woods to see floating red kites, familiar at my home near the Chilterns, but rare here. It is one of those days that make up for months of disappointment scanning skies for eagles in Scotland. If you tread carefully through the landscape, all manner of wildlife emerges. I find my observation skills improving, in tune with the natural world around me as if some remnant hunting skill is awakening. I plod through the forest, recently churned and harvested, trees felled and dragged into stacks awaiting transport. It is heavy going and unpleasant until I reach open moorland ascending to almost 500 metres above Dylife and a possible campsite. I can see the Star Inn, nestled in the valley below. I heard it is not a place to stay, but I'll take a chance; if it is terrible, I'll wild camp.

Sure enough, the landlady is blunt.

'We're closed.'

'Do you open later? Can I camp in the field?'

'Use the paddock,' she huffs.

I scrape the horse dung off the grass for a pitch on a slope. It is not ideal, but not much will dissuade me. There is no horse to be seen. I walk to the pub at opening time. I can get a meal, and join a couple from Wolverhampton, who must have had an afternoon nap. The decor is tired, the room unswept and the furniture in need of replacement; my expectations of service and food quality are low. Dan, the chef, a rather sizeable, bubbly chap, appears and starts a monologue of quick-fire jokes that defuse the tension. He could easily be a stand-up comic; I recall one of his jokes:

> *A tourist sauntered into a pub in Llandrindod Wells and said,*
> *'What's the quickest way to get to Brecon from here?'*
>
> *Rhodri, the landlord, answered, 'Are you walking or going by*
> *car?'*
>
> *The tourist answered, 'By car, of course.'*
>
> *Rhodri said, 'Well, that's the quickest way.'*

Once the jokes settle down, it is time to order food.

'You'll be having steak and chips,' says Dan; there is no menu to hand.

'Peas too?' I jest; he starts to lock into my dry sarcasm and fires back, 'Green or orange? We serve all types here.' I like this man (he means baked beans).

The beer is good, and Dan produces a delicious meal. The campsite is free when I come to pay the bill. The couple retire to their room; I dare not imagine the bed linen. Dan carries on with his jokes and monologue. I tell him he is in the wrong career, but he explains the pub will soon change hands, or even close. Dan is a natural front-of-house raconteur and talented chef – an undiscovered Jamie Oliver.

I bed down to sleep in my tent and hear Dan start a souped-up, highly tuned Subaru Impreza. He screams down the road in pure Welsh rally style. I listen to the turbo pops until they fade in the still night air, the silence restored to a remote, desolate former mining town.

I later read that the 'Y Star Inn' (renamed) is now very different, restored and busy again. So the pub life cycle repeats: decline and regeneration, and decline as the novelty and enthusiasm wear off – customers are so fickle. For me, it will have lost its character, but others will be happy. I wouldn't trust Tripadvisor. I had a great time, but it is a Marmite experience.

I climb back up to the ridge and unobstructed views under a low cloud base. I am near the watershed and the source of the River Severn (Britain's longest river at 220 miles) and the source of the River Wye (134 miles). Both watercourses have been close friends since leaving Chepstow, yet take very different routes to the sea.

I check Glaslyn (a mountain lake) for any unusual birdlife, but decide not to dwell and ascend Foel Fadian for the views. Just below the summit lies a memorial to Wynford Vaughan-Thomas, the BBC wartime radio and TV broadcaster (and the man who opened the Pembrokeshire Coast Path), who loved the views over Wales from this point. Who could disagree? I wonder, is that Yr Wyddfa (Snowdon) in the distance? To the south, somewhere near Hyddgen, lies a famous battleground marking a notable victory for Owain Glyndŵr in 1401, against the odds. To the west, I can see the Dyfi estuary and a storm approaching, marked by a deep black underbelly, a cloud base set just above my eye line. It is time to move. Jogging down to a farm track, I overbalance and tumble down a slope – a potent reminder to take it easy in the hills when carrying a heavy load.

At Talbontdrain, a notice gives a warning:

If you are walking through, and a black cat follows, please could you shake a little cat food out of the plastic milk bottle by the shed door onto the ground. Not too much, he'll get fat! Make sure you put the lid on firmly. Then make a run for it while he is eating. He has followed someone for two miles, and seems a bit clueless about getting back home.

I do not see the culprit, which is unsurprising, as it is raining heavily, so heavily I decide to take a direct route into the town of Machynlleth, following a single-track lane. I'm soon sitting soaked at the railway station. The forecast is abysmal, and flood warnings are in place. A week-long storm is about to break – a remnant of some Caribbean hurricane. I chicken out and catch a train home, delighted that an extra £1 will bring me back here later to complete the walk into Welshpool.

* * *

With hindsight, I made the right decision. Heavy rain and flooding make walking unpleasant, often impossible. The River Severn north of Welshpool has a fearsome reputation, confirmed by a high-tide mark of debris, deposited by massive flows. I return in spring to walk the section from Knighton to Welshpool on Offa's Dyke and then catch a train back to Mach (as Machynlleth is known colloquially). My journey with Owain continues.

I walk out through the town. Every house displays a pink ribbon, with a few blunt notices asking the press not to call. Tributes to April Jones, a five-year-old local girl murdered in October 2012, cover the doorways. I cannot comprehend such a horrific act in such a beautiful town, the grieving made all the more painful by the lack of a body. The police conducted the most extensive missing person search in UK history, without results.

I step thoughtfully towards Penegoes to ascend into the rolling hills that overlook the Afon Dyfi. The low cloud and overcast day have stripped the landscape of colour. I walk within my world, lacking a frame of reference. Navigation requires discipline, but a new smartphone app is working a treat. It is easy to press a button to see precisely where I am. My right foot is developing a blister, which is annoying, as I have no idea of the root cause. These are the same boots I have worn for two years without problems. At least I am carrying less weight now, having made a decision not to camp after researching the possibilities for the remainder of the journey to Prestatyn via Offa's Dyke (see Chapter 5). I arrive at Llanbrynmair and a clean B&B, with pub opposite. A quick check of my heel reveals a developing blister, which I cover with a Compeed patch after letting it breathe overnight.

After a salty breakfast, I'm walking again into the hills and a fantastic section along Cerrig y Tân into woodland and along smooth forest tracks and paths along Afon Gam into Llangadfan. I meet the Glyndŵr's Way ranger.

'Good morning, lovely day. Can I ask, are you married to the Offa's Dyke ranger?' I say, perhaps being too forward.

'Er … no, I'm not,' she says. 'Why do you ask?'

I have said the wrong thing, but explain how I met a man on the way into Welshpool on Offa's Dyke who said he was the ranger, married to the ranger on Glyndŵr's Way. I should have taken a name, as I have stuck my foot in it.

'It might have been Tim you met,' she says. 'He was married recently.'

'I'm so sorry to intrude. It's a great walk, by the way, but I bailed out recently because of the heavy rain.' My interrogation technique needs improvement.

'Good decision – the going can be rough in places when the ground is sodden.'

I'm guessing volunteers call themselves rangers on the first contact. Nevertheless, she is busy putting in marker posts for a section across the Pen Coed featureless moorland; the wild ponies have a habit of knocking them over when scratching their behinds. As punishment, I get lost. Eventually, I find the bridge at Llangadfan and stop for lunch. I must have added a mile to my journey. Paying closer attention to navigation, I reach the Dyfnant Forest and a network of single-track lanes into Ddôl Cownwy. One last ascent and I can see Llyn Efyrnwy (Lake Vyrnwy), another vast reservoir serving industry and homes in Liverpool. I have wanted to view this site for many years, having once worked for the civil-engineering company Thomas Hawksley (later MWH), which designed and built the dam in 1888.

One of the former engineers' cottages is now a B&B, run by a local farmer, Ieuan. He welcomes me in, unconcerned about my muddy boots, to sit down for tea. Tea that is, in the Welsh style: porcelain cups and cake stands, with a selection of homemade cakes. The table is laid with pride and speaks volumes to tradition. We drop quickly into a conversation, talking about my journey through Wales and my loose connection to the very cottage I am sitting in. It is a real pleasure to talk and listen to this wonderful man, full of wisdom and knowledge of an environment he has lived in all of his life. I am corrected on the pronunciation of Welsh names and learn about his daily life. He is charming, modest and full of humour. The cottage is neither modified nor extended. He leads me through a dining room, complete with Welsh dresser and collection of personal keepsakes; the fire is ready to be lit, matches to one side. The stairs open to a luxurious bedroom. It reminds me clearly of visiting my grandparents as a small child:

there is great attention to detail and it is spotlessly clean. Objects are acquired for life, maintained and not replaced continuously, in sharp contrast to the throwaway consumer society we live in today.

Breakfast is fit for a king, expertly cooked by someone who has perfected the art over many years. It is hands down the best I have ever tasted, a result of superb ingredients and skilful cooking. The tableware is the finest Spode and the cutlery of bone-handled knives with flexible blue steel blades that make spreading butter a delight.

The highlight of the day has passed, as I head east. Just before I ascend again into woodland, Ieuan stops in his Toyota truck, complete with sheepdog, to offer advice on the path ahead.

'Take the next left and go through the gate,' he says. 'Take care now.'

'Thank you so much.' I almost choke up with gratitude.

I struggle to find more words; the brief stay has affected me more deeply than I know. My faith in kind nature is restored, modelled on old values and traditions lost to future generations.

Perhaps the hymns and poetry of Ann Griffiths can explain. She was born in 1776, near Llanfihangel-yng-Ngwynfa, not far from a walk named after her, that follows the River Vyrnwy. She is the most prominent Welsh hymn writer and became a national icon. So it is fitting to walk through Dolwar Fach, her former home, before descending to Dolanog and crossing the bridge to follow the south bank riverside path into Pontrobert – a pleasant day's walk under gentle trees along a babbling stream.

The walk into Meifod is short, but tough going, along muddy paths. My blisters are making their presence known as my boots twist and squelch through the ruts. I am happy to arrive at the Kings Head for a large bowl of macaroni cheese and a pint. The pub is full of local farmers watching the final football score on the television, playing pool and proceeding to get as drunk as possible. It is their day off.

I have to walk roadside to a local B&B. It is comfortable and welcoming, as I am beginning to expect. My blister is a mess;

something is seriously wrong as it smells of rotten fish. A deep clean and dry-out while watching television helps, soaking the wound in alcohol (ouch!) before bandaging it the next day. It is way beyond maximum Compeed size. I am pleased I have the basic first aid kit, but I am not happy about cutting the journey short. To continue would be folly; it is time to take the train home. It is such a disappointment. One walker told me his story of Morton's neuroma: permanent nerve damage in the foot after failing to rest and diagnose the root cause of his foot blisters. Listen to your body, my wife would say.

My predicament is put into context over breakfast, as I learn about the difficulties finding meaningful work in this area. Most people are on the basic minimum wage and hold two or three jobs, some travelling across Britain each week to work. Welshpool is a livestock market and gateway into the Mid Wales agricultural economy, keenly sensing the health of the region. It will occasionally suffer a sore throat, the hand of the economy gripping the neck of central Wales.

It is only ten miles into the town, and I can sense space-time adjusting to normal again. The clock resets a hundred years forward and starts running faster. I have one last chance to reflect on the walk from the top of Y Golfa. Leaning against the trig pillar, I scan the horizon, looking deep into Wales. I'm sure that I can see Snowdonia and Cadair Idris in the distance. This landscape is timeless, mystical and friendly.

I dawdle into Tesco to grab some food for the train journey home, inadvertently missing the 11 a.m. service; I now have to wait for two hours. I need to get my mojo back and wake from my depressive dark cloud of failure. I should be setting off north along Offa's Dyke, not sheepishly bailing out to fix an errant blister. I change at Shrewsbury, Birmingham and Leamington Spa, the latter waiting room beautifully restored to its interwar glory. A collection of magazines and journals is available to read. I casually pick up a copy of the *FMC Bulletin* – the official quarterly of the Federated Mountain Clubs of New Zealand, issue 189. Inside is written clearly 'PLEASE LEAVE IN HUT'. How this document reached Leamington Spa from a mountain bothy halfway around the world is a mystery. Did someone leave it as a joke? I certainly chuckle.

A week later, I am cleaning my boots. It dawns on me that I changed the footbeds, raising my heel a few millimetres. This new geometry is the root cause of my blister. My recovery is rapid, and in a few weeks I return to Welshpool to complete Offa's Dyke (see Chapter 5) without any complaints. However, I have protected my heel copiously with Hypafix tape, just to be safe.

Better a mistake that makes you humble than an achievement that makes you arrogant.

7

PENNINE WAY

Distance: 268 miles
Days to complete: 14 days
Mileage so far: 1,395 miles

THE SPINE OF ENGLAND

A pedestrian is a man in danger of his life.
A walker is a man in possession of his soul.

– David McCord

If you ask anyone to name a National Trail, this will be the one; this is the first. In 1935, two American girls wrote to a local newspaper, asking if there was anything like the Appalachian Trail in the UK. Tom Stephenson picked up the letter and started a campaign that led to the opening of the first seventy-mile route in 1965. In 2021, over 5,000 miles of National Trails will be available when the England Coast Path is completed.

The Pennine Way has been on my mind for several years. It wraps its legendary status in tales of heroic deeds and efforts. It follows a range of mountains and hills from Edale in the south, to Kirk Yetholm on the Scottish border, crossing three National Parks – a total of 268 miles, much at high level through remote moorland. It is rightly considered a challenge for any enthusiastic walker and deeply rewarding.

The Pennine Way is a beautiful thing
In summer, autumn, winter, spring.
As the clouds dance across the Pennine sky
And the wild birds wheel past the walker's eye.

– © Ian McMillan @IMcMillan[5]

I am always anxious when I set out on a long walk. It is an irrational state of mind. Do I fear failure? Do I feel guilty? The train journey to Sheffield gives me plenty of time to reflect on the enormity of the task ahead. 'Just break it down day by day,' I say in my head. 'As time passes you *will* make progress.' As soon as I am walking to the youth hostel, my worries subside. Is it the rush of endorphins from new exercise, nulling my doubting synapses?

It is great to be outdoors in the Peak District National Park, amongst the hills and moorland. I am fortunate to have the time to do this before the autumn nights draw in; the trains were busy with business travellers and students returning to university. I alight at Edale and breathe in the chilled air; it invigorates my soul and flushes out my doubts.

A Danish *Sprogskole* adventure trip has overrun the hostel. The warden kindly puts me into a remote shed, together with another middle-aged walker. He has so much gear he needs two bunks to sort through it all to find his pyjamas! … Pyjamas! Pots and pans hang on the side of his backpack, like a comedy sketch. It is a heavy pack.

'Walking the Pennine Way?' I ask.

'That's the plan, what about you?'

'Yes, I'll start tomorrow.'

'You're travelling light – are you camping?'

'Well, I thought about that, then I realised there are lots of ideally spaced youth hostels on the entire route. I just need a few B&Bs to fill in the gaps. I usually camp.'

'Perhaps I should have done that, but it's cheaper with a tent.'

'Maybe. YHAs are £12 to £15 a night at most, plus some have good kitchens, so I can keep the cost of food down too.'

'Hmm, maybe I'll get my brother to pick up some of my gear.'

'It's worthwhile – they won't be too busy at this time of year.'

I wake early and manage to get to the head of the breakfast queue as a horde of schoolkids explode out of the dorms. The noise in the dining room reaches a crescendo but then a teacher demands calm. The Danish kids will be getting muddy and wet on the adventure course today and are too excited – marginally more than I am.

My smartphone map cannot pinpoint my location. It is trying to download assisted GPS satellite coordinates still set for London, without a mobile data signal. I can't be bothered to work out how to fix it, and walk in the direction of the Edale visitor centre. The map on the wall shows the entire route and the enormity of the task ahead. A copy of Stephenson's newspaper article is attached to the first fingerpost. 'WANTED – A Long Green Trail,' it demanded on 22 June 1935. The final words read:

Whatever the cost, it would be a worthy and enduring testimony – bringing health and pleasure beyond computation, for none could walk that Pennine Way without being improved in mind and body, inspired and invigorated and filled with the desire to explore every corner of this lovely island.

There, in one long sentence, is an answer to why I like walking the National Trails. If any further persuasion is required, a wooden bench further along the path reads:

Office bustle for leaves' rustle
Mobiles ringing for birds singing
Lover's rejection for water's reflection
Twenty-first century for glimpse of eternity.

– Unknown

This poem is more than enough inspiration for a misty morning as I make my way towards Jacob's Ladder and start an ascent on to Kinder Scout. It is tough going, but my walking poles help. I pass 600 metres into a warm sunny day and a stunning temperature inversion. The thick misty blanket covers the valleys. The peaks and cairns of Kinder Scout poke into a blue sky, criss-crossed with contrails. I can hear intercontinental aircraft making their final approach to Manchester airport. They disappear into the cloud as they descend. It is such a breathless sight that I can only stop and stare before I have to make progress along the flagstone path that points northward. Luckily, the atmospheric effect continues for several miles, as I walk along the ridgeline. I'm in a heavenly landscape above the dreary mass of civilisation below.

The red grouse have taken elocution lessons from Donald Duck: 'g' back, g' back, g' back,' they call as I disturb them from the heather. Perhaps they could learn 'nae shoot, nae shoot' instead, for that is almost certainly their fate. Shooting parties will line the grouse butts this weekend and blast them from the skies. For now, it is peaceful and quiet, and I pay tribute to the pioneers who fought for the right to walk and share this moorland: I pluck some heather and wedge it into my backpack strapping, for luck and to remind me of them.

The birds are busy flitting from twig to twig and they are my only company until I turn right at Mill Hill. 'No Mill and not much Hill,' as Alfred Wainwright would say. A group of students are searching for a Second World War plane wreck, not the famous B-29 Superfortress still evident on Bleaklow Ridge ahead, but a lesser-known aircraft. These cloud-covered hills even claim victims to this day – a dangerous landscape on foot or in the air. The flagstones are a welcome sight, helicoptered from dismantled mills and laid together in paths, to manage erosion over the deep bog. I adjust my gait to synchronise with the interleaving stones, which offer grip, even when wet. I cross Snake Pass, the first of many trans-Pennine routes across the high moorland. A community science sign asks for help with a bumblebee survey. I start seeing these high-speed black–yellow marbles whizzing across the moorland – too fast to count.

There is a charming B&B in Crowden, and I am offered a lift to the Peels Arms pub in the evening. Soup, a roast dinner and water cost £9; no London prices here. I'm not drinking alcohol on this trip, having recently lost a good friend to alcoholism. Many would argue that it is not possible to walk this path without a good pint or two, but I remain determined to honour his memory. His loss is still raw and my grief unprocessed, something I want to do in a sober state, walking it out over the next two weeks.

It is shorts and a T-shirt the next day, much to the amusement of the landlady. There is still hill fog, but I am hoping for a repeat of yesterday. It is eerily quiet in the mist, only the sound of babbling brooks, draining their way to a river or reservoir. Wainwright got stuck in the bog here, adding to his dislike of the Pennine Way, not something you would expect. Were it not for the flagstones, I too would be buried up to my knees in thick black fibrous peat. I eat the two sausages stolen from my breakfast and wrapped in foil for lunch to keep my energy levels high as I reach Black Hill, a desolate spot with a welcome trig pillar, freshly painted white – like the capital letter I on a blank black page.

I descend, crossing the dangerous Dean Clough (river gorge) into Wessenden Moor. More torrential rain would undoubtedly demand a wide detour to reach the A635. I read a campaign sign, seeking help to find the Moors murder victim Keith Bennett, buried here somewhere in 1964. Further north, a plaque recalls the Black Flood in Marsden, a disaster in 1810 when the inky black water in the reservoir burst its banks and drowned six people. I try to purge morbid thoughts from my mind as I approach Standedge and my accommodation for the night. I can see the lights of the hotel piercing the mist. I have time to read about the four parallel tunnels, each five kilometres long, that convey canal boats and railway traffic under the Pennines. Quite a feat of engineering, yet unseen from the moors.

It is a delight to be served a Turkish meal instead of the usual chips with everything. I rest well and wake to meet a fellow Pennine Way walker, Alan. He completed the path some years ago and is back for the highlights. We walk together as he recalls his journey and gives me advice, stopping for exceptional views of Manchester and its conurbations. We summit White Hill, Black Hill's twin sister, a sentinel in a landscape of foreboding names. Bleakegate Moor lies ahead of us.

We cross the M62 over a footbridge I have wanted to cross for decades as I have passed underneath it on many an occasion by car. The road noise penetrates the tranquillity of the moorland, accompanied by a toot or two from lorry drivers as we wave at them. Blackstone Edge, a gritstone escarpment, stands in defiance of the encroaching urban spread. We cross a drove road signposted by the Aiggin Stone, a marker of indeterminate origin, perhaps earlier than the Roman way it sits beside. There is a beautiful poem etched in gold on the face of the gritstone, recently completed. It is worth a couple of readings. My companion reads it aloud; I reread it to myself afterwards, trying to absorb all of its meaning.

RAIN

Be glad
of these freshwater tears,
each pearled droplet
some salty old sea-bullet
air-lifted out of the waves,
then laundered and sieved,
recast as a soft bead
and returned.

And no matter how much
it strafes or sheets,
it is no mean feat
to catch one raindrop
clean in the mouth,
to take one drop
on the tongue, tasting
cloud-pollen,
grain of the heavens,
raw sky.

Let it teem, up here
where the front of the mind
distils
the brunt of the world.

– Simon Armitage (2010)[6]

This is a poem in the location it describes – an escarpment that will force the rain out of the southwesterly clouds, eager to shed their burden at the first opportunity.

It is a short walk to the White House public house on the A58 and a pleasant pub lunch. My legs are sore; I fear shin splints, which I hate. Alan has come prepared and gives me some ibuprofen gel, which works a treat. The next section is not strenuous and leads through a network of reservoirs serving the cities below, towards the imposing Stoodley Pike. This monument also lies on the Pennine Bridleway, a path I will walk in a few years' time. A few horse riders are enjoying the end of the day; it looks like an ideal mode of transport on the moors. I walk to the monument's base, climb to its balcony, and read the graffiti etched in the gritstone, before diverting back into Mankinholes and the youth hostel nestled in the valley. Alan came off the path earlier, and we meet later, to walk a short distance to a local pub, the Top Brink Inn in Lumbutts.

The pub is buzzing, and Alan is meeting a few friends, a motley crew of adventurers. One is walking from Land's End to John o'Groats, another cycling the same; several have already completed the Pennine Way. It is a pleasant gathering of like-minded souls, and we enthusiastically share our experiences. Even alcohol-free, I enjoy the evening, but not the walk back through the dark lanes without a torch. I sleep erratically in a bunk that is six inches too short, knowing that tomorrow is a long haul to Earby, the next hostel on the route, twenty-five miles away.

We have now traversed the gap that lies between the great northern cities, heading for the Yorkshire Dales. Alan peels off towards Hebden Bridge, and I climb back into moorland after crossing the Rochdale canal. A black cat crosses my path, so it is going to be a lucky day, or so I think until I come across a dead sheep and a murder of crows feasting on it.

I am met by a three-legged dog, wagging its tail with joy as it hops up the path to meet me. It is utterly indifferent to its disability and easily outpaces its owner, who joins me for a chat.

'He's happy,' I say.

'He loves this walk, does it every day, whatever the weather.'

'My friend told me to stop at May's shop, is it nearby?' I continue the conversation, keen to pet this lovely Labrador a little longer.

'You're close. Turn left on the lane ahead, you can't miss it.'

Alan was right. May's Aladdin's Cave is full of everything a Pennine Way walker could need. Pies, sandwiches, cake, beverages, blister repair, painkillers, bandages; the list is endless. This farm shop has been open fourteen hours a day, 364 days a year for the past forty years. The wonder gran who runs it has been a godsend for many a weary walker. I buy an ice lolly as it is a beautiful day and progress on to Heptonstall Moor and yet more reservoirs. There is a grouse shoot underway, and I can see the line of beaters flushing out the poor things from the heather. It is big business and a significant contributor to the rural economy. That explains the traps I can see at regular intervals, controlling any predators that would eat the chicks. Another predator, paying £1,000 or more, will slaughter the bird, in the prime of its life, with the brutal efficiency of a twelve-bore shotgun.

I reach Top Withens. A plaque describes its significance:

> Top Withens. This farmhouse has been associated with
> 'Wuthering Heights', the Earnshaw home in Emily Brontë's
> novel. The buildings, even when complete, bear no resemblance to
> the house she described, but the situation may have been in her
> mind when she wrote of the moorland setting of the heights.
> – Brontë Society, 1964

It is a favourite spot for tourists; the signs from Haworth are written in Japanese to guide enthusiasts over the moorland. I pass a few dressed in transparent plastic macs, more Mary Quant in style than your regulation Gore-Tex. Their footwear is entirely unsuitable as they pick their way through the sheep droppings. White plimsolls take on a new colour and smell. Not as they perhaps intended when buying them at the fashion store in Tokyo.

The route descends and ascends again into the natural moorland and into what seems to be a hobby farm at Cowling. Notices pinned to the gates warn you not to feed the animals. A shaming list names the naughty pigs and sheep who will happily follow you on to the moorland if you do not close the gate. Closing it tightly, I continue at a relaxed pace to Pinhaw Beacon and stop for a while as the day draws to a close. I stare at the endless desert moorland and close my eyes. I stop and do nothing, resting on a comfortable rock. There is no wind or sound; nothing is happening; I am thinking about nothing as I enter a state of meditation. All I can hear is the passing of time as my heart beats. A shiver wakes me. I must follow waymarks to a very cosy youth hostel at Earby before I catch a chill. I arrive at the same time as a mountain bike group who stayed at Mankinholes last night. They recognise me.

'Have you walked here?!' they exclaim. 'We covered the same distance, and we're exhausted.'

'You must have taken the long route, or spent too much time in the pub for lunch?' I ask.

'Er, yes that's it.'

They must have got lost too; I confirm the twenty-five miles, and we chat in the common room for a while, before I have to rest. The dorm is a man cave of beer-fuelled snoring trolls. Earplugs have little effect. Getting up early seems the only solution, even though I only plan a short walk to Malham youth hostel, eleven miles away. Today I cross the Aire Gap, a natural glacial pass through the Pennines. The route is pastoral, following the Leeds and Liverpool canal towards Gargrave. Smoke from the canal-boat wood fires drifts gently into the air. *Rosie and Jim* puppets stare out of the windows.

Having skipped breakfast, I make amends at the delightful insti-tution that is the Dalesman cafe tea rooms – a magnet for cyclists and walkers. The full Yorkshire all-day breakfast is a treat, served in a room with an open fire, next door to a sweet shop that would keep any kid (or adult) happy for a month. The decor is eccentric and full of Pennine Way memorabilia; even the mugs show the route ahead to Malham.

The Yorkshire Dales landscape of drystone walls and pasture emerges as I approach Malham along the River Aire. I'm early, so sit and sleep on the slopes above the village, and nibble on the cake I bought yesterday. I have no desire to join the tourist crowds in Malham just yet.

I read everything in the visitor centre, waiting for the youth hostel to open at 5 p.m. The entrance is marked with a mosaic of stones, depicting the head of the iconic Swaledale sheep. It is a large hostel with a restaurant and washing facilities. I read in the dorm, as more adventurers arrive to fill all the bunks. One late arrival is running fifty miles a day for a month, aiming to visit every county in Britain – an astonishing goal. He is an ultrarunner from France and has secured the services of an ex-army logistics guy to support him – a good business, he tells me later. The routine seems to be: up at 4 a.m., drive to start point, feed on the route, and then run until 7 or 8 p.m., for a month! The runner is complaining of a sore ankle, so I give him some ibuprofen gel – day one for him. I suggest he buys a big tube.

At breakfast, the kitchen is full of other adventurers, but not the ultrarunner, who left hours ago. We chat about what we are doing. Everyone is very knowledgeable about both Scotland and this area, so we share tips and recommendations. Using the hostels and being in the company of like-minded people is far more friendly than wild camping.

I'm on the path to Malham Cove early, before the crowds. A mighty waterfall eroded the broken-cup curved limestone feature during the last Ice Age, some 12,000 years ago. Now a mere trickle flows over the lip, spraying the trees that cling to the rock face with minerals. I scan the cliffs for peregrine falcons and little owls, which I read live here, but without success. The climb to the limestone pavement summit reveals a molar-tooth-like surface, which requires concentration to walk on. The path leads to Ing

Scar and Malham Tarn, which I assume to be the remnants of a once-mighty glacial river. I am met by six collie puppies at Tennant Gill Farm, just before the long-drawn-out ascent of Fountains Fell. They fuss around my feet, nibbling my laces as I talk to a young farmer.

'In a few days we'll select one of these to work on the farm,' he says. 'You can always tell after six weeks. The rest will become pets.'

I guess which one it may be, but get it wrong.

'This is the current favourite – keen-eyed, intelligent and responds readily to my voice,' he adds. 'The father is a champion sheepdog. I'll start his training soon.'

One of them follows me up the path. I briefly consider dog-napping, but the farmer has to round them all up. How ironic – I thought that was their job.

The heights of Fountains Fell reveal the full glory of the National Park, like being a low-flying pilot over the expanse of moorland and fells. Proudly overlooking Ribblesdale, and the peaks of Whernside and Ingleborough, is Pen-y-ghent, the three hills being collectively known as the Yorkshire Three Peaks. Its name sounds Welsh, and indeed the Cumbric language had a connection to that Celtic culture. I start the steep ascent to its summit, joining a crowd of people who have parked along the roadside. I climb over the last drystone wall to touch the trig pillar and see a posse of cyclo-cross bikes carried on the backs of very focused cyclists. They immediately turn after checking in, to descend like madmen down the steep slope. I now have to battle against a tide of competitors using the same path, so I stop for lunch to let the leaders get on with their race. I do my best to pick a route to avoid a collision, but these guys and gals are on a mission. It is the annual Three Peaks Cyclo-Cross race, conceived in the 1960s. A good time for the forty-kilometre course is three hours. The atmosphere is excellent; the cyclists appreciate me getting out of their way.

I'm happy to have arrived in the village of Horton-in-Ribblesdale and the Pen-y-ghent cafe. It is time for a pint of tea and a hefty portion of fruitcake. An old timing clock can measure your attempt on the three peaks. The record is faster than the cycling times: an astonishing two hours and thirty minutes, although the course is slightly shorter. The challenge is almost like a coming-of-age event for any Yorkshireman. Photographs cover the walls: bicycles up to their saddle in water, exhausted skinny-limbed runners splattered in mud – legends of the moors.

The bunkroom is surprisingly empty, considering the weekend events, but I can gather why when I sit at the bar. The meal is awful, and the customers are abusing the poor bar girl. It is an unpleasant feeling; the landlord is absent. I skip breakfast, choosing to return to the cafe, which opens on time to serve up a perfect bacon butty and another pint of strong tea. This owner knows his customers' needs.

The route follows stone-filled farm tracks and is hard going; the wind has picked up. I need gloves. The clouds are racing north-east as if filmed in time-lapse, casting their shadows on the fells. The Ribblehead viaduct is at one moment beautifully lit by the sun's starburst rays. I meet several enduro riders on motorcycles, and they too are making slow progress along the rough tracks. Their engines resonate with a pair of RAF Tucano T1 trainer air-craft racing down the valley. Buzzards and kites hover in the air, unconcerned, focused on hunting.

I descend into Hawes. A couple of older American women have ventured into the fells, dressed in expensive outdoor gear – all brand new. They look like escapees from the cast of *Cocoon*, with a vitality that belies their age. The town is full of tourists until the coaches depart. I find the local youth hostel and settle in for an afternoon nap. I am joined in the dorm by Colin, who is cycling in the area on a beat-up mountain bike, in essential outdoor gear made from modified clothing. He is touring around the Dales across the moorland passes. I admire his wisdom and knowledge; he can travel without effort, unencumbered by material possessions.

It is a delight to meet an old friend that evening who has moved to the Yorkshire Dales from the hubbub of London. We spend a few hours over a pleasant meal, catching up on events. She en-courages me to write a book, which I dismiss as a crazy idea, but she has sown a seed which will grow into this manuscript.

'Why not?' she asks. 'Everyone has a book in them. Send me your first chapter.'

'Really? I'm an IT guy used to programming and numbers. Words are not my thing.'

'Write it as you would speak it. I'll send you a few tips and tricks.'

'Mmm ... OK.'

I depart after an excellent breakfast to walk through the town, setting up for the Tuesday market. I ascend Great Shunner Fell into the thick cloud to spend a pleasant few hours traversing Thwaite Common. I need my compass at the summit to navigate to the village in Swaledale. Cloud obscures what would be a marvellous view in clear weather. No picture-postcard photographs today. The Kearton Tearooms extort an unbelievable £9 for tea and toastie from my wallet, clearly pricing to a different clientele; they too know their market. It is a picturesque hamlet, the inspiration for the Kearton brothers, Richard and Cherry, early pioneers of wildlife photography at the turn of the century. They were born in the village.

I depart lighter than expected, paying with every scrap of change I can find. Walking alongside Kisdon Valley, I note a sequence of beautiful waterfalls. The path is rough and overgrown until I can ascend again into native moorland and reach the remote Tan Hill Inn, Britain's highest inn at 528 metres, or 1,732 feet in old money. I receive a warm welcome and sit by a roaring coal fire, still in my shorts. The direct heat does wonders for my weary muscles. Tracy, the landlady, is a real character and full of tales of epic lock-ins, due to heavy snow. She knows that people study the forecast, to time such 'happenings' to perfection. There is always enough beer and coal to last. The Theakston Old Peculiar (5.6% ABV) hand pump stands centrally on the bar. It must be one hell of a party. The thought of that exquisite nectar tests my resolve, but painful feelings remain of my dear departed friend.

Local customers include the gamekeepers and the moorland sheep, who will barge through an unlatched door and sit in front of the fire; I thought sheep were stupid, but they are not daft on Stonesdale Moor. If ever there is heavy snow in England, you can be sure a photo of this pub will be on the front page of the tabloids. I recall a stunning photograph of the building bathed in the *aurora borealis*. Some describe the Tan Hill Inn as the *Fawlty Towers* of the north. I love it, and so do many others, as the range of newspaper articles and postcards pinned to the wall testify.

But I have no love of the heavy rain that starts the day. Tracy advises avoiding the Sleightholme Moor route (which runs alongside Frumming Beck), due to flooding and deep bog. I'm not to argue and take the road towards the farm before crossing underneath a very busy A66 that connects the north-east to the north-west. I'm in the North Pennines now, heading to Middleton-in-Teesdale and a warm B&B. My waterproofs and boots are holding out against an onslaught of rain and wind. I arrive at High Birk Hatt Farm, the home of Hannah Hauxwell, an English farmer made famous by a series of articles and television documentaries. She endured poverty and hardship over the decades. Her story became so well known that she attended the Woman of the Year gala at London's Savoy Hotel. 'In summer I lived, and in winter I existed,' she is quoted as saying. I can begin to imagine the hardship as I walk through her meadows in the torrential rain; this is a remote and inhospitable place when the weather turns for the worst. I trudge on into Middleton, over Harter Fell. The 1618 cafe is a welcome stop for cake and tea. I don't want to arrive at the B&B too early and need to acclimatise to life indoors. A second mug with two sugars brings my body back to life. A fish and chip shop completes my transformation into a normal human being, presentable for the B&B and ready for a good night's rest.

After perhaps the best breakfast I have had on this trip, I set out to walk alongside the River Tees, after recrossing the road bridge. In a few miles, I can hear the sound of Low Force ahead, a prelude to High Force (*High Fosse* in Nordic), the largest waterfall in England, by volume of water. The Durham County footpath gates are quite different: far more straightforward to open than the mantraps in Yorkshire. Teesdale is lovely on an overcast day, the dark skies reflecting in the peaty fast-flowing river. A stone sculpture announces 'A wonderful place to be a walker'. I heartily agree as I continue to the impressive waterfalls.

A Natural England control post insists that I disinfect my walking boots to prevent the spread of a tree-killing disease called *Phytophthora austrocedrae*. Juniper trees are rare, so I am happy to oblige, my boots now clean of mud and infection. I turn west to endure a problematic riverside section of awkwardly spaced polished rocks, to reach my third waterfall: Cauldron Snout, the longest in England. That is two ticks in the book, even though it appears to be an unnatural feature, a man-made overflow from a reservoir above. I can hear thunder, but the signs warning of military activity suggest gunfire. The land to the south is active with an exercise, or maybe it is thunder, I cannot be sure.

I'm happy to reach the isolation of the open moors again and walk contentedly west until High Cup Nick assaults my senses – an enormous symmetrical gouge in the Pennine ridge as if dug by some mythical monster dragging a giant beach spade through the sand. It is undoubtedly the most exquisite view on the Pennine Way. I have to stop and gawp, feeding crumbs of cake into an open, dribbling mouth. The feature is so unexpected; I thought the Lake District, Scotland and Snowdonia had a monopoly on beautiful views.

The descent is exhilarating into Dufton. My fitness levels are high; I am skipping over the rocks to a farm track that enters the village. Perhaps it was the joy of seeing such a sight that has given me levitation. The youth hostel is a diamond: friendly, comfortable and quiet. The pub opposite is even better, with a roaring coal range and a kitchen that produces a humble, yet delicious pork belly meal. I am gasping for a pint to join in with the banter, but my resolve continues. This self-enforced abstinence is proving harder than walking.

Ten days have passed since I left London; the walk has become my new life. I am feeling full of energy and ready to tackle one of the hardest days. I started from the south for two reasons: to keep the sun behind me, so it lights up the landscape I am walking into, and to keep the tough sections to the end. Cross

Fell beckons, the highest point on the Pennine Way. It's a cloudy day, but it's not raining. I take a farm track, but miss a signpost and end up following *A Pennine Journey* – Alfred Wainwright's route around the Pennines in 1938. This route from Settle to Hexham is a tribute to his work and an excellent publication, but he was not a fan of the Pennines compared to his love of the Lakeland Fells. I use Dufton Pike as a guide to get me back on track, where I meet a farmer on his quad bike setting off into the hills.

'What will the weather be like today?' I ask. 'The forecast is rain.'

'Don't trust the forecast, lad; it'll be fine, although cloudy. The wind direction is all-important,' he replies.

I trust his judgement. He points to the radar station on Great Dun Fell, clearly visible in a patch of blue. The next time I see it, I will be standing twenty metres in front of it. Now the cloud draws in. His sheepdog is running in the adjacent field, hiding behind the drystone wall to gather sheep ahead. The flock is oblivious to his approach until he pops over a stile and startles them in the direction he wants. The farmer does not need to whistle; this intelligent dog knows the plan.

I start my climb along Swindale Beck, reaching the imposing Knock Old Man cairn, 500 metres above Dufton. This navigation aid is the signal to turn north-west, and I check my smartphone to confirm which path to follow. You do not want to get lost on this route as it is littered with shake holes and hashes (gullies used to flush out minerals) from the former lead mining industry of the nineteenth century. I double-check my position with map and compass. Sure enough, the enormous Buckminsterfullerene dome emerges in the mist, a surreal white monster football protecting the air traffic control radar. I'm walking in the right direction, but it would be all too easy to take a sheep-track path and end up hopelessly lost. I recheck compass and smartphone, noting a crossroad ahead as my next navigation point. It is marked by a beautifully carved flagstone, clearly indicating the way to Cross Fell.

I reach the trig pillar at 893 metres. This isolated peak is home to the only named wind in England, the Helm Wind. When a strong northeasterly is blowing, the vortex off the lee slope builds a howling wind that tears down the gullies. Wind speeds can reach 130 miles per hour on Great Dun Fell; it is not a place to linger. One of England's few bothies lies a mile north, beneath the scree slopes. Greg's Hut is a welcome shelter if conditions are poor. This former mining hut has a wood-burning stove (bring fuel) and sleeping platform. I give my ears a rest from the strengthening wind and enjoy lunch. I am glad I packed a thermos flask of tea. Navigation now is simple. You just follow the corpse road east and north to Carrigill. Grouse butts and vermin traps are everywhere along the seven-mile slog into the village. I walk alongside the River South Tyne, starting its journey to Newcastle on the east coast; I have crossed a significant watershed even though I am nearer to the Irish Sea.

The youth hostel has a note pinned to the door. They have decided a lone walker is to be a casualty of a subsequent block booking – a commercial consideration that makes my blood boil. There is no one to remonstrate with as the door is locked. I have to walk into Alston town centre and ask around. The Cumberland Inn has a vacancy. It is a delightful stay: lovely food, a welcoming host and a lively bar. I have to climb the stairs on my hands and knees to bed; it has been a long, hard day.

I grab lunch at the local Spar before continuing through South Tynedale. A cycle track offers an alternative route, but I stick to the path. A farmer on a quad bike with a sheepdog stop for a chat – the usual pleasantries.

'Good morning, are you lost?'

'Maybe, I'm walking the Pennine Way.'

'You need to cross the gate over there.' He points to the corner of the field.

'Thanks. I notice your bike is a diesel engine – that's unusual.'

'Aye. It's much cheaper to run. I can use lower-duty red diesel, but the bike is not as reliable. I struggle to find ways to save money nowadays. There's no profit in sheep farming now. I'm divorced, and the children have all got good jobs in the city. I've no idea what will become of the farm,' he adds.

The sheepdog stares at me with piercing eyes – one blue, one green. There is an almost uncanny sense of connection and understanding between us, as if he reads my mind. The heterochromic stare is bewitching.

'By the way, Spot agrees you're going the wrong way.' The dog barks once to confirm.

Sure enough, I have drifted off the path, but we continue to chat for a while. I sense the farmer hasn't spoken to anyone for a few days and he is glad of the company. So am I.

I haven't seen any walkers for a while either, but suddenly they are everywhere – a long line of day walkers on the ridgeline, another group of women ascending the hill. I hear the telltale thrum of a BMW motorcycle on the A689, a sure sign it is Saturday; everyone is out to enjoy the day. It is energy-sapping bog into Greenhead. A rude sign blocks my path, stating clearly, 'NOT Pennine Way'. I check my map and then proceed to another gate. I open it to be confronted by a bull in the field. My navigation has gone to pot today. I question my skills as I delicately walk around the beast, almost tripping up into a cast-iron bath repurposed as a water trough.

My boots are caked in peat as I enter the village. The Greenhead Tea Room is unconcerned as I ask to join other customers; they have seen enough walkers over the years. I enquire about the youth hostel, and they direct me to the pub opposite. They appear to own it too, so I settle in and return for a meal. The same woman who served me in the tea room is now working behind the bar. This family have a monopoly on Greenhead facilities. I can see the synergies as the hostel fills up with inebriated customers at closing time – a sensible approach, but not in the usual spirit of youth hostelling. The kitchen is next to useless – not even a kettle to use.

The Pennine Way joins up with Hadrian's Wall Path for a few miles. I'm walking before dawn and ascending to a Roman fort, passing Milecastle 46. The walk now takes a rollercoaster ride along the escarpment. Birdsong fills the still air, celebrating a new day. The deep red dawn fades to orange, igniting the moors in a beautiful soft light, revealing the texture of the land and the stunning archaeological features. It is a joy to be up so early walking through such a transcendental landscape.

I count off the milestones until I reach milestone 37A – a signal to depart from the wall and head north. That brief eight-mile Roman section gives way to bog and forest. The fields ahead are full of rams and horses, and it is breeding season. The sheep sporting fluorescent marks on their backs have had their turn. The stallions haul their genitalia between their legs; something is in the air that morning, and the sun has tickled everyone's pituitary gland (I am wearing a hat for protection). The path passes close to pretty cottages, some with overhanging fruit trees. The plums and apples are ripe and taste delicious. I am careful not to gorge on them, biting the flesh and spitting out the pips as I walk.

Bellingham appears after reaching the earthy-named Shitlington Crags. Crossing the North Tyne, I head for the hostel; a wood-burning stove crackles in the common room, but no one is around. Leaving my gear, I explore this busy Kielder Forest gateway town. The local Chinese takeaway has a menu of 400 dishes, but I have no energy to choose, so I copy the order from the customer ahead of me, on the basis that they might know more than I do. Returning to a spotlessly clean hostel kitchen, I devour the meal. A Danish fisherman turns up; he has been coming to this place for years.

'It is so far from the sea; I could not ask for more.' He has the smile of a man who has been looking forward to this week for months.

The warden arrives and checks us in. It is a relaxing place to stay: clean, comfortable and quiet. Forcing myself to have a lie-in, I leave late after breakfast. It is the penultimate day, and I know the real test is tomorrow. The moorland now seems like a second home; although featureless, there is always something of interest if you keep your eyes open. I have become attuned to any movement: a shy grouse, soaring buzzards, lizards and insects. A lonely hairy caterpillar is making steady progress across the open ground, its destination lost in a vastness of moorland. I get on my hands and knees to imagine my walk at its scale; this wee beastie is running an ultramarathon.

The landscape changes as I enter Kielder. A network of tracks and paths built with industrial efficiency overlay a vast forest. In between the precise array of trees lie huge volumes of fly agaric mushrooms, with their dark red caps and white spots. The shade provided by the fir trees means the path cannot dry out, so it is deep bog and ponds all the way. Health and safety diversions don't help either, directing me into the impenetrable forest. It is unpleasant walking into Blakehopeburnhaugh (eighteen letters), which I read is the longest place name in England, but someone missed Cottonshopeburnfoot (nineteen letters), a short distance further on.

I am met by Joyce, waving from the door of Forest View Lodge, my accommodation for the night. This well-known Pennine Way establishment is the only option in the area. The welcome is warm and friendly; she knows the routine by now. She places my boots in a drying room; tea and cake are served and stories told. I can listen to her comprehensive knowledge and wisdom for hours. She sees patterns in customer visits: teachers arriving two weeks after school breaks for the summer; clusters of Land's End to John o'Groats and Pennine Way walkers (up to sixty stayed this year). She thinks the recession has increased bookings from those who have lost their jobs. She goes on: the fastest completion is … , the most times completed is … , and so on. I'm one of the last she expects to see this year; the snows are due soon on the Cheviots.

The conversation continues over a simple evening meal. The house is covered in 'Please do not … ' notices; the 'shop' is a cupboard full of simple goods priced to the nearest penny, each labelled with a handwritten ticket. For 89p I can buy a tin of tomato soup. It is very quirky and charming. Joyce knows I will have to leave before dawn, so she pre-lays a simple breakfast. Someone has cleaned my boots; they are unrecognisably bone dry too. I set off into the pitch-black night, barely able to see a black cat cross my path – a good omen. Today is a twenty-seven-mile walk to the finish.

Last night's briefing from Joyce included which flagstones have broken, where the boggiest sections are, and where the escape points are. It is a long, remote, high-level section and not usually completed in one day. I consider an overnight contingency at Auchope bothy if the weather turns. As I ascend to Bryness Hill, some joker has placed a television on the fence, like some surreal, funny-ironic comment on the nature of reality; I wish I had taken a photo. Another bright red dawn emerges. The biblical rhyme 'Red sky in the morning, shepherd's warning' is not encouraging as I reach open moorland and look east over an ominous sky.

Instructions to follow fence lines and divert along ridges are perfect. I can avoid the worst of the bog. Soon I am on firmer grassland heading towards Chew Green, a substantial Roman camp. The Cheviots are covered in ancient paths and drove roads, connecting Scotland to England. The ridge follows the border over a sine wave of peaks and passes. To the south-east lies Otterburn camp, an enormous army training ground which extends into the distance. The first mountain hut I arrive at is full of young soldiers, a staging post for today's yomping competition. They puff on their cigarettes and give me a stare that clearly says I cannot come in. A mile later, a squad of heavily laden soldiers is pacing up the hill, carrying heavy Bergen backpacks and fully armed with rifles and general-purpose machine guns and tripods. The staff sergeant stops to talk.

'Aye, these lads are doing well, only another thirty clicks to go.'

'How much weight are they carrying?' I ask, curious to compare with my fifteen-kilogram load.

'Maybe forty kilograms, depending on how many rocks their mates have sneaked into the packs,' he says, laughing. 'What are you doing up here?'

I explain that I am finishing the Pennine Way today, a twenty-seven-mile walk into Kirk Yetholm, setting off at 6 a.m. this morning.

'Aye, nae bad. By the way, we have left a few whizz bangs on the bridges ahead, be careful of the trip wires! They're to wake up the sleepyheads.'

A quick look at his map confirms I will miss these bridges, but it is good to know.

'Gotta go.' He is off, running up the hill to catch his squad and make sure they are not cheating (or smoking).

I meet another squad a few moments later and stop the leader to mention missing flagstones. Joyce had warned me that some have broken and sunk into the bog, hidden with inky black water. I have a habit of testing each suspect step with my walking pole. A few hundred yards earlier, it unexpectedly disappeared at least three or four feet into the ground – a dangerous hazard that could easily break a leg.

'Mind the sunken flagstone ahead. It's hidden in a pool of water.'

'Thanks, mate,' he says, unwrapping another Snickers bar.

Mozie Law and Windy Gyle follow another wonderfully named Beefstand Hill. The clouds are clearing, and I can see the North Sea and into the Southern Uplands of Scotland, perhaps from the most utterly remote part of England, with rolling fells and moors in all directions. I know I am miles from civilisation, yet two gentlemen turn up dressed in kilts. They are on a day walk and parked their Land Rover on the col that leads to Cocklawfoot or Trows Farm – one of the escape routes off the path and an option for walkers who will take two days on this section.

I clatter on, using my poles for purchase as I ascend towards the Cheviot, but I leave the optional summit diversion for another day, preferring to take the route to the Auchope bothy to fuel up for the final stretch. It is good to be out of the wind as I finish my flask of tea and sandwiches. I sign the visitors' book, full of amusing graffiti, and set off north. I don't want my legs to seize up now, but I have to stop at the Schil for one last look as I descend wearily into Kirk Yetholm, taking the low route. After one final climb, which must have been cursed by many, I reach the Border Hotel, in Scotland.

I call Joyce to let her know I have arrived.

'Good time, well done,' she says. 'I'm glad you're safe.' Having her know my itinerary was reassuring.

The independently run Friends of Nature hostel is delightful, with a chatty warden, Simon. We talk for an hour before my stomach starts making rude noises. It is mandatory to visit the

Border Hotel, but the evening meal is expensive, and the long tradition of a free half pint has faded. Wainwright put up £15,000 of his own money to fund it, but that has long since lapsed, I assume. I sign the book, but the staff are indifferent, so I am happy to return to the common room, for a cup of tea and a chat. A young girl arrives late. She is staying for a few weeks, counting bats.

Simon tries to persuade me to run a hostel, as we discuss the politics of the youth hostel organisations. He is fed up of people booking the place just because it is the cheaper option, and then expecting televisions and full evening meals. He mentions that Kirk Yetholm is the start of the unofficial Scottish national trail, another 500-odd miles north to Cape Wrath, the most north-westerly tip of the Highlands.

Now there's a thought to ponder on the train home.

8

COTSWOLD WAY

Distance: 102 miles
Days to complete: 5 days
Mileage so far: 1,663 miles

SPRING DASH

I am a slow walker, but I never walk back.
– Abraham Lincoln

I have a week to spare and check through the National Trail possibilities. The Cotswold Way fits perfectly at 102 miles in length, and is close to home. By way of a train to Stratford-upon-Avon and a bus to Chipping Campden, I am standing beside a stone pillar which marks 'COTSWOLD WAY – THE BEGINNING AND THE END'. My pedantic mind wonders how it can be both at the same time. Is this a Schrödinger's cat thought experiment, the answer unknown until the presence of an observer? A new marker stone was installed in 2016; its inscription offers one explanation:

> *In my beginning is my end. Now the light falls*
> *Across the open field, leaving the deep lane*
> *Shuttered with branches, dark in the afternoon,*
> *Where you lean against a bank while a van passes,*
> *And the deep lane insists on the direction*

Into the village, in the electric heat
Hypnotised. In a warm haze the sultry light
Is absorbed, not reflected, by grey stone.
The dahlias sleep in the empty silence.
Wait for the early owl.

– T.S. Eliot, from *Four Quartets* (1943)[7]

Chipping Campden is a dusky Cotswold wool-market town, with an elegant terraced high street. The buildings are constructed from a warm Jurassic limestone – a distinctive motif that is pleasing to the eye. The golden hue of the stone walls and farm buildings complements the broad green fields and azure skies perfectly – a colour match an artist would use.

I climb up to the ridge to views across Evesham Vale, before turning south towards Broadway Tower, at 313 metres' elevation. On a clear day, you can see sixteen counties from this superb viewpoint, conceived by Capability Brown and built by James Watt, in 1794. It is an imposing self-indulgent structure featuring battlements, gargoyles and turrets that serve no practical purpose; they are purely aesthetic.

I'd prefer to maintain height, but the path descends steeply into Broadway, a popular tourist destination in this area of outstanding natural beauty. It is not as busy as it can get; but the shops and cafes are full, making it difficult to find lunch unless you explore the back streets where the locals go. A simple sandwich and I'm on my way, ascending on to the ridge with views now encompassing the Severn Valley. The village of Stanton lies ahead; in comparison to Broadway, it is unspoilt. The golden-stone cottages jealously guard their original patina, without a hint of restoration or modernisation. Old oak doors nestle underneath the lintels, protecting hidden rooms of incredible beauty and comfort.

I meet Alex a few miles out of the village, and we walk together for a while. She is an artist who has walked a few National Trails and enjoys wild camping. We spend a couple of hours exchanging life stories, which make the miles go by. She too walked the

Pennine Way a few years earlier, and we laugh at the shared experience and trials we faced.

'Nice walking poles,' she says. 'Do you think they help?'

'Yes, in many ways. They are fall arresters, dog defenders, fruit pickers, cattle prods, bog testers, bushwhackers and turn me into a 4x4 walker.'

'I agree,' she says. 'You travel light – where's all your gear?'

'I'm not camping for this trip, I prefer a fast walk and comfortable stays. I couldn't find any campsites in the right locations.'

We walk past Stanway House, a stunning yellow-stone Jacobean manor house, and home to the tallest fountain in Britain, at ninety metres. It also holds the record for the tallest gravity-fed fountain in the world, supplied by a reservoir in the hills 180 metres above. Only the turbine-powered fountain on Lake Geneva is higher. Such amusing facts add to the conversation, but we say our goodbyes before Winchcombe. She is off to find a campsite, which makes me feel guilty about the room I have booked at the White Hart Inn.

Ascending the next day, I reach Belas Knap Long Barrow, an early Neolithic burial chamber, some 5,500 years old. I descend again through woodland and see three shy roe deer, observing me intently before leaping away through the trees. It is a stormy, sometimes sunny, rainbow-like day, casting a regal light on Postlip Hall, a co-housing community living in a manor house nestled in a gully in the hillside. They have found a secret for sustained social harmony and living for over fifty years.

The path now follows the ridge around Cheltenham, a Regency spa town cuddled by the Cotswold Hills. Every detail can be seen: the racecourse, numerous churches, colleges and schools. A Gloucestershire Warwickshire Steam Railway train puffs away, marking its passage with plumes of steam rising in the cold morning air. The views give the impression of walking above a model village. I spend a while at Cleeve Hill studying the detail and identifying features against my OS map, confirming my sightings with a compass (usually buried deep in my rucksack). Further on, you can see the mountains of South Wales and the River

Severn, which meanders out to the Bristol Channel towards the horizon.

Outside the town lies the Government Communications Head-quarters (GCHQ) – an enormous doughnut-shaped spaceship nestled in the suburbs. This organisation superseded the Government Code and Cypher School (GC&CS) in 1944. During the war, the industrialisation of intelligence gathering gave birth to the earliest computers, imagined by Alan Turing, and built by Tommy Flowers in 1941. Both the early electromechanical (Bombe) and later electronic valve-driven (Colossus) computers can still be seen in the museum at Bletchley Park. Based on the same principles, modern systems with exponentially more power analyse data in real time. New-generation artificial intelligence and quantum computers are perhaps in use today too (it's top secret, so we don't know). How ironic that a humble smartphone can track GCHQ employees on their lunchtime Strava runs.

I have plenty of warning of rain showers as they arrive, donning my waterproof just seconds before the heavens open. The light is intense and fresh, illuminating the bright yellow fields of oilseed rape. The electricity pylons accurately follow the path, making navigation easy and keeping my map dry. The road noise directs me to Birdlip. The hotel is dreary, like a budget business bed block, devoid of character. At least it has a deep bath to soak my weary legs, but I wish I had brought my bivouac gear.

The evening meal and breakfast are mediocre. There seems to be an inverse correlation between price and quality in this area. Unless you wild camp (problematic in tightly managed dog-walking countryside) you have few options. Finding a campsite is difficult. Prices can escalate dramatically during the Cheltenham Festival or Badminton Horse Trials, so timing is all-important. It is perhaps the one National Trail where it is wise to book ahead.

The day starts bright as I walk along a woodland path. The bluebells and wild garlic have exploded under the beech trees. The pungent aroma is overpowering. Deer are a common sight if you tread lightly and keep your eyes open. Stop, stare and study them, until they turn into the woods. Their eyes rely on movement to detect a threat, and if you stay still, they are unsure of your intentions. The dappled light under the tree canopy enhances their camouflage. I'm sure I'd see more if I wasn't wearing a red waterproof.

I stay with the contours to Cooper's Hill, the site of the famous annual cheese-rolling competition held on the spring bank holiday. The event was traditionally for the village folk of Brockworth. It may derive from the pagan habit of rolling large objects down steep hills. In this case, a four-kilogram Double Gloucester cheese is released from the top of a very steep concave incline, chased by a line of competitors, who launch themselves recklessly after it. The objective is to catch the cheese – a somewhat unachievable feat unless you exceed seventy miles per hour. The event has been summarised as 'Twenty young men chasing a piece of cheese off a cliff, tumbling 200 yards to the paramedics who scrape them up and pack them off to the hospital!' Health and Safety have recently intervened, and a foam cheese is now used after someone realised it could veer off course and seriously injure someone. What would England be without this mad eccentricity?

The frantic nature of the competition is in contrast to meditative walking: a cadence of breath, motion and heartbeat blend with the birdsong and rustling leaves. My mental rhythms harmonise with woodland sounds; it is a joyous state to be in. I am walking without effort and without thought, almost floating. The experience can be sustained for hours if the conditions allow, but it is rare for this to happen.

Dodging golf balls at Painswick golf course, I enter the historic wool town in search of lunch. The churchyard is resplendent with ninety-nine yew trees, neatly trimmed, standing like lost souls in the graveyard. A strict building code protects the soft-yellow stone buildings. You are viewing a scene unchanged in 200 years; the only foreign objects are motor vehicles and people wearing unnatural colours. Bluebells and wild garlic are replaced by fields of buttercups as I pass a sign indicating fifty-five miles to Bath. Almost halfway now. I stop at a topograph, which shows the relief of the landscape and my position in it. The brass ridges on the dial are polished by the touch of a million human fingers, revealing the famous landmarks – the top ten views, as voted by generations of walkers. The panorama is extensive: both Severn bridges can clearly be seen to the south-west of the escarpment, deeper Wales to the west, Herefordshire to the north – the land carved by the Severn estuary, which runs to the Bristol Channel.

Dropping into Stroud to cross the River Frome I walk past private school playing fields. The girls are playing rounders, the boys cricket, confirming stereotypes. All of them follow a strict dress code. It is like a fashion prison with no possibility of deviation. I only have a few miles to go before reaching a B&B in Middleyard. The landlady is very welcoming, and I can relax in her conservatory, overlooking the fields. The house is spotless. It is time to book one more night's accommodation and catch up with some reading. The chair envelops me in comfortable cushions almost to the point where I cannot stand. A cuddly toy drops on my lap, one of a selection that rests on the furniture.

My walking meditation continues the next morning through superb woodlands that blanket the steeper sections of the landscape, the trees unspoilt and intact purely because the land cannot be cultivated. Long barrows and ancient hillforts command strategic views across the River Severn into Wales. Iron Age communities established defensive strongholds on isolated geological anomalies, somehow detached from the main escarpment, floating out to sea. I hitch a ride on Cam Long Down into Dursley – a popular centre for walkers.

My relaxed pacing ends. I must climb steeply out of the town on to a downland tabletop peninsula that hosts a golf course. A circumnavigation is rewarded with exceptional views. Who could argue that 'golf is a good walk spoiled' with such an outlook? It is a pity to lose height again into a valley peppered with freshwater springs, to climb once more to the Tyndale monument on Nibley Knoll. This structure commemorates the life of William Tyndale, the scholar who first translated the Bible into English. I stand two metres in front of a building that has piqued my curiosity for two days; it occupies such a prominent position on the ridgeline.

En route to Wotton-under-Edge, I take lunch beneath a cluster of pine trees. Planted initially to mark the Battle of Waterloo in 1815, they were chopped down and burnt at the end of the Crimean War in 1856 and replanted again for Victoria's Golden Jubilee in 1887. Death and rebirth. I add a small pine cone to my backpack, one of a thousand that litter the ground – a good luck charm with excellent ancestry.

The town is busy with shoppers and traffic, but I have no reason to stop. I meet a trio of walkers in training for the Yorkshire Three Peaks; I have to up my pace to stay with them. They circle back, and I then meet another group, who are uncomfortable crossing a field with cattle blocking the path. The cows are with calves, so we give them a wide berth. A dog off its lead doesn't help, and the cows are intelligent enough to take up the matter with the pet's owner. Several years spent working on farms has taught me enough to understand their basic behaviour, but they still frighten me at times. Safely across, I head for Hawkesbury Upton and the Fox Inn. It is a comfortable stay with an excellent embedded Italian restaurant, managed by welcoming hosts. A glass of red is more than enough to initiate deep sleep to finish my day. I forget to write up my journal.

Now I have a twenty-five-mile sprint into Bath to catch a train home. I'm in the mood for a fast-paced march, without regard to the views; it is rare for me to be an athlete and not a rambler. I wolf down the bacon roll that has been left for me, with instructions on how to let myself out. I'm on a mission – starting now at 6 a.m.

The heavy dew soaks my boots thoroughly, but I don't mind. I love being up this early before the villages wake. The route is mostly arable farmland now, with few woodland areas. This is not a day for meditation. I am striding out, breathing in the dense dawn air with eyes forward and arms swinging.

Dropping down into Horton Court, there is a grand pepperpot folly, designed to provide a home for swallows and owls. Asterisk-shaped windows discourage pigeons from squatting. I progress through sleepy villages and fields, past yet more Iron Age forts towards the unmistakable white-noise drone of the M4. I reach the motorway via Dodington Park, another landscape designed by Capability Brown. It is full of ancient oaks and clumps of woodland laid out like a well-composed painting.

I cross the motorway and walk under enormous pylons, launching their high-tension cables off the hill to span the estuary towards South Wales. A strip-lynchet field system leads past Dyrham Park, an impressive baroque country house and deer park. I stop briefly at a petrol station on the A46 for Snickers bar fuel, which I need to negotiate the rugged hills ahead towards Lansdown Hill. On this tabletop-shaped down, contour lines stop at 230 metres, as if a potter has shaved off the wet clay peak with wire before firing the Cotswold Hills in the oven. The flat grasslands are ideal for a racecourse or a conflict. The Battle of Lansdowne, in 1643, is marked by a simple stone which depicts a looting soldier, to add to the many monuments in England that commemorate bloody conflict between Royalists and Parliamentarians. Today, Bath racecourse hosts regular flat races – horses for leisure rather than at war.

Bristol is laid out below and can be read like a map. Prospect Stile topograph explains the view to the south and east, where I can see the Roman spa city of Bath, my destination. For the last time, I descend from the ridge into the outskirts, stopping at a trig pillar to orientate my mental compass towards the centre. I emerge from parkland into an expanse of Georgian architecture, the crowning glory of the Cotswold art. Some buildings are six storeys high. The Royal Crescent is a masterpiece: thirty terraced houses built in a sweeping crescent, audacious and opulent.

The city is packed with tourists and commercial life. I have to adjust to the melee of people, bicycles, cars and buses. I am heading for Bath Abbey and the end of the Cotswold Way. The churchyard is packed. The marker stone reveals itself as a crowd of Japanese tourists move along after they have been briefed by their tour guide. The outer ring reads:

Stand ye in the ways and see, ask for the old paths, where is the good way, and walk therein, and ye shall find rest for your souls.

I'm exhausted. I count off the names of features etched in the circular Irish blue limestone which recall the places I have walked through over the past five days – an odd choice of stone colour, but the perfect punctuation for a fantastic walk. This is my end.

I am sitting on the platform at Bath station waiting for the InterCity 125 and overhear a conversation. An American woman has lost her husband. They arrived at Heathrow a few hours ago from Boise, Idaho; it is the first time they have ever left the US.

'Can you help me find my husband?' she asks the station manager.

'Yes, when did you see him last?'

'He went to explore the train half an hour ago, but he didn't get off at Bath.' The manager gets on her radio.

'Crrcch. George. We have a missing person. Get on to control and see if we can call the guard on the 15.50 from Paddington. Crrcch.'

He has no identification, passport or money, and the Great Western Railway staff are busily trying to work out where on earth he could be. As time passes, the possibilities multiply. I wisely set my alarm to wake me before I reach Reading, lest I fall asleep and wake up in Paddington. Even a local can make such a simple mistake.

9

NORTH DOWNS WAY

Distance: 125 miles
Days to complete: 5 days
Mileage so far: 1,765 miles

PILGRIMS' WAY

To go fast, go alone; to go far, go together.
– African proverb

Another opportunity opens in the summer of 2014. I have a gap in my work schedule, and my wife has booked a course for a few weeks. The plan is to walk both the North and South Downs ways in one continuous journey, as fast and as light as possible, starting at Farnham and finishing at Winchester within two weeks. I'll be walking through the prosperous commuter belt with few campsites and expensive B&Bs. Stealthy wild camping with a bivvy bag will allow flexibility. I book a train ticket for Monday morning.

A fatality on the railway line, announced thirty minutes after leaving Waterloo station, scuppers my plan for an early start. I do not reach Farnham until midday, almost three hours late. It is a baking hot day, over 30 °C, with very little wind. My lightweight pack doubles in weight with the three litres of water I am carrying, using two Platypus bladders and a Nalgene water bottle. I take no cooking gear and a bare minimum of clothing, together with a light sleeping bag, foam mat and bivvy bag.

The initial fingerpost points to Dover, some 153 miles away, but that assumes you complete the Canterbury loop. My route is 125 miles, the more direct southern option. I get going towards Guildford, with no fixed plan other than to reach Newlands Corner for something to eat. I am going to leave the accommodation to chance; what is the worst that can happen in such warm weather? As long as I am fed and watered I can walk to my schedule. I am glad of the shade for the first few miles, walking alongside hedgerows, with a few trees in full fruit. The cherry-sized yellow and red plums are delicious and abundant; it is a variety I have never seen in a supermarket. I shake the branch, and a rainstorm of delicious foraged food falls to the ground. I could not have timed the harvest more perfectly, but caution against eating too many, like some Labrador-brained schoolchild who will later regret a sick stomach.

The footpath follows a dry valley, beneath the Hog's Back ridge towards the southern outskirts of Guildford, a sizeable commuter-belt town, rejoining the Pilgrims' Way. This path is a historical route between Winchester and Canterbury, named by an imaginative Ordnance Survey surveyor who recognised ancient ways between two crucial religious centres. The high and low paths weave in and out of the chalk, greensand and clay, forming the northern boundary walls of the Weald (an enclosed area of sand once covered in an ancient forest). The southern boundary is the South Downs Way. I will, in effect, circumnavigate this distinctive geological feature.

Earlier pilgrims would make the journey east to pay homage to Thomas Becket's shrine in Canterbury Cathedral. Murdered by Henry II's men in 1170, the archbishop is venerated as a saint and martyr by both Catholics and Anglicans, sealing his high status. By making such a journey, you were demonstrating your faith or seeking absolution (or completing a shorter pilgrimage, for Catholics avoiding the trip to Rome).

I am climbing through the sand to St Martha's Church, perched on an enormous dune, as if by the sea. The views are not of the English Channel, but the western extent of the Low Weald towards the South Downs. It is a glorious place to stop and rest, to soak in the modern arable and woodland landscape. The fields are tinder dry and golden in the midsummer drought. I finish a litre of water to quench my thirst, knowing I can replenish soon at Newlands Corner. 'Yellow or straw, must drink more' will be my mantra for the weeks ahead (referring to the colour of your urine – an indicator of dehydration).

> Have you not heard of the road that we long ago travell'd with
>   Chaucer,
> Here on the Pilgrim's Way, spanning the length of the Downs?
> Have you not seen these yews, still green in their sæcular glory,
> Marking the course of the route – older than Edward the Third?
> Well, we are with them now, on the height that faces St Martha's,
> Thus on a summer eve watching the sunset awhile;
> Watching the golden moon, as she rises afar to the eastward,
> Over the Silent Pool, over the hollows of Shere.
>
> – Arthur Joseph Munby,
> from 'Then and Now – The North Downs' (1899)

The cafe serves a diverse group of walkers, cyclists, motorcyclists and daytrippers, keen to take in the glory of the Surrey Hills. I order a high-calorie burger and chips for my evening meal and refill with water for the next stage. I pour a litre over my head to cool down, before a second refill. I have been walking for five hours and can slow down and find a suitable wild-camping spot in the woods. I eventually hide behind a bramble hedge on a south-facing slope, trying not to snooze too early. I can lay out my sleeping kit and relax as the sun starts to set.

The deep amber dusk is a signal for wildlife to emerge. In the silence of the evening, I can see a barn owl drift across the field below. A roe deer stag announces its territory, with a loud drawn-out bark, like a dog with a chest infection. It cannot see me in my prone position as it leaps up the hill, without effort, followed by its harem. The owls keep me awake as I soak in the night sky, counting shooting stars and early evening satellites in the moonless heavens.

It is lovely to sleep exposed to nature; I drift off to sleep. Strange noises fade to dreaming.

If anyone will catch you wild camping, it is a cocker spaniel, out for an early morning walk. Fortunately, I am up and decamped, but at 5 a.m. it is quite a surprise to see anyone. The owner is sitting on a bench as I rejoin the path.

'Up bright and early,' I say.

He is unconcerned at my camping exploits.

'Yes, every morning, since my wife passed away a few months ago.'

'Oh. I'm so sorry to hear that. Does your dog miss her too?'

'Yes, quite a bit,' he says as I pet his spaniel.

'Another hot day by the looks of it; at least it is cooler at this hour.'

'Oh yes, perhaps for the rest of the week too.'

I am not one to intrude; his early morning walk and faithful companion are ideal bereavement therapy. His dog has finished exploring every last square metre of the surrounding woodland and returns to demand they move along, just as we conclude our conversation. I have about six miles to reach the A24, where I know the famous Ryka's bikers' cafe will serve breakfast. Even at a relaxed pace, I arrive too early – a half-hour wait for two mugs of tea and a bacon and egg roll.

They kindly fill up my water containers before I set off south along the A24 once more. Just a short few yards and I'm cautiously crossing the stepping stones across the River Mole, a picturesque spot that marks the beginning of a steep 120-metre ascent to Box Hill. The summit is marked by Leopold Salomons' memorial just above a trig pillar – in memory of his gift of Box Hill to the nation in 1914. The area seems to be sponsored by SIS (Science in Sport) as their customers have thoughtlessly left hundreds of empty fuel-gel squeeze tubes by the roadside, having just climbed the Zig Zag Road. They have cornered the market with an inspired marketing campaign: their brand and used products are littering the very landscape their customers enjoy. It is such a shock to see, but nowhere near as shocking as a gang of high-speed mountain bikers racing through the woodland at breakneck speed. I have to dive into the hedge to avoid a collision. They are like kids on a glucose-tartrazine-caffeine hyperactive rush. I must check the ingredients of these gels; they induce mania – not a condition I wish to emulate on a relaxing walk.

The path follows the base of the ridge before ascending above the Weald to the Inglis memorial: a striking drinking fountain at the summit of Colley Hill. The views are extensive and not what you expect a few hundred metres from the M25 motorway, which thrums away in the background. I can see the ridgeline for several miles east. I do not need a compass or map to navigate.

Gatton Park is a welcome stop for a nice meal and a rest. I can see Gatwick airport in action. Skies of aircraft circle and land at two-minute intervals; aircraft take off between arrivals, into the wind. I have a second ice lolly and fill my water containers again. A blocking high pressure is sitting on south-east England, creating hot and humid conditions. The thermometer is still in the thirties, and I drink at every opportunity to avoid dehydration. I add a packet of crisps for minerals and nutrients.

The M25 will be a friend now for a few days until I turn east alongside the M20. The new highways of commerce follow the old, seeking the same geological advantages through the valleys and hills. Both the North Downs and Pilgrims' Way have chosen a high ridge route which attracts golf courses and radio antennae for the commanding views and radio coverage. A rare and welcome water tap allows me to cool down and wash before I start my search for a wild campsite. There are no accessible woodlands to hide in, so I lie in a rough field amongst the wildflowers, hidden from view.

I count the endless fleets of articulated lorries heading for the ports, thankful I have earplugs, as they will continue through the night. I sleep surprisingly well on a bed of grass, but I'm woken early by a keen jogger and his dog, getting in five kilometres before breakfast. It is an excuse to get walking soon in the cold air; I will have a midday siesta later. After a good ten miles or so I arrive in Otford, with a lovely tea room which I can sit in for a while and work my way through the menu. A duck pond opposite looks inviting, the temptation to dive thwarted by common sense. I can get a shower at a B&B near Cuxton, which has a vacancy. It is going to be another twenty-seven-mile day, but I know I can pamper myself this evening. I climb on to Otford Mount and a trig pillar that marks magnificent views yet again. I walk at a pace adjusted to the heat, just fast enough to break a sweat, but no more, conserving body fluid.

I join walkers at Trosley country park, taking an afternoon stroll in the shade. I head north through a land of lost villages and timber-framed cottages, untouched by time. The last mile descends through fields ripe for harvest. Fine-barbed barley grasses pierce my socks. It takes a while to pull them through before I knock on the door of my B&B.

It is a beautifully converted barn, and the hosts could not be more welcoming. I can shower and then relax in their living room, drinking tea and eating home-baked cake. I sleep like a baby and wake late to a superb cooked breakfast. My energy and hydration levels have been reset, after a seventy-five-mile sprint over two and a half long days' fast walking in a heatwave. The landlady tells me a story of two American walkers found suffering from heatstroke. Their water bladders split on a remote part of the trail; in only a few miles, they became weak and had to rest. Somehow this story made the local press, the sort of story they like to feed on: tales of misfortune and foreign interest.

I now drink at least a litre of water before starting the day, forcing it down. It is so hot, the three litres I am carrying seem insufficient without a refill at lunchtime. Suitably hydrated, I ascend into Ranscombe Farm nature reserve, to views over the Medway Valley. Both the M2 and a high-speed rail link cross the river, which drains the north part of the Weald into the Thames estuary. It is the second-largest catchment area in the south of England and the first major river crossing since Farnham. Just as I reach the railway bridge, an HS1 train flies through on its way to London from France. This section holds the UK rail speed record of 208 miles per hour (335 kilometres per hour), set in 2003 by another HS1/Eurostar train.

The motorway crossing offers extensive views towards Chatham. The tide is out, stranding vessels on the mudflats in the marina. The drone of the M2 is intense until the path turns inland and ascends once more on to the chalk ridgeway. I pass Kit's Coty House and Little Kit's Coty House, two long-barrow dolmen burial chambers with views south across the Weald, a view they have enjoyed for over 4,000 years. The name could mean 'Tomb in the Forest' at a time when the land below was impenetrable woodland rather than the arable landscape of today. My route is an ancient motorway and railway line.

Dean, a fast walker, catches me up on the path. He is taking his weekly constitutional from Rochester out into the downs and back, some twenty miles. He has been unemployed for several years, and this is the cheapest form of exercise he knows. I up my pace to maintain conversation until we reach Jade's Bridge, which crosses the A249 near Detling. He explains its significance.

'Jade and her grandmother were killed when crossing the dual carriageway on 16 December 2000,' he reads. 'It took a twenty-year campaign to get a bridge built, something that should have been done when the new road severed the village in half in 1962. It took the deaths of four people to persuade the council to act finally,' he continues.

We are both grateful for a crossing which now bears both the Pilgrims' and North Downs ways. Dean carries on his route home, and I finish the last of my water supply before ascending again on to the ridge and a superb viewpoint from the White Horse Wood country park. I take a well-earned rest; trying to keep up with Dean for the past couple of hours has exhausted me. I drift dangerously into slumber under an old tree. A skylark sings above, unseen, an evocative summer tune.

> He rises and begins to round,
> He drops the silver chain of sound,
> Of many links without a break,
> In chirrup, whistle, slur and shake [...]
> For singing till his heaven fills,
> 'Tis love of earth that he instils,
> And ever winging up and up,

Our valley is his golden cup,
And he the wine which overflows
To lift us with him as he goes.
        – George Meredith, from 'The Lark Ascending' (1881)

I slow the pace into Hollingbourne, which has a pub called the Dirty Habit, an ancient watering hole. It is impossible to pass. I enter and order a pint of fruit juice and water, topped up with ice, which I down before the barman can return my change. A second pint doesn't touch the sides, but a third is joined by a packet of crisps and consumed at leisure. The locals are laughing.

'Thirsty, mate? Don't you fancy a proper pint?' said in a tone that means, 'like a real man.' I decline. They are clearly on a roll, with the telltale red noses of seasoned drinkers; they have been at it for a few hours, it seems.

'Where are you walking?' one asks.

'Along the North Downs Way. I left Farnham on Monday.' (It is Thursday lunchtime now.)

'Seriously? In this weather?' another mutters, sipping more beer. They now have an explanation for my thirst as I ask the barman to fill up my three litre containers to supplement the three pints of chilled juice I have just downed (keep up, boys).

'Watch out for the black panther,' they say. 'There have been rumours of a big wild black cat in the woods around here.' They cackle, now laughing at their own jokes.

I set off on the Pilgrims' Way, marked by the first scallop shell sign I have ever seen – similar to those on the Camino de Santiago in northern Spain. The scallop shell has been a symbol of pilgrimage for centuries. The radiating lines are a metaphor for the routes pilgrims follow to their destination. They serve a practical purpose as a scoop, to receive food once offered by people supporting these religious journeys. More likely, they were an artefact to prove completion – a representation of the setting sun on the day's effort. My favourite explanation relates to the goddess Venus as a symbol of love and rebirth. She possesses an authentic and shameless self, beautifully depicted in Botticelli's painting *The*

Birth of Venus. She emerges from the sea, fully grown, aboard her protective mother scallop shell. This image mirrors the experience of self-awareness and discovery when walking.

The harvest is in full swing: an enormous CLAAS combine harvester comes towards me down the bridleway. Fortunately, it turns into a field before it unfurls its massive wings and commences to sheer the corn. I gawp in wonder at the brutal efficiency; attendant tractors pull grain bins that fill in moments. This task used to be done by hand with a scythe; it must have taken a dozen men a full day to do one field.

I only have a few miles to reach Lenham and the accommodation I have booked for the evening; I am in no hurry. I stop to rest and meet Percy.

'Pilgrim bound by staff and faith, rest thy bones!' Percy is Brother Percival, a wooden carving of a monk at rest on a bench. A couple are feeding cats with titbits on the picnic table next to me.

'Are you taking the cats for a walk?' I ask.

'Oh no. They live here. We come out and feed them occasionally,' she replies. It is a strange sight and a routine that seems perfectly reasonable for them.

'Can we take your picture?'

'Of course. Can you take one of me too on my phone? I want to mimic Percy, with eyes closed, resting.'

They have seen something that is not apparent to me: the striking resemblance of my number 1 haircut and head shape to Percy's. I mirror his closed eyes and resting palm as they capture a picture that has me in stitches when I view it later that day; it is uncanny how alike Percy and I look.

At the Dog & Bear Hotel, I treat myself to a cracking good evening meal and comfortable bed, with a pint or two of Shepherd Neame, from a brewery claiming to be the oldest in Britain, having brewed at Faversham since 1573. It is a delightful summer evening, watching the local Morris men perform in the square opposite, holding a clean pint and nursing legs that have taken 46,000 steps over twenty-one miles (according to my new pedometer).

The Chalk Cross, above the village, is sitting in a field of poppies that have finished flowering. The memorial commemorates forty-two (that number again) men who fought and died in the Great War. During the Second World War, it was covered in soil to remove it as a navigation aid, but it returned to its original function afterwards, adding a further fourteen names to the list. It is a poignant reminder of the sacrifice made by so many men.

Powered by a full breakfast, I am making good progress along a byway that would make an excellent off-road cycle route – an ancient trackway that retains rights as a thoroughfare for commerce, long since diverted to the A20 and M20. It is easy walking into the Kent fruit farms and orchards until I reach Wye, a lovely village on the Great Stour. The Tickled Trout pub is catering for a busy Friday lunchtime crowd. It is very tempting to stop, but I find the Co-op in the centre of the village. I walk around the chilled aisles, enjoying the air conditioning for longer than necessary. I snack on a bench in the churchyard, studying a map. I have passed the point where the North Downs Way diverts to Canterbury, and I leave the Pilgrims' Way to head south-east to Folkestone on the more direct route to Dover.

The view from the Floreat Wye millennium stone on the ridge above Wye gives no hint of the enormous chalk crown carved below on the face of the downs. The views south to the Weald have not changed for several days now. The same golden fields ripe for harvest, or shorn of their crop, fit into a pattern of woodland and village that is recognisably England. The path hugs the ridge for several miles, descending briefly into Stowting to pass yet another welcoming pub, the Tiger Inn. I know a visit will severely curtail my pace, but what an excellent pub crawl this walk would make.

It is fortunate timing, as when I reach the ridge again, I can hear the unmistakable sound of a Rolls-Royce Merlin engine approaching. Sure enough, a Supermarine Spitfire roars overhead at a low level, then climbs into a roll above the downland landscape. Here is *the* iconic warplane in the very skies it fought over, during the summer of 1940. It sends tingles down my spine, and I have to sit and watch the free display. It swoops down low over the hills, and I can see it land at an airstrip that you would not believe existed in the valley below – what luck, what emotion, what a privilege to witness!

At Etchinghill, I am hoping to get a meal, but yet another pub has succumbed to commercial reality and closed. I take a chance at the local golf club; they are more than happy to serve a simple meal for a walker. I will have to find a wild-camping spot in the next few hours, so stock up on snacks and fill my water containers. One last climb on to the ridge and I find a field with long grass, an ideal spot to lay my bivvy bag. It is a warm evening, but the cloud formations foretell changing weather conditions. I recall the words I learnt on the farm as a boy:

Mares' tails and mackerel scales make lofty ships carry low sails,
or
Mackerel sky, mackerel sky, never long wet, never long dry.

True to form, it rains overnight, after a glorious orange sunset (I wonder what happened to 'Red sky at night ... '). The views over the English Channel are sublime: smooth seas and un-obstructed views until the rain starts. The weather is changing: the blocking high is on the move; the hot spell will end with dramatic thunderstorms and heavy rain. I hunker down in my bivvy bag to keep dry until morning.

It is a short walk to the stunning rail terminal that marks the entrance to the Channel Tunnel. I am startled by a vicious dog, but hold my ground with walking poles pointed forward. The owner appears, apologises and collars the German shepherd. He was not expecting to see another walker at 6 a.m; nonetheless, we chat for a moment as we observe freight and passenger trains exit and enter the tunnel below.

'These trig pillars are unusual,' I say, pointing to a roughcast concrete cylinder.

'They were put in place to survey the tunnel entrance and civil works we can see,' he replies. 'You'd be amazed by how the land-scape has changed here, with the spoils of the tunnel works. I've lived in and walked these hills for twenty years; you're not too far from the coast now.'

I walk over the Channel Tunnel entrance and then under the A20, dug deeply into the last remnants of the chalk-down ridge before it submerges beneath the sea, only to re-emerge again just south of Calais: an unexpected geological link to Europe that mirrors the road and rail links. It is astonishing how geology shapes the movement of commerce, both ancient and modern.

It is a joy to reach the coast and the white cliffs that overlook the English Channel. A profoundly moving Battle of Britain memorial commands views south-east to the French coast, making the channel crossing seem trivial. A lone pilot sits in the middle of a three-bladed mosaic wrapped in his sheepskin jacket, expressionless but reflecting on the trauma of war. A new cafe is under construction, in the shape of a Spitfire wing; until then, an old volunteer-run shack opens just as I arrive, to serve a simple snack and obligatory cup of tea.

> *Here inscribed the names of friends we knew,*
> *Young men with whom we often flew.*
> *Scrambled to many angels high,*
> *They knew that they or friends might die.*
> *Many were very scarcely trained,*
> *And many badly burnt or maimed.*
> *Behind each name a story lies*
> *Of bravery in summer skies;*
> *Though many brave unwritten tales*
> *Were simply told in vapour trails.*
> *Many now lie in sacred graves*
> *And many rest beneath the waves.*
> *Outnumbered every day they flew,*
> *Remembered here as just 'The Few'.*
>
> – William L.B. Walker, 616 Squadron, 'Our Wall'[8]

The path now teeters on the edge of the cliff face, with a hundred-metre drop to the shore below. Somehow a railway line clings to the coast, occasionally tunnelling through the cliff face where it cannot see a route around the shoreline. Samphire Hoe country park is a new gravel platform built from the chalk excavations of the Channel Tunnel which lies somewhere below me. The last hump-back chalk ridge takes a breath before diving into Dover harbour, busy with docking and departing passenger and cargo ferries. The artefacts from the war litter the hills, including an odd-shaped concave concrete listening dome, a rudimentary audio radar. I stand at the focal point, in a vain attempt to hear a French voice.

Dover is too busy, as I commence my final descent, past the massive defensive buildings of the Western Heights and on to the Drop Redoubt. The solid structures signify the strategic importance of the port. In a moment I am in a strange world of shoppers, as I march down King Street to the Marine Parade and the final marker stone of the North Downs Way. Holiday crowds pack the beach; a funfair is in full swing. I feel uncomfortable and anxious after the peace and tranquillity of the coastal path. I make a snap decision to return home. The forecast is dreadful, with violent thunderstorms and heavy rain forecast. I don't want to be walking along the South Downs in such conditions. I reach the ticket counter at Dover station.

'Single to London, please,' I ask.

'Fast or slow?' she replies, as if this is some pub joke.

'Er … fast, please.'

It is worth the extra £8, as the service is non-stop to St Pancras, using the same HS1 line I crossed two days ago. I can't believe how quickly I am transported back across the countryside I have just walked through, reaching London in just over an hour. It is like someone has pressed fast-reverse on the videotape machine. Sites I recognise flash past the window: first the downs, the chalk crosses, memories of the Spitfire, then the Medway estuary, before the unrecognisable city landscape of London. I am sucked into the underground to reach my connecting station. I'm in shorts, with a deep tan, unwashed, unkempt and weary, like some alien from the countryside, entirely out of place amongst the commuters in the city.

No one bats an eyelid.

10

SOUTH DOWNS WAY

Distance: 100 miles
Days to complete: 4 days
Mileage so far: 1,890 miles

WALK, TALK, CHALK

When I rest my feet my mind also ceases to function.
– J.G. Hamann

Violent thunderstorms raked through the south-east the week after I completed the North Downs Way, so it was the right decision to delay the circumnavigation of the Weald along the South Downs to Winchester. Minute-perfect train connections swiftly bring me back three weeks later. My arrival is signposted by the Long Man of Wilmington, a chalk carving on the north-facing downland, Europe's most significant artistic representation of the human form. He is bald, tall and holding poorly adjusted walking poles – not unlike me.

I walk from Eastbourne station to Grand Parade to find that I have arrived in time for the annual Eastbourne International Airshow. The beach is packed with an expectant crowd waiting for the display to start, prime bench seating jealously guarded by enthusiasts with binoculars, cameras, thermos flasks and homemade sandwiches. I squeeze on the edge of a seat, next to a guy reading the programme.

'When does the display start?' I ask.

'Soon,' he says. 'I can't wait to see two Lancaster bombers flying together.'

'Oh wow. What time are they due?'

'About one o'clock.'

The newspapers have been covering the visit of a Vera, a Canadian-built Lancaster Mk. X that has flown from Hamilton, Ontario to join the Battle of Britain Lancaster PA474 Mk. I for a season of air displays. I grab some lunch and stroll westwards until I reach the Kiosk cafe and start an ascent on to the downs for a better view of the show. Lynx helicopters do backflips in the sky; grown men are standing on the wings of biplanes; jets scare you witless with unannounced low-level passes. I wish I had brought my binoculars as the two Lancasters, with their Spitfire fighter escorts, approach from the east. It is a memorable experience; the crowds around me fall silent as the sound of ten Merlin engines thunder along the coastline. My hairs bristle on the back of my neck, as they did weeks earlier on the North Downs Way. It seems daft to leave the airshow early, so I find a comfortable spot to relax and wait for the RAF Red Arrows finale. The formation makes a grand entrance over the crowd and ascends, smoke on, into the skies. It is an unusual experience to see the show from above, sitting on the cliff edge, overlooking the display line. A singleton aircraft roars below the cliffs to corkscrew around an opposing colleague. Everyone is standing in awe at their skill and precision.

I have to get a move on to reach the campsite at Alfriston and continue my ascent to Beachy Head overlooking the red and white lighthouse below, lost in a sea of murky chalk at high tide. The rollercoaster green cliffs are a joy to walk along, with extensive views across the English Channel. The Belle Tout lighthouse offers exclusive accommodation and unparalleled views along the Seven Sisters, the sequence of cliffs that mark an abrupt end to the South Downs as they erode into the sea – a blindingly bright white curtain of chalk. Now my journey begins:

The Weald is good, the Downs are best –
I'll give you the run of 'em, East to West.
Beachy Head and Winddoor Hill,
They were once and they are still.
Firle, Mount Caburn and Mount Harry
Go back as far as sums'll carry.
Ditchling Beacon and Chanctonbury Ring
They have looked on many a thing,
And what those two have missed between 'em
I reckon Truleigh Hill has seen 'em.
Highden, Bignor and Duncton Down
Knew Old England before the Crown.
Linch Down, Treyford and Sunwood
Knew Old England before the Flood;
And when you end on the Hampshire side –
Butser's old as Time and Tide.
The Downs are sheep, the Weald is corn,
You be glad you are Sussex born!
                – Rudyard Kipling, 'The Run of the Downs' (1910)

I am hyperventilating as I reach Cuckmere Haven; the fresh air is intoxicating. It is a disappointment to turn inland and miss the photogenic coastguard cottages, but I have no choice other than to walk along the meandering River Cuckmere. I thought the path would follow the coast, but I cross the busy A259, clogged with airshow traffic, to weave my way through woodland and along the riverbank towards the only footbridge into the next village. It is closed for repairs, but I ignore the health and safety signs and clamber over the scaffolding to the opposite bank.

The restaurants and accommodation are out of my price range. But I find a campsite (£7 a night) and pitch my tarp and bivvy over my walking poles, eating noodles for dinner. I'm startled by a fox, looking for food in the middle of the night, a downside of not using a tent with walls. It is sure to find a feast at one of the barbecue pits. I watch it in the moonlight, trotting through the campsite detritus, snacking on discarded chicken bones, licking tubs of coleslaw.

The village shop – a post office and delicatessen – opens at 8 a.m. They serve a mind-boggling array of goodies, which I am happy to stock up on as compensation for a cheap night. I ascend again on to the downs, briefly severed by the river. The route is already busy with horse riders and cyclists, out in force for an early weekend. Groups of cyclists wear their tribal South Downs sponsored jerseys – a branded line of bodies against staggering views of both the Weald and the English Channel. I'm on the deck of an aircraft carrier, sailing through the countryside, taking (in my mind) an occasional diversionary low-level flight across the downs and valleys. The views are as dramatic as the Cheviot at the end of the Pennine Way, 600 metres higher than where I am now standing.

The path descends once more to cross another river draining the West Sussex catchment area to the sea. Canals and locks tame its flow and provide commercial navigation to the inland ports of Lewes and beyond, bringing goods to the port of Newhaven. In no time I return to the ridgeway above Lewes, the traditional county town of Sussex. I cross the Greenwich Meridian, marked by a sign that indicates the divide between western and eastern hemispheres, before a further descent to the busy A27.

Housedean Farm has thoughtfully provided a water tap for walkers, a commodity that is difficult to find on the downs. I replenish my water containers before the climb north to Blackcap, through gorgeous sunflower fields, whose heads rotate to follow the sun. The slope terminates abruptly as the chalk ridge meets mudstone and greensand, a geological feature that has shaped my walking since I started in Farnham.

Turning west, the broad chalk path leads to Ditchling Beacon and one of the few roads to traverse the ridge, the nemesis for many a London-to-Brighton cyclist. I stay a moment at the trig pillar (an almost religious requirement) to take in endless views north. You can practically see the curvature of the planet, not something I'd thought possible over land. A couple of empty dew ponds line the route, dug by farmers to provide water for their livestock. I visit the Clayton windmills, known locally as Jack and

Jill, two distinctive yet different nineteenth-century structures. Jill still occasionally produces stoneground wholemeal flour, but not today in the still, warm air.

Two busy A roads weave through dry valleys, isolating the village of Pyecombe. A busy BP garage is a source of food and air conditioning, so I stock up and cool down before walking the final few miles to Saddlescombe and a National Trust campsite. A £5 donation seems fair to stay in a working-farm hamlet. By chance, a local folk band are entertaining a family gathering. It is someone's birthday; not a riotous affair, just cakes and Ovaltine, a nightcap that lives up to its advertised benefit of inducing sleep.

After picking a few slugs from my damp groundsheet, I ease into a bright morning and climb up to the rim of Devil's Dyke: a hundred-metre-deep U-shaped valley dredged from the chalk down by a fictitiously large hot scoop in a vanilla ice cream tub. Hang-gliders are up early to enjoy the perfect wind conditions on a summer weekend. A short jog downhill and they soar into the sky, gently drifting along the ridge in the updraft until boredom brings them down to earth again.

As I approach Edburton Hill, I meet two families from the Netherlands. Each set of parents has three or four children, ranging from a few months old to early teens. Everyone has a broad smile on their faces.

'Are you walking the South Downs Way?' I ask.

'Yes, we start in Winchester a week ago, perhaps a few days now to Eastbourne.'

The youngest sit cosily in trailers modified for the outdoor terrain; others snooze in snuggly carriers around their parents. The younger children are twirling wildflowers and seem happy walking. The whole menagerie has enjoyed the walk so far.

'How do you keep the children amused?'

'They are thrilled to be on the hills, exploring the wildlife and plants. When they get tired, we carry them in the trailers.'

They have found a successful formula. It is a delight to see such happy, hippy-like families enjoying the pure pleasure of a long-distance walk. I suggest the National Trust farm ahead as a place to camp, as I can see they are pulling their tents and cooking pots with them to feed their mobile community.

'Why the South Downs?' I ask a silly question and get a simple answer.

'We have no hills in der Netherlands.'

It was such a life-affirming encounter. I hope those children grow up with the same sense of adventure as their parents.

The route descends once more to cross the River Adur, contained within its embankments as it flows towards the sea at Shoreham. I am walking at a good pace now, covering twenty-five miles a day with ease. I'm wearing lightweight walking shoes that increase muscle endurance at the expense of foot protection; I might have plenty of energy, but aches are developing. Is it plantar fasciitis? Perhaps I have been walking too fast? I had no problems walking the North Downs Way in my Meindl boots in sweltering conditions. What is going wrong? I start to worry.

I reach Chanctonbury Ring, a prehistoric hilltop fort dating from the early Iron Age. Legend suggests you can summon the devil by running seven times around the tree clump in an anti-clockwise direction. I have read it is not a place to wild camp or you will be disturbed by ghosts and demons. If the timing were right, I'd dare to pitch for the night, but there are plenty of miles left in the day. A group of Duke of Edinburgh walkers throw off their packs.

'This looks like a good place to camp,' an enthusiastic leader announces.

'Chase you around the trees,' shouts a boy.

I haven't the heart to tell them.

I can now see the Isle of Wight in the distance, isolated in the Solent, asleep in the haze. I am still coming to terms with the glorious coastal views, so unexpected and intense; they are at times overwhelming. I descend to the River Arun, the fourth such incursion into the chalk downland, to take lunch at Amberley station. A decent fish and chips will keep me going for the remainder of the day, providing fuel for another 200-metre ascent of tumuli-covered hillside (it was a trendy place to bury the dead in the Neolithic and Bronze ages).

Over the downs there were birds flying,
Far off glittered the sea,
And toward the north the weald of Sussex
Lay like a kingdom under me.

I was happier than the larks
That nest on the downs and sing to the sky,
Over the downs the birds flying
Were not as happy as I.

It was not you, though you were near,
Though you were good to hear and see,
It was not the earth, it was not heaven,
It was myself that sang in me.

      – Sara Teasdale, 'On the Sussex Downs' (1924)

At Bignor Hill I turn off the South Downs Way to walk to Gumber bothy, a National Trust camping barn that cannot be reached by motor vehicle. The route follows the arrow-straight Stane Street, a Roman road that connected Chichester to London. The line of sight directly intersects the 1,000-year-old cathedral spire. The bothy is a converted flintstone barn and stables for cyclists, horse riders and walkers, with necessary facilities and warm showers. Silence envelops the site as the sun sets and the stars come out. Planets glow with colour in a clear sky unpolluted by artificial light.

I sleep deeply, under a roof for a change, but wake early to an alarm call of crows pecking and cawing loudly at the windows, like a scene from Hitchcock's *The Birds*. A simple breakfast and £10 in the honesty box and I'm away, only to be accosted by three sheepdogs. One bites my arm, another distracts me, while the third tries to mount me from behind. It is an organised gang, only called off by the farmer in time for me to reach the safety of a gate. That gets my adrenaline running as I rejoin the ridge and head west on to Graffham Down. I take a wrong turning into Charlton Forest and meet a group of women cycling in the opposite direction.

'Walking the South Downs Way?' they ask.

'Er … yes, that's right.'

'We're all going the wrong way, then. We must have all missed a signpost. There's only an oil well down this road.'

'No worries,' I say, getting out my smartphone.

They study maps, and we spot a shortcut back to the ridgeline and the comforting sight of a trig pillar. My bearings reset to familiar compass points, the Weald to the north and the Channel to the south; I'm back on the deck of the HMS *South Downs Way*, the National Trails' finest aircraft carrier.

The path continues for a few miles before descending through Queen Elizabeth country park to a car park and cafe. It is a busy Sunday and cyclists and walkers are everywhere. The woodland is a pleasant change from those extensive views and marks my departure from the Weald. The cafe serves a tasty venison burger and cake, which should be enough now for the day. I have a steep ascent to the summit of Butser Hill and a short walk to HMS *Mercury*, a former naval communications and navigation school which is now home to a sizeable sustainability educational centre.

The climb is tough but rewarding, across smooth green slopes, occasionally used for downhill grass-slope skiing – a sport which is sure to wreck your knees. The skis are lightweight tank tracks of a design that is in search of a problem. The sport is now super-seded by off-road skateboarders or mountain boarding; each to their own as trend follows trend. I prefer activities with a low risk of injury. Ironically, I have developed sore feet walking at such a pace, covering some eighty miles in three and a half days since Eastbourne.

The hostel is comfortable, ideal for larger groups staying to study one of the many eco-oriented subjects available at the centre. You can learn about beekeeping, bushcraft, hedge laying, jam making, deer butchery, coppicing, timber-frame buildings, natural remedies, cosmetics and trug making (wooden baskets). There is a good crowd in the common room, notably an over-excited group of sixth-formers cycling to Barcelona before uni-versity, with no fixed plan other than to carry debit cards and a toothbrush. What they lack in experience is easily compensated for by attitude and energy. One guy pulls out his smartphone.

'Anyone fancy an Indian tonight?' says one lad.

'Yeah, great,' comes a chorus of support.

'Join us?' one asks me.

It takes thirty seconds to order the meal, and thirty minutes later, a scooter delivers a feast. These guys will survive, no doubt about it. I couldn't rustle up a treat so quickly; this convenience is a new normal. These guys are still growing and can eat like dustbins, and seem resourceful in ways that would not occur to me. Their bicycles are a motley collection of childhood wonders, sporting derailleur gears and cantilever brakes from a different era. Give them a few years before they turn into gearheads. For now, they are blissfully innocent.

They have left long before I wake, to catch an early ferry from Portsmouth. I am wishing I had their energy levels as I nurse my feet, which are aching uncomfortably. It is a steady march into Winchester. A last delightful view of the downs ridge can be seen from an Iron Age fort, before one final descent to the River Meon and the beautiful villages of Meonstoke and Exton, a retirement cottage paradise with neatly trimmed gardens and borders. Wild watercress waves in the clear chalk streams, home to wild otters now returning to their habitat after many decades.

All this tranquillity shatters as I approach Winchester. A scene of devastation unfolds soon after I spot the first abandoned tent, blown into a field by a freshening breeze. After that, field after field of abandoned camping gear, tents, sleeping bags, plastic bottles, beer cans and tin tray barbecues litter the grasslands, well beyond the original boundaries of the Boomtown festival, which has just concluded. I am shocked at the sheer volume of mass-produced material so casually left behind; the volunteers at the last hostel diligently recycled every last scrap of food packaging. This scene is not how I imagined the walk would end. I'm almost tearful with sadness, only ameliorated by teams of people clearing up the mess – a litter-crop summer harvest.

I drift aimlessly down through the streets into the city centre, crossing the busy M3 which carves its way through Twyford Down, the scene of a vigorous protest in the early 1990s. The chalk-down ridge has been torn apart by explosion and digger; there was no other option to address a chronic bottleneck through the Itchen Valley. I meet walkers heading east and warn them of the devastating dumpsite ahead, but then also describe the sheer magnificence of the South Downs Way journey beyond.

Alfred greets me to mark the final yards of my journey. The imposing statue to King Alfred the Great, King of the Anglo-Saxons and of Wessex, holds his sword aloft in defiance of western Viking armies. Under his protection, I walk along the High Street to meet some close friends for a cup of tea and cake. Their boisterous Labrador, Wallace, goes bonkers, licking my smelly socks as if they are a tasty sour treat. My aching feet revived, I catch the train home and reflect on a nine-day sprint of the North and South Downs Way. While I can celebrate my fitness, it is a journey I should return to at a more leisurely pace, maybe even on a bicycle.

11

HADRIAN'S WALL PATH

Distance: 81 miles
Days to complete: 4 days
Mileage so far: 1,990 miles

THE FAMOUS B6318

Walking is man's best medicine.

– Hippocrates

On a trip to the USA, I read an article in the Alaska Airlines in-flight magazine; it was a four-page comprehensive guide to Hadrian's Wall. There I was, flying at 40,000 feet over the Pacific Ocean, reading about a local walk. The route is of such international renown you will find it listed with the Great Wall of China and Offa's Dyke in the top ten walks in the archaeological world. It is justifiably famous; how lucky we are in Britain to have two.

The remnants of Hurricane Gonzalo have delayed my start for a week. Yes, it is true, we have such conditions in the British Isles, although by the time it had crossed the Atlantic, the Met Office and Met Éireann had downgraded it to a tropical storm. It is late October and not the best time weather-wise, with muddy conditions underfoot, but I want to get another path done before the winter.

Hadrian's Wall is the second northern boundary of the Roman Empire. They built the Antonine Wall further north, between modern-day Glasgow and Edinburgh, but it did not get much use. Construction began on Hadrian's Wall in AD 122, some 1,900 years ago, and was completed six years later. The Romans abandoned all northern fortifications around AD 410. There is some evidence of continued use for the remainder of the fifth century, until its ultimate decline; details are sketchy.

At eighty-four miles, Hadrian's Wall Path stretches from Wallsend, Newcastle to Bowness-on-Solway near Carlisle. I chose to walk it in this direction primarily due to lower travel costs and accommodation logistics. The entire journey will take five days, but I could have stayed for two weeks, or even two months, to fully explore this archaeological wonder. This trip is a luxury tour, staying in B&Bs and inns; if it had been summer, I would have camped.

The east coast mainline train to Newcastle is a pleasure, with few passengers and plenty of room to lay my map out on a table. I connect quickly with the local Metro network to alight near the start in Wallsend around midday. If you were to extend the path five miles east to the North Sea, you could call this a coast-to-coast route. The wall terminates where the River Tyne widens, at Segedunum, a significant Roman fort. I should pause to look around the excellent museum, but I have to get to my accommodation, ten miles west. So I set off along a litter-strewn path through the aptly named Walker estate to Newcastle centre, passing daytime dog walkers.

As I approach the city, the beautiful bridges over the River Tyne stack up one behind the other. I find myself whistling Lindisfarne's 'Fog on the Tyne' as I reach the Gateshead Millennium Bridge, an eye-achingly beautiful foot and cycle bridge that blinks as it pivots to allow shipping traffic to pass. There follows a civil-engineering museum of pedestrian, road and railway bridges, overlooked proudly by St James' Park football stadium.

I leave Newcastle behind and head into the countryside, climbing a hill into Heddon-on-the-Wall village, north of the mighty Tyne. A local cafe is about to close, but they are more than happy to serve me a meal. It nestles inside a housing estate, primarily serving a local community.

'Pie, beans and chips OK?' the owner says. She disappears into the kitchen, as her friends, devoid of her conversation, turn in my direction.

'What brings you to Heddon?' they ask.

'I just started walking Hadrian's Wall Path.'

'You'll love it at this time of year, but it is a bit muddy in places. Where are you staying tonight?'

'At the farm down the road. Not far now, I think.'

'Oh, that'll be Paula, she'll take care of you. Just walk through the estate and follow the road until you reach the farm.'

After tea and cake for pudding, I say my goodbyes and seek out the farmhouse B&B. I cannot imagine having such a warm chat in a cafe where I live in the south-east. Most people here naturally fall into conversation with you and love to natter. I am met by Paula, who takes me across the yard to a purpose-built bunkhouse. I am the only guest tonight.

'Which pub do you recommend? I hear there's a microbrewery nearby.'

'Ah! That'll be Wylam's. You'll get a pint at the Swan back in the village.' She gestures in the direction I have just walked.

'I'll be back at eightish, I expect.'

I can't resist a few real ales, served with a thick foam head, northern style. It is a struggle to walk home – not, as you might think, due to excessive consumption, but because my legs have seized up; I am not used to the day's feverish pace on unforgiving pavement.

A full fry-up appears through the serving hatch the next morning, and an empty plate is returned moments later.

'Thanks, Paula, that was just what I needed. How much do I owe you?'

I pack and pay, but the farm dogs don't want me to leave; they want to play with a ball. I oblige by kicking it across the yard, and it returns seconds later. This behaviour is so ingrained in the canine species, I wonder if they have a specific gene for ball fetching, like I might have a gene for wanderlust.

'Phhheww … Phewwwit.' A quick whistle and the game is over.

The dogs jump into the back of the Land Rover, and the farmer is away to the fields. Time for work for them, and time for me to start my walk.

I cross the A69, a busy dual carriageway between Newcastle and Carlisle, to reach Milecastle 13. These are small forts or lookouts, spaced at one-mile intervals. I am not sure where numbers 1 to 12 went; they lie buried or forgotten, somewhere towards the city. Heading west, the wall is evident, as is the Vallum, a defensive ditch and mound. This earth structure runs parallel to the stone wall defending the southern boundary, as does the nearby B6318 – a minor military road built in the eighteenth century, using materials from the Roman structures. This archaeological vandalism, which continued as farmers sought building materials, was eventually curtailed by John Clayton, in the 1830s. He had the foresight to buy up the land and farms to protect the monument.

It is a cold morning. There must be more road building ahead, as a Tarmac lorry passes by every fifteen minutes. The intense pine tarmacadam perfume wafts in my direction, not unpleasant by any means. Mixed with the fresh air, it smells like a Fisherman's Friend lozenge, adding another sensory dimension to an enjoyable day. The grass path is kept in peak condition by champion natural lawnmowers: sheep – lots of sheep.

I continue on the path, elevated above the road, and cross the River Tyne into Chollerford. To my delight, an unexpected tea room is attached to the local garage.

'Fish and chips and a cup o' tea, please.'

'Coming up,' the waitress replies, pleased to have a customer.

' … and a slice of cake for later too.' I choose fruitcake.

'Do you want a pot of custard with that?'

'Oh, lovely, yes.' What an excellent idea.

The meal fills my boots like topping up a hot water bottle; the energy returns, as the water level rises in your legs. I can relax a bit now as my B&B is only an hour away; no need to rush. Eventually, I walk past Chesters Roman Fort, built to defend a bridge crossing the river between Milecastle 27 and 28. The farmhouse B&B is along a track, a mile away. Two cats greet me as I knock on the door, purring through my legs and cleaning my dirty boots; what excellent service! They seem to like the texture of dry mud.

The farmer's wife shows me to an empty bunkhouse which could host a dozen walkers, a sign that the path gets busy at peak times.

'Anyone else due tonight?' I ask.

'No, you're on your own. We only get a few walkers at this time of year, but we were fully booked over the summer with walking groups,' she is pleased to say. 'I'll just switch the heating on for you … I'll bring breakfast over in the morning. Help yourself to tea and coffee.'

I turn the thermostat down as she leaves; it seems a shame to waste energy in a large dorm, and I'm still warm from the walk. It also seems a shame to keep that chocolate bar in my pack until tomorrow. The tea can wait for a moment; I'll make a pot before I write up my journal.

The next morning, she brings over a full breakfast wrapped in foil and sits down for a natter. They are near retirement. It is difficult to pass on the farm to their children, who have long since left for more lucrative work. She laments the last of a generation, those who take care of the land that surrounds the farm.

'You'll enjoy the walk today – it's the best bit of the wall,' she says, nodding. 'You can take a shortcut back to the path through the farm.'

So I set off, passing the farmer, who is busy clearing out the barn with his tractor. I am grateful to them for providing such peaceful accommodation. They probably profit more from walkers than from the farm and cattle they tend to daily. I follow the B6318 road for another five miles, passing sections of the wall and Milecastles 29 to 34, plus a few camps and a fort or two. The road then separates from the path to follow the contour of the land, while the wall ascends towards Sewingshields Crags at 325 metres. I should take the time to visit a fort, but I will be back next year to see friends and can take a morning to visit one, but which? I do some research that evening.

Vindolanda and Vercovicium are superb examples of Roman forts on Hadrian's Wall. Archaeologists are thrilled to recover artefacts in an excellent state of preservation: leather shoes, swords in scabbards, boxing gloves and wooden toilet seats give an insight into how the garrison lived nearly 2,000 years ago. Incredibly, actual written letters and script survive, offering an unprecedented first-hand account of daily life: personal notes, invitations to birthday parties, requests for more beer, orders and reports; some of these form an outstanding exhibit at the British Museum in London. Vindolanda pre-dates the building of Hadrian's Wall, but Vercovicium (know locally as Housesteads, after a nearby farm) is contemporary, a garrison fort sited between the Vallum and stone wall structure, housing a cohort of Tungrians, 800 fighting men of a German-speaking tribe. These details, and more, are known from the written records. An unsent letter from a Roman soldier reads:

I'm lonely here
the places I didn't go
to defend this place
have given me a headache
for twenty years or so.

The underpinnings in gorse
tiny flowers of thyme
grow through it, these stones
have bled more blood than men
and yet I'm full of hope.
It's willow weaving time,
at Christmas we will decorate:
celebrate Saturnalia, drink
toasts to spill into the new year
hope for a changing of the guard.

The men it posted here
from Syria to Africa
who stood as sentry
through winter's outnumbered days
wish you were here, and here, and here.

If I picture-frame the landscape with thumbs and forefingers, I can replicate postcards found in most local shops. The wall zip-seams along the Whin Sill, a horizontal table of hard dolerite rock. This major geological feature throws up crags and rock cliffs, which can be seen in the middle distance – a natural feature requiring no masonry to be an effective barrier. To the north, barren brown moorland counterbalances the green pastures to the south, enhancing the dividing image of the boundary. I am scratching my head, trying to work out why. Do cattle graze the north and sheep the south? Is it the wind direction? I expect each landscape is managed differently according to soil type, but I cannot be sure.

The quality of the light is exceptional. So it is no surprise when I meet a professional photographer, overloaded with packs, cameras, lenses and tripods.

'Good morning, nice day,' I say.

'Oh, hi.' He turns around to face me.

'You can't fail to take a good photograph today.'

'It's lovely, isn't it.'

'You must be professional with all that gear.'

Indeed he is; Alan is a freelancer from New York who makes a living supplying stock photographs for the travel industry. I tell him the story of my experience on an Alaska Airlines flight. Did he possibly take those photos? While I look with envy at his camera gear compared to my humble smartphone, he is looking at my boots with equal envy.

'I could do with a pair of those boots; my shoes have no grip at all. It has taken me an hour to reach this point through the muddy paths.' He flips a leg up to show me the smooth leather soles on shoes more suited to fashion than function.

'You can pick up a decent pair in most outdoor shops. You need to do that before you end up on your arse.'

Alan turns to show me his mud-stained trousers and jacket.

'Ah. I see.'

He shrugs in agreement.

Several thousand pounds' worth of camera gear, but what he

needs is a decent pair of boots. At this moment I wouldn't have swapped my Meindl Bhutans for his Nikon camera gear.

Ahead of me is the sea swell of the Whin Sill crags leading to Greenhead. To my left lies Housesteads fort, noted for a later visit as the ride ahead is too exhilarating to stop. I surf endless ascents and descents, pumping my lungs so full of oxygen that it triggers euphoria. I don't want to stop; I'm in the zone today. I force myself to pause and observe the tree at Sycamore Gap, and later Milecastle 39 at Steel Rigg. If you had just two photographs of Hadrian's Wall, I'd bet they would depict these scenes. The tree famously appeared in the film *Robin Hood: Prince of Thieves* and has since become known as 'Robin Hood's tree', even though Sherwood Forest is 150 miles to the south.

The trig pillar ahead is an excellent place to stop for lunch before I get dizzy. An expectation of peace shatters when an RAF Tornado punches a sound tunnel in the sky. I can follow it for miles as it hugs the landscape; a red light flashes from its enormous tail, its engine leaving a smoke trail behind. Re-energised, I descend to join the Pennine Way – a familiar path, but now I'm walking in the opposite direction to my earlier journey. The ride continues into Greenhead, but I do not stop until the Samson Inn at Gilsland. I can justify steak and chips and a few pints to mark a fitting end to a glorious day.

It is raining as I wake; I knew my luck would run out. Never mind. After breakfast, it is the full waterproof kit, worn over yesterday's base layers. The scenery changes too. I walk alongside a well-preserved section of wall to the River Irthing. I sense I am descending slowly towards the sea, interrupted by an occasional short ascent. A plaque is attached to a farm building – an original Roman script or graffiti, I cannot tell:

CHO V

D G PILIPPI

FROM THE FIFTH COHORT

THE CENTURY OF GELLIVS

PHILIPPUS (BUILT THIS)

I retreat into my waterproof hood with only my thoughts for company, and I get into a marching rhythm. Without much external stimulus, I ponder the life of a Roman centurion. How fast did they march, I wonder. What type of shoes did they wear? How long did it take them to walk from Rome? How on earth did they stay warm and dry?

> *For me this land, that sea, these airs, those folk and fields suffice.*
> *What purple Southern pomp can match our changeful Northern skies,*
> *Black with December snows unshed or pearled with August haze –*
> *The clanging arch of steel-grey March, or June's long-lighted days?*
>   – Rudyard Kipling,
>   from 'The Roman Centurion's Song' (1911)

The rain continues, but a wonderful honesty cafe provides a brief respite. The small wooden shed is warm and dry. It contains all you need for a tea break: electric kettle, fridge with milk and cake, chocolate, tea bags and so on. Thank-you notes from all over the world cover the interior, bearing witness to the gratitude of weary walkers. Several taxi companies see a business opportunity and have left their cards, just in case. Very tempting on a day like today as the rain starts to permeate my meagre defences; no waterproof can endure this deluge. I have to keep going to stay warm. I retreat again into my waterproof hood and start marching. A rhythmic earworm strikes:

'Car wash, car wash, dooooo … dod did diddy did do dooo, car wash, car wash … ' With a subtle change of lyrics it morphs into: 'Walkin' through a car wash, boy … whoa whoa whoa … car wash.'

Where did that tune come from? What's worse, I am not sure if I am singing the original 1970s version by Rose Royce, or the later duet between Christina Aguilera and Missy Elliott. It has a nice tempo: 120 beats per minute – perfect for marching.

Weird, but at least mile after Milecastle disappears as I approach Carlisle and the River Eden. I get chased over the bridge by a dog that objects to my walking poles, as I aim for the centre of town. The owner says he is a rescue dog who regularly got beaten by a broom. How was I to know? I stumble upon a great coffee shop, John Watt & Son; they welcome weary walkers.

'What is the most calorific meal you have?' I ask.

'Ah, you'll be wanting the stottie,' the waitress replies. I have no energy to ask what that means. I needn't have worried as she brings a roast dinner in a bun, complete with a jug of gravy. 'Anything for pudding?' she asks. The main course is followed by a hefty slice of Dundee cake, floating in a bowl of custard. I have come to the right place.

I wonder how I will now rise from the chair, having taken on so much weight. When I try I find my legs have seized solid – again. I topple towards the counter to pay, looking like an animated scarecrow.

'Thank you so much,' I say, with heartfelt warmth.

I stumble towards my B&B, about a mile away, in Warwick Road. It is a relief to get out of the rain and to be dry.

Breakfast is epic, about as good as you can get, served in a breakfast room with so much bric-a-brac you cannot see the wallpaper. The owner has been in this business a while. We chat about what customers like and don't like and how difficult it is to please everyone.

'Tripadvisor doesn't help,' he says. 'One man's pleasure is another man's poison.'

I find the place delightful and full of character; others would complain about the decoration. The landlord takes a great deal of pride in the house; he has just started to decorate *everything* with Christmas lights. I hope it doesn't blow a fuse, but I sense he knows about such things. Sadly, the following year, the River Eden floods, inundating Warwick Road with filthy muddy water to the first-floor windows. The evening news catches my eye; I am shocked and saddened to see the breakfast room, so carefully curated, under several feet of water.

The rain has eased, but the paths are very muddy. I reach Mile-castle 73 and the Solway Firth. There is an ethereal quality to the light, with views north to the snow-capped moorlands in Scotland. I cannot linger, as a high spring tide is due shortly. The road can flood when a combination of tide, pressure and river flow conspire to raise the water level by three metres. A picture of a local bus, wading axle-deep, qualifies the warning notice. Today, the road is clear and leads me into Drumburgh: a village on a hill, complete with an imposing fortified manor house. Only a few miles remain as I enter Bowness-on-Solway to find a beautiful shelter built by the local community. There is a Romanesque mosaic on the floor, designed by the primary schoolkids, depicting the local birdlife and announcing, '*AVE MAIA*' (Hail Maia) – Maia being the last Roman fort of the walk.

I wait by the bus stop for a connection to Carlisle and a train home. The lamppost timetable is at odds with my smartphone search. A resident pops out of her house to say the bus will be along soon.

'Ignore the timetable, it's wrong. The kids will be home from school soon. It's always on time,' she shouts. 'They never get around to changing it, even though the bus passes every day.'

'Thanks, good to know. I'm getting a bit cold waiting.'

She is right, and soon I am whizzing past the paths and roads I have walked, to reach the city railway station with minutes to spare before the express service to London.

I spend my time on the train googling 'Roman soldier marching'. The benchmark is twenty miles in five summer hours carrying a fifty-pound pack; that's four miles per hour! 'No way!' I exclaim to myself. A little further research tells me that a Roman mile is shorter than an imperial mile and daylight is divided into twelve equal hours. So a quick recalculation shows that to be three miles per hour!

That's the pace I have been walking. I'm chuffed to bits; I can sign up to a legion tomorrow.

12

YORKSHIRE WOLDS WAY

Distance: 79 miles
Days to complete: 4 days
Mileage so far: 2,071 miles

HOCKNEY COUNTRY

The soul that sees beauty may sometimes walk alone.
— Goethe

I catch the 07.26 into London as if going to work, looking somewhat out of place with boots, backpack and bobble hat. Within the hour I depart from King's Cross, enjoying a complimentary full English breakfast in a first-class carriage I booked months ago – a rare indulgence, but the price was keen. The connecting line from Doncaster races across the marshland of the Humber estuary towards the road bridge emerging from the morning sea mist. It is going to be a good day to start the Yorkshire Wolds Way, from the historic town of Hessle.

Within a few minutes, I am walking under the Humber Bridge, an immense superstructure that spans the River Humber, connecting the Lincolnshire and Yorkshire Wolds. For seventeen years it held the record for the largest single-span bridge in the world. It still holds the record for the longest foot and cycle span. The vertical supporting towers are thirty-six millimetres further apart at the top to compensate for the curvature of the Earth.

When viewed from underneath, the aerofoil wing-shaped roadway launches across the estuary to its vanishing point on the southern bank. The scale is incomprehensible.

Plastic cable ties secure bunches of flowers, in various stages of decay, to the riverside benches. It is not immediately apparent what they are for until I read a few of the attached cards. This location is a notorious suicide spot, where over 200 people have ended their lives since 1981 (the year the bridge opened). Samaritan notices offer counselling support to anyone who can dial just six digits (116 123) on their mobile. It is a sobering start to the walk.

The path heads inland, along glutinous clay paths yet to recover from their winter state, to the busy A63. Estuary wildfowl birdlife changes to squabbling gangs of chaffinches arguing in the hedgerows. I stop for lunch at Welton, a charming village without pretension, neat and tidy with a Yorkshire Wolds Way bench and unusual cream-coloured telephone box; they are usually post-office red. It is an indication that I am in the boundaries of the only independent municipal telephone network provider in the UK, KCOM (British Telecom otherwise has a monopoly).

The mud gets squelchier and deeper. I meet a dachshund, gliding along the deep sections like a penguin unable to contain the joy of a deep snow slope. His owners are not far behind.

'Someone is having fun,' I say.

'He won't let us pick him up until we get to the car.'

'Best not to, in that state.'

'We'll have to get the hose out when we get home; he's not going to like that,' they add.

A little yelp of pleasure punctuates the encounter. My boots now weigh double, covered to their cuffs in thick grey mud, which does not shed easily, accumulating until the sheer weight makes lifting your legs difficult. I try to ascend along Welton Dale into the woodland, sliding backwards at times. I'm happy to be using walking poles to keep my balance and prevent a fall. Deer and buzzards watch in amusement as I progress; I stop to stare them out until they nonchalantly move on, giggling at this stupid human, I imagine.

A new elevation opens up a foretaste of the Wolds landscape. It is strangely familiar, almost *déjà vu*; then the penny drops. Four years earlier, in 2012, I visited David Hockney's A Bigger Picture, his exhibition at the Royal Academy of Arts. Usually, I recognise the landscape in art; but now I see the art in the landscape. It is a pleasant effect to have seen a preview, so accurately captured in the mind's eye: perspective, form, shape, colour and texture all recognisable. The exhibition had a profound impact on me; now I can experience it in real life.

After walking past a lonely twelfth-century parish church nestled in the valley above Brantingham, a red triangle sign reads 'Caution Walkers', sponsored by HM Prison Service, so I do not know what to expect ahead. No doubt the participants have to stick to the chosen route, not unlike my journey on the Yorkshire Wolds Way. I assume the event is for the prison staff, but would also imagine any inmate would not get far, like Abel Magwitch in irons, knee-deep in the mudflats of the Thames estuary, in Charles Dickens's *Great Expectations*. The conditions are similar today, at times.

I pass beside a south-facing vineyard, producing a variety of wines. With changes in climate, wine production in England is increasing, but to find one so far north is a surprise. What they have in common with their southern counterparts is the chalk bed-rock, a seam that will terminate thirty kilometres further north when the Yorkshire Wolds Way turns eastwards. One of many poetry benches allows a momentary rest. I read the wooden slats:

We shed them one by one, by shattered field and barley seas,
until the way is open for echoes of us
made strange by wind, deserted barn, the shifting trade
of shadows on the Humbri, Humbre, Humber,
our mouths to springs that speak in tongues of thirst.
                                        – John Wedgwood Clarke[9]

Back into the woodland, the going is awkward until I reach a B road near a trig pillar. The local motel has agreed to pick me up, so I phone for a lift while I clean my boots. I'm floating in a boiling hot bath within ten minutes, emerging as pink as a lobster to change for a good meal – quite a different disposition to an hour ago.

I have seventeen miles to cover the following day, to a pre-booked B&B in Millington. I'm not camping on this trip; it is early March and what few campsites I can find remain closed until Easter. I can cover that distance in less than six hours, so I lie in and take a late breakfast, before getting another lift to the start. It has turned wintry, with a light dusting of snow and an icy easterly wind; the mud at least has hardened a little. I welcome cover as I descend into the first of many chalk valleys, a distinctive feature of the Wolds. The grass vales carved by Ice Age rivers now run dry, the chalk bed efficiently draining away the rainwater. Swin Dale is an excellent example, a deep meandering V-shaped contour that carves its way through the hills.

Soon I am up on the Wolds again, at a height of 144 metres. Another phallic-looking Yorkshire Wolds Way signpost marks the completion of a five-mile section, the National Trails acorn carved suggestively on top of a wooden post. This marker is the fourth, so I am twenty miles from Hessle. Walkers jam good-luck coins into the splits in the wood. I have picked up a similar habit of collecting feathers as I walk to decorated gateposts, copied from an unnamed walker a few years ago. It is a pity the local farmer has to cover one gateway in warnings: 'BULL IN FIELD' followed by 'COWS WITH CALVES CAN BE AGGRESSIVE' to discourage progress. I half expect I must sign a waiver before I continue into Goodmanham past another poetry bench.

> From dark to dark the bird flies through the fire-lit hall,
> flies through the axe that strikes the shrine,
>   through burning that grows once more in stone and coloured light,
> through rain as it amazes chalk
> and flowers in this latest cup of breath.
>
> – John Wedgwood Clarke[10]

A full apology for the grumpy farmer warnings appears as I reach the village: a sign invites walkers to partake of their ales and pies

– a perfect temptation. Still, I carry on to the privately owned estate village of Londesborough; I have enough food in my pack. There are a large number of country estates in the Yorkshire Wolds, privately owned since the mid-sixteenth century when the ancestors of the present owners enclosed common land into titled or deeded estates – in this case, the Clifford family and a succession of dukes, earls and barons. The village and surrounding areas are unchanged, retaining a character that might otherwise surrender to the modern world if they were not subject to the estate's restrictive covenants.

This illusion vanishes just moments later as I read an information topograph. Reading left to right it marks the horizon to the west: Doncaster power station, Drax power station, Eggborough power station, Ferrybridge power station – four hungry coal-fired power stations, presumably near the east coast for reasons of pollution. The artist drew an ironic skylark flying above the landscape; as if one little bird can adequately compensate for this industrial intensity.

Only a few minutes later (they like their signs around here), another information bench explains the Pilgrimage of Grace. In 1536, Yorkshire folk thought Henry VIII was mad, trying to decide whether to honour or behead his wives, raise taxes, close monasteries and cancel public holidays, and generally execute anyone who disagreed with him. Wishing to retain their devout traditions, they rebelled, marching to York and capturing the city. By now the rebel army had grown to 50,000 men, more than a match for Henry's 8,000 royal soldiers at Doncaster, so Henry granted a pardon. The rebellious army went home; but they should have carried on to London, for Henry broke his promises and executed the original leaders. The signs do not discourage my progress or dishearten me, but should I need emotional support I can always call in at the World Peace cafe, a meditation centre at Kilnwick Percy Hall. I wonder what Henry VIII would have thought of such a Buddhist community, diametrically opposite to his religion.

One last ascent for the day leads me towards Warter Wold, into a Hockney art gallery landscape again, immediately recognisable.

York Minster is fifteen miles away, seen clearly from another poetry bench, with a poignant few words:

> *The straight line breaks into the mutterings of a track,*
> *the body's unfolding way from dale to dale.*
> *Our muscles burn in its common knowledge,*
> *our breath its song above springs as they pour villa into village,*
> *marsh marigolds into God's chrysalis.*
>
> – John Wedgwood Clarke[11]

I can see the village of Millington, asleep below in the valley, a short descent away. I can wash my boots thoroughly in the stream before meeting my host at the Ramblers' Rest, a walking, cycling-friendly B&B.

'You'll want to pop across the road for a meal. Our tea room is closed, but breakfast at eight OK for you?'

I emerge from the room after the sun has set, to see the warm, friendly glow from the windows of the Gait Inn. The landlord serves me a foaming pint and hands me the menu.

'You'll be having the pie tonight,' he says, in a tone that suggests I'd be stupid to choose otherwise.

'Looks good to me.' As if I am one to argue with a Yorkshireman.

The pie, mash and peas are served as I browse over my map and guide. What appears to be simple pub fare turns out to be a Michelin three-star meal. Unknown to me, it is a pie competition night. The pastry is sublime, the meat like fillet steak, swimming in a gravy that would send a *MasterChef* judge into raptures. A crowd arrives: the judges and competition entrants, I assume. They only have to get their beers from the bar, no need to order food. They politely observe me in my sensory bubble while they mumble away about the thickness of the gravy and the colour of the mash. I finish my last spoonful (as the gravy demands).

'Aw'right, lad?' comes the question with a knowing look.

'Superb' is the only reply, but no words are needed, they can judge my happy face alone. Their dishes arrive; the hubbub conversation stops, replaced by the clatter of cutlery. The last dregs consumed, the pub is once again buzzing. The Gait Inn must have this one in the bag; it certainly gets my vote.

A full English stokes my boiler for breakfast. I am ready for a long hard day; the forecast is dreadful. It will be wet and cold, but not cold enough to snow. Back on the ridge, a vicious easterly drives horizontal rain. Time to set a fast pace into the wind to keep warm. The aptly named Cold Wold is the first ascent, quickly followed by an 'up hill and down dale' ride through the enigmatic dry valleys. No wonder this area is popular with walkers, who have a wide selection of circular walks to choose from (plus pies and ales, of course). My path is linear, following the lip of Pasture Dale past Huggate to the magnificent Horse and Holm dales. I stop long enough to read another pleasant bench poem:

We have rippled the earth with our desire to be here not there.
We have driven the dale's wedge of hush home between us.
But you move, as we moved, in the ghost of water:
a hare rips away from the dead, thuds down the dyke
and out into everywhere the grasses foam.

– John Wedgwood Clarke[12]

Holm Dale is almost a hundred metres deep and kept neatly shorn by hungry sheep – as pleasant as any country house lawn. Their walking tracks cover the slopes, like wrinkles on a weathered face, as they meander north. The precise V-shaped geometry is a remnant of a different time, when Ice Age forces chiselled channels for pleasure, as a map shows no other reason for their existence; no streams or rivers are flowing in their depths.

Fridaythorpe's claim to fame is marked, tongue in cheek, by a blue heritage plaque: 'LANCE MOXTON – The first person in the Wolds to start collecting vintage washing machines – resident here since 2009.' My mind wanders, and I start playing the claim to fame game too: 'My ex-girlfriend's best mate's mother used to have milk delivered by Sean Connery.' The more obscure, the better: 'I went to a U2 concert in the 1980s at Kingston Polytechnic and when the band finished no one clapped.'

The village has a new glass-fronted bus shelter, a perfect place to dry out and have lunch. Rain pelts against the glass panels like a drum skin, making thought or conversation impossible. It is time to move on, through Brubber Dale towards the village of Thixendale, in the grip of gentrification. The faux tranquillity of the village gives way to electric-fenced animal enclosures, packed with miserable-looking muddy sheep, perhaps off to slaughter. A moment later, I come across pheasant cages. I assume they are used for breeding birds for sport. The crows have got inside; it is a bloodbath as they feed on their helpless victims. I am tempted to lift the cage and let them free but know better than to interfere in country matters.

I pick up an ear tag, most likely discarded by a calf brushing against a fence post. UK 142919/100294 is missing his or her identity, subverting a farmer's computerised record-keeping system. On a later holiday in Shetland, I notice the calves on Eday have tags with names, like Lucy or Herbert, attached to their ears. It starts a thought stream in my mind about the question of identity: will I wear a digital label or barcode one day? What if I lose it? Do I exist without it? Am I being objectified, like poor UK 142919/100294? Can we live without labels? What are the chances of the farmer reading this book and checking his records? I trip up as my thoughts take flight, bringing me back to earth, but I am reminded daily by the yellow tag that hangs from my desk lamp: who am I without a label of a name and national insurance number, in a digital world? Am I being commercially farmed for profit, like that poor calf?

My spirits soar when dramatic views emerge as the heavy black clouds lift above the Wolds. My Hockney-infused synapses are firing once again as I scan folded hills and leafless tree lines, unspoilt by power lines or wind turbines. The views fade as I descend into Deep Dale and the deserted medieval village of Wharram Percy, abandoned in the mid-fourteenth century. It is one of the most thoroughly studied and perhaps well known of several hundred 'lost village' archaeological sites in England, villages which fell out of use during the Black Death. While not a direct cause, it seems the village ceased to be a viable concern as farming practices changed. The graves contain mutilated bodies, decapitated and cut to prevent the dead rising in a zombie apocalypse. It is an eerie place, with a roofless church, overlooking fields with decaying foundations of homes and farm buildings.

It is not far to North Grimstone and my accommodation at the Middleton Arms. The door is locked when I arrive, but two guests relaxing in the bar see a fellow walker and let me in. Ian and Jeff are walking the Yorkshire Wolds Way in sections. They are two old school friends from Hull, on a jolly for a few days, and are already on their second pints from a self-service bar.

'Terrible day – we finished early. Too cold and wet for us,' they say. 'Where have you walked from?'

'The Gait Inn, Millington.'

'Great pub is that,' they agree. 'Good beer and fab food.'

So the conversation starts. I disrobe my outer layers and take a bath before joining them. My waterproof has worked too well; the pockets are full of water, but I am generally dry, and my boots have done an excellent job of keeping water out.

Ian and Jeff are excellent company; we can chatter away for hours with the natural conversation that flows between walkers. The landlady arrives, having entrusted the pub to the guests.

'I see you have found a straggler,' she says. 'You must be Martyn. Are you joining us for dinner tonight?'

The food is wholesome and filling, washed down with foaming pints that appear without the need to order; your drained glass signals another is needed, you need not ask.

'This must be my round,' I insist.

'No need, lad,' says Jeff.

No one is counting. I'm tired and make my excuses, confirming I'll join them for breakfast at 8 a.m. I wisely set the alarm in case the alcohol has reset my internal body clock.

The chalk ridgeline will soon turn east, marking its last days before reaching the sea. Ian and Jeff will set off a few hours later and promise to meet me in Ganton.

'A free pint for every hour's delay,' I say, teasing them to keep pace.

'You're on.' Ian seals the bet with a handshake.

The landlady's Labrador sniffs my boots as I get ready to depart. It knows by scent alone that a pleasant walk is on offer and is getting overexcited. The path is easy going with one rough descent and then a shockingly steep ascent after Wintringham. The finger-post points at an angle of forty-five degrees to the top of the hill, warning of the climb. I engage four-wheel drive (two legs and two walking poles) and select low gear until I reach the summit.

Another artwork installation – like the bus shelter in Friday-thorpe, I later learn – is part of a series in the WANDER pro-gramme, the first planned art installations on a National Trail. This one is a mix of Iron Age guardian figures, long-barrow struc-tures and a dew pond, aiming to capture ancient forms in a hill-top setting. It overlooks the Vale of Pickering, a former lake, long since drained into the sea and now marshland. Large settlements formed along its southern shores, concentrating important arch-aeological sites, that together build a picture of habitation and industry over millennia. Chalk gives way to clay soil and rock similar to the Jurassic belts on the south coast: a geological boundary between northern and southern England that starts in Lyme Regis in Dorset and loops around to this point, via Hun-stanton in Norfolk.

I remember the fable of the tortoise and the hare; I have a bet to secure and cannot dawdle. The ridge above East Heslerton enhances the views north. The RAF is taking advantage of the clearing weather as a pair of Panavia Tornadoes scream down the vale to the North Sea. One more poetry bench is a good time for a breather and to fully drink in the views. I forget to note the poem, and I am missing the Wolds Way five-mile-interval phallus markers too; I must be relaxing more, unconcerned by schedules and collections.

This section runs with the Centenary Way, a route created to mark the hundredth anniversary of Yorkshire County Council; it should be a hundred miles long, but runs for only eighty-three, between York Minster and Filey Brigg. One little seventeen-mile loop would have completed the distance, exploring deeper into the Wolds. The path descends to the vale along a muddy track, beside a field of soggy flattened crops, much to the disappointment of the gathered starlings. I have only a few miles to reach the Ganton Greyhound, through a village of white cottages and another convenient gravel stream to clean my boots before arrival. I'm checking in, confident in victory, when Jeff saunters in from the bar.

'I'll line them up, shall I?' he says calmly.

'B ... bu ... but, you never passed me. How did you get here so soon?'

'The 843 Coastliner bus,' he says with a smile. 'I never said we were walking all the way!'

It is great to be back in their company; we can have a real laugh and banter as if we have been friends for years. The food quality and service are high, and the beer flows. I do not lack in calories or company on this walk. Even the decor is fascinating: a collection of porcelain jugs of all shapes and styles hang from the ceiling, rather like Toby jugs in a London pub. I sleep deeply once more; mind rested, legs filled.

It is a leisurely twelve miles into Filey and the end of the Wolds Way. I aim for RAF Staxton Wold radar station and then along field boundaries to the last dry valley of the walk. Hares are rampant in the fields, occasionally running at an unreal speed. Lapwings make their presence known with a loud 'pwaay-eech' call, defending their nests. The final fingerpost and poetry bench coincide with one last view of a dry valley, Camp Dale, seven miles from the end:

Find the barn's astounding echo,
the space between your hand and shadow, beacon and leaf,
this sprung wood and the axis of that spire.
And in this place you've made, this hidden dale,
let nine chalk springs compose their Whitestone harmony.

– John Wedgwood Clarke[13]

Wild garlic is starting to bloom, and I can smell the sea, now visible on the eastern horizon – one final weary descent into the bustling town of Filey, past lines of ponderous cars and idle pedestrians. The last elevated grass walk brings me to Filey Brigg: an outcrop of limestone and sandstone, the remains of a fictional dragon, drowned as it washed from its teeth local parkin that the townsfolk had tricked it into eating. A triangular pillar marks the end of the Wolds Way and the start of the Cleveland Way, my next National Trail.

13

CLEVELAND WAY

Distance: 110 miles
Days to complete: 5 days
Mileage so far: 2,150 miles

PIES AND PINTS

The secret to living well and longer is:
eat half, walk double, laugh triple, and love without measure.
– Tibetan proverb

Within moments of completing the Yorkshire Wolds Way, I set off along the coast to Scarborough on the Cleveland Way. The difference is dramatic. I swap lapwings for gulls, dry valleys for the North Sea, chalk for sandstone, and up hill and down dale for a gentle coast path. I've missed coastal walking since completing the South West Coast Path in 2007; there is something about the convergence of the classical Greek elements – earth (the path), water (the sea), air (the sky) and fire (the sun) – that stimulates the subconscious mind.

Although the sun is out, the path is sticky and slippery; it is hard going into Scarborough. I meet a man walking towards me wearing waders. Surely the conditions are not that muddy? He is a fisherman, carrying a plastic bag full of fish, returning to his caravan after a morning in the surf below.

'Good catch today?'

'A couple of wrasses. Enough for tea.' He opens the bag to show me.

'They're beautiful fish, such stunning colours. Are they good to eat?'

'Not really,' he answers, 'I'd prefer a nice bass.'

He is sweating profusely in his non-breathable dungaree waders. The campsite is a few hundred metres away, the static caravans spread over the cliffside fields, organised in loops and cul-de-sacs, modelled on a small housing estate.

The coastline falls readily into the sea – an unstoppable erosion, lubricated by streams and winter storms over centuries. The path frequently diverts inland to avoid the dangerous sections – ominous cracks opening up along the cliff edge that could give way at any moment; the millimetre motion of rock and soil will reach a sudden frightening conclusion. I keep my eyes on the path, not the sea tempting me to a watery grave.

Ahead lies Scarborough Castle, an unmistakable landmark. I do not have far to go to end a twenty-four-mile day from Ganton. The Victorian and Regency promenade comes into view, dominated by the Grand Hotel – a magnificent facade. My accommodation is a modest yet spotlessly clean B&B under new ownership by a couple from London.

'We love it in Scarborough,' they declare. 'Not unlike Brighton, really, and the weather is surprisingly mild.'

I cannot disagree; my love of the town is confirmed after a great evening at the Highlander, a pub buzzing with locals and tourists alike, with a no-nonsense approach to good beer and food. The B&B is busy with couples here for the blues festival. There is always something on in Scarborough: Elvis tributes, northern-soul gatherings, corporate conferences and motorcycle racing – you'll never get bored.

After breakfast, it takes a while to walk out of the town, past the fishing port, castle, amusement arcades and beach huts. Art Deco tea and coffee stands remain closed, but no doubt make a roaring trade in summer. Finally, after Scalby Mills, I am back on the coast path, entering the North York Moors National Park (which I will remain inside until Helmsley, a hundred miles further on the Cleveland Way). The track is starting to dry out, so going gets more manageable. I am enjoying the quiet paths until a local hunt approaches at speed, horns blaring. A pack of hounds are heading straight for me! I can either jump off the cliff or scale a barbed wire fence to avoid them; I hope there is no fox poo on my boots.

'Morning,' I call.

'Morning ... Mornin' ... Hi there ... Morning.' Each rider greets me in turn.

'Lovely day,' says the last in line, trying to keep up on a smaller horse.

They pass without incident. It is an anxious encounter; my heart rate and fight or flight responses briefly escalate. The path remains level, with occasional forays into wooded gullies, but always with a continuous view of the North Sea. Closer observation reveals a multitude of seabirds, rafting on the water, or gliding alongside. The more you look, the more you see. I must bring binoculars and ignore their weight; I'd see even more. A former Second World War radar station lies derelict, now in the care of the National Trust. This coastline has a long history of watchtowers, from Roman times to modern-day air defence networks.

On reaching Ravenscar, the ugly cliffside hotel assaults my eyes, a prison-like structure. The Raven Hall Hotel bar, within, is the finishing point for the Lyke Wake Walk, and will be a welcome sight for those who have just completed the gruelling walk, a fortymile trek from Osmotherly. The famous event is never taken too seriously, yet walkers receive awards, called 'degrees', for multiple crossings: three crossings entitle you to a black neckband and the title Master or Mistress of Misery; some addicts have crossed the route a hundred times, earning them the title Senile Centenarian.

I stop for lunch on a North Sea Cycle Route bench, celebrating a 6,000-kilometre circumnavigation that runs from Dover to Shetland, Bergen to Calais. A thought is hatching in my mind to attempt this at a future date. The section in Britain follows National Cycle Network Route 1. A nearby sculpture in garish colours confirms the direction – another intricate network of possibilities for cyclists, to complement national, regional and local paths for walkers.

Moving along the path, I enter the coastal alum works, an eighteenth-century industrial complex that manufactured this valuable fixative, used for dyeing. It was a dirty process, first burning shale rock before mixing it with urine. The landscape is ugly, so it is a surprise to learn of Victorian plans to build a massive resort in this location. The misguided venture lacked any attributes to attract investors and failed dismally in bankruptcy; traces of the initial road infrastructure overlie a scarred industrial landscape. The vegetation competes with the sea to reclaim the land.

Robin Hood's Bay, just a few miles north, is beautiful. Delightful red-roofed fishermen's cottages tumble down a ravine to a rocky shore – rare access to the sea. Walkers are everywhere; the village streets are full of people dressed in outdoor gear and walking boots. It dawns on me that this is the finishing point of the Coast-to-Coast Walk that starts at St Bees Head in the west, beyond the Lake District. It is a popular route, far more so than the Cleveland or Yorkshire Wolds ways – the two least used of the National Trails. This popularity explains the eye-watering prices of the B&Bs: low supply matched to high demand. The local YHA at Boggle Hole is full, packed to the gunnels with young families, so I am lucky to secure any bed. It is one last calf-burning thirty per cent gradient until I can relax in a very comfortable B&B that can justify its extortionate tariff. The landlady suggests a table at the seafood bistro opposite if I lurk by the entrance at opening time. I am starving and do not want to descend again to the village.

'I'm sorry, we're fully booked,' the waitress says, as she opens up.

'I'm a fast eater.'

'Let me see what we can do.' She returns a moment later.

'Can you vacate a table before 7 p.m?'

'Yes, no problem, thank you.'

The locally caught fish is fresh and cooked superbly. The food quality over the past week has been a revelation: first champion pies on the Yorkshire Wolds Way, now sublime seafood on the Cleveland Way: delicious crayfish, hot and tender meat that falls from its carapace; cream lobster soup soaked up with buttered rye bread. These menus would be double or triple the price in London.

The forecast is excellent – a bright sunny day. I am up early to join a crowded breakfast room of rail enthusiasts, eager to depart for a trip pulled by engine 60103, the *Flying Scotsman*. It is one of the first passenger journeys since its significant refurbishment; tickets sold out months ago. It is like a room of schoolkids, so excited as to be unable to eat breakfast. It is a brilliant way to spend a day on the North Yorkshire Moors Railway. I secretly wish I was joining them.

The paths are now dry, the sun is out, and I'm in shorts for the first time this year. The route is busy with Sunday walkers who diminish in number along the later remote sections. The blue sea merges seamlessly with the blue sky, removing the horizon. The cliffs increase in stature, covered in nesting seabirds wheeling around the skies. Fulmars, kittiwakes and herring gulls chatter away in an endless cacophony of squabbles, waiting to breed. It is a happy few hours to Whitby Abbey, sitting proudly, but forlorn, on the headland above the town. If the Pope had agreed to the annulment of Henry VIII's marriage to Catherine of Aragon, we might now enjoy a thriving Benedictine abbey with a deep history stretching back to the seventh century. Instead, we have a Grade I listed building in need of modernisation, a victim of the dissolution of the monasteries.

I pause to read the inscription on a memorial to Cædmon, the earliest known English poet; it reads 'Fell asleep hard by, 680.' I assume this means he died 1,340 years ago. The distinctive Celtic cross is richly carved on all four sides and coated with a lichen patina. It does not record his indecipherable poetry, some of the earliest in Old English.

Nu scylun hergan hefaenricaes uard
metudæs maecti end his modgidanc
uerc uuldurfadur sue he uundra gihuaes
eci dryctin or astelidæ
he aerist scop aelda barnum

heben til hrofe haleg scepen.
tha middungeard moncynnæs uard
eci dryctin æfter tiadæ
firum foldu frea allmectig.
Primo cantauit Cædmon istud carmen.

– 'Cædmon's Hymn'

Not an easy poem to commit to memory, but I'll have a go at counting the 199 steps that descend into the town. If my counting concurs, I will treat myself to fish and chips. If I fail, then I'll clean my food bag of scraps. The port is as busy as one might expect. The *Flying Scotsman* is in town, it is Sunday, and the sun is shining. I count precisely 199 steps, but every chippie is packed, with queues in the streets of England's capital of fish and chips, so I have to be satisfied with a hotdog with mustard from a shed stall. There is a proliferation of shops selling Whitby jet, a gemstone of fossilised coal formed by ancient compressed monkey puzzle trees. This gemstone (found locally on the beaches) was made fashionable by Queen Victoria, on the death of her husband, Prince Albert, in 1861.

Whitby inspired Bram Stoker's *Dracula* and hosts numerous gothic festivals, but it is the town's connection to Captain Cook that interests me. Many locations on the path record significant events in his life. Both HMS *Endeavour* and HMS *Resolution* were conversions of sturdy merchant collier sloops, originally built in Whitby. His statue is a counterpoint to Cædmon's Cross, overlooking the entrance to the harbour, alongside a signpost with improbable distances marked. The place of his death, Hawaii, is 13,970 miles away; Botany Bay is 13,325 miles – an antipodean location, measured by a great circle that points in an unexpected direction.

It is a humbling perspective to the 200 miles I will walk on this trip.

It is a short road walk to Sandsend and into a disused quarry and abandoned railway tunnels. The path rejoins the cliff edge to Runswick Bay and a beach walk to the quayside. A steep climb out of the village passes a desperately tempting hotel bar, with chairs lined up for the sunshine. The customers are savouring their drinks in front of a parched walker.

'You look like you could do with a drink,' one man says.

'Very tempting,' I answer, but then they tease me.

'Nice pint is this, Tim. Cool, refreshing taste, ideal for washing down these salt and vinegar crisps.'

'Aye, Jezza, just what you'd fancy after a *long* walk.' They take a long sip.

'I think I might have another,' says Jezza, laughing.

I shouldn't have stopped to catch my breath. The locals are like predatory timeshare sales associates in the pay of the landlord. But they are actually engaged in friendly banter – an attractive characteristic in this part of the world.

'I only have a few clicks to Staithes,' I reply, before moving on.

'Enjoy your walk. Cheers, mate!' they reply, raising their glasses.

Within the hour, I stop to absorb some exceptional views of the village, embraced by Cowbar Nab, a spit of land that provides a natural sea defence. The red-roofed white-walled cottages make a picture that would frustrate the most patient jigsaw fan. The Cod & Lobster pub looks inviting, but I need to secure a B&B first. It is not quite Whitby standards and is missing the breakfast bit, but a cheap cosy room suits me and is more than compensated for by the Captain Cook Inn nearby. Once again, the food is unpretentious and tasty, washed down by a deep dark porter that settles from bubble to nectar as I warm my legs against a real coal fire. When I leave, a blood-red sunset darkens the western sky, a positive sign of good weather tomorrow.

I empty the contents of my food bag for breakfast: dusty gorp (good old raisins and peanuts) and half a Mars bar. There will be a good cafe in Saltburn eight miles away. First, I ascend to the summit of the highest cliff on the east coast of England, 203 metres above sea level, passing Boulby potash mine. This complex crowns a vast network of tunnels under the North Sea. The mine is the second deepest in Europe, extending 1.4 kilometres below the surface. Here they mine mega-tonnes of fertiliser, but it is also the location of a particle physics experiment to detect evidence of dark matter. Isolated tanks are quietly waiting for weakly interacting massive particles (WIMPs) to tickle their detectors, confirming an almost unmeasurable event to support the existence of a phenomenon that makes up an estimated sixty-eight per cent of the universe.

Sea fog is pushing up the cliff face and rolling inland, requiring a waterproof to stop a chill. It is a lonely and eerie scene, as if walking a mountain ridge in the Lake District. The sun returns at Skinningrove, a fishing village with a few Yorkshire coble boats still in use, but many rotting. One has been restored as a sculpture, complete with wooden fishermen, setting out to sea on a green lawn. Fake Banksy artwork depicts a spaceman with an ironic life-support system containing sea air. Not something I need as I ascend once again to the cliff edge to skirt round Warsett Hill, following the coastal railway line. A delightful rusty steel charm-bracelet sculpture features trinkets that reflect heritage and landscape: a shark egg purse, starfish, hammer and marlinspike dangle in the wind.

Saltburn-by-the-Sea comes into view; sadly, I will soon turn inland, my coastal walking completed. It is time to stop for brunch at a riverside cafe. My mind solves a complex price versus calorie versus taste equation to fuel up for the long section ahead (answer: bacon and egg roll). One last photograph of Yorkshire's last remaining seaside pier and I enter a wooded valley, walking under a viaduct to Skelton and on into the Cleveland Hills. Motorcycle tracks scar the trails; the ascents look unachievable by foot, let alone two wheels, but no one is on hand to demonstrate. The path progresses deeper into Guisborough Forest, where logging operations are in progress. A Ponsse harvester is stepping through the forest, turning trees into logs with frightening efficiency. I stare in awe at a scene from H.G. Wells's *War of the Worlds* as an alien operator, enclosed in a comfortable life-support capsule, casually slaughters life forms below. This beast could clear a hillside in an afternoon. At a safer distance, I stop for lunch at Highcliffe Nab, a yellow outcrop of sandstone, to take in the panoramic view across Guisborough and the industrial landscape of Middlesbrough, further north. Smokestacks discharge out to sea to form strange unnatural clouds of pollutants, adding to the planetary stock of CO_2 and other poisons.

Roseberry Topping, a pyramidic outcrop that overlooks my final destination at Great Ayton, comes into view. It is a steep climb to the trig pillar to join a crowd at the summit. It is a popular local walk, in one case obsessively so: a local legend, Keith Heaviside, climbed it six days a week for twenty years from the village below, in all conditions – equivalent to climbing Everest 220 times. This ascent is my first; I would need to complete another 6,239 to match his record.

This distinctive geological outcrop punches above its weight, resplendent in the surrounding landscape – a geological anomaly. In true Yorkshire style, Margery Moorput, a character in a 1761 Joseph Reed farce, exaggerated by saying:

> Certainly God! ye knaw Roſeberry? I thought ony Fule had knawn Roſeberry! – It's t' biggeſt Hill in oll Yorkſhire – It's aboun a Mile an a hofe high, an as coad as Ice at' top on't i't hetteſt Summer's Day – that it is.

While we are on the subject of local folklore, we can add a fisherman saying:

> When Roseberry Topping wears a cap, let Cleveland then beware of a clap!

I assume by clap, they mean thunder. Fortunately, the weather is clear, which is more than can be said about mobile coverage. Even though I have a signal, I cannot contact the owners of the hotel below, who said they would give me a lift. So I resign myself to a long walk via a sensible exit from the Cleveland Way. I could just drop down into town on a route that Keith would have taken, but I don't want to reduce my target to 6,238 with a climb in the morning to summit the 320-metre peak and rejoin the path. I should have done so at that moment, for the gamekeepers have lit the moorland to burn the heather. I have to skirt upwind around the boundary of the flames which are now enveloping the path. I stop to chat.

'Getting ready for the season?' I ask.

'Aye. At this time of year, we control-burn the gorse and heather. Everyone's at it tonight.' He points south to a sequence of black smoke clouds that confirm more activity. 'It's not often we get the right conditions: low wind, dry heather but wet ground.'

The burn encourages new growth and new shoots for red grouse to feed; the more, the better, ready to be blasted out of the sky at the start of the shooting season – 'the Glorious Twelfth'.

Grouse shooting is a significant employer in the National Park, supporting communities who do much to preserve the landscape I am enjoying – something to contemplate as I pace out the last miles down the lanes to the Royal Oak. The new owners are decorating, and the place is in chaos. They show me to an occupied room, which is an embarrassment for a guest in the middle of changing. After a twenty-five-mile and 60,000-step day, I am beyond complaining as they show me to a half-decorated smaller room. Fortunately, the kitchen is on top form, and it is cosy in the bar. A local couple are having a night out without their five children; they join me in a conversation for the evening. I'm noting all of their recommendations.

'You must try Suggitt's ice cream.'

'The pies from Stokesley's are the best.'

'Don't forget to climb Roseberry Topping!'

I explain my more extensive journey; they are envious of my free time.

I sleep well after a deep, late bath (no one else is bathing in it, fortunately). The landlord apologises for the mix-up and gives me a discount and a lift to my starting point. Today is another long twenty-three-mile day, to Osmotherly, mostly along the edge of the North York Moors, at times above 400 metres. On a good day, this would be spectacular, but the cloud base hovers at 300 metres. I reach the Captain Cook monument on Easby Moor. It starts to rain.

James Cook was born in 1728, a Yorkshireman. His father's employer paid for him to attend school in Great Ayton and he too would regularly climb Roseberry Topping. At sixteen, after moving to Staithes, he fell in love with the sea, but bored with his work as a grocer's boy, he moved to Whitby to start a merchant navy apprenticeship. With an aptitude for mathematics, navigation and astronomy, he joined the Royal Navy. He progressed through the ranks to command a scientific voyage in 1768, having impressed his superiors with his surveying abilities. For the next eleven years, he completed three significant expeditions, circumnavigating the oceans, discovering unknown lands and one continent, until his untimely death in Hawaii. To this day the Hawaiian flag features the Union Jack, a symbol of the friendship established between the two countries. An Australian industrialist bought James Cook's Great Ayton family cottage for £800 in 1933 and shipped it brick-by-brick to Melbourne, where it stands today in Fitzroy Gardens. What an extraordinary life he must have enjoyed; I'd have loved to swap places with him.

Properly togged up, with map and compass to hand, I follow tracks through the moorland. There is only one channel on landscape TV: a white-static view (someone pulled the aerial cable out) with the volume turned up. The wind is fresh, and the mist is impenetrable. My only frame of reference is a three-metre section of flagstone or track ahead of me. The map shows critical junctions at Bloworth Crossing, which, if missed, will lead me deep into featureless moorland, so I check my bearings and use twenty-minute pace to measure one mile, a rehearsed deadreckoning technique (I can sense when I am walking at three miles per hour).

Red grouse are startled by this strange creature walking in their territory. I am not sure who is the more startled, as the birds flap away into the mist calling a 'g' back ... g' back' warning. I have seen no one and nothing for three hours when I reach a gate precisely at the same time as another walker, heading east.

'Morning – Morning.' A synchronised greeting.

'Walking the Cleveland Way,' we announce like parrots together.

'Yes, also the Yorkshire Wolds Way,' I interject before this turns into an awkward dance.

'It's not the best day for this section. It's a pity about the conditions, as I'm sure the views are fantastic.'

'It is kinda strangely pleasant,' I add, sounding optimistic.

We manage to get through the gate and carry on, losing sight of each other in seconds. It is a ghostly encounter.

The path is now rugged, with frequent tough ascents and descents. I feel I am a few metres away from a cliff edge; an inner sense warns me to watch my step. Soon, I am amongst the Wain Stones, to meet a gaggle of schoolchildren having rock-climbing lessons; what an enlightened curriculum. They gleefully abseil down the rock face under the careful guidance of their instructors, clearly enjoying the day and somehow oblivious to the conditions; they are having too much fun.

I am just in time again, to open a gate for a gamekeeper on his quad bike. He stops to say thank you.

'There's a good cafe a few miles further on,' he says. 'It looks like you could do with a cuppa.'

'Oh yes. I need a break.'

I left my water bottle behind at the hotel, and I am quite thirsty. At Lord Stones country park is a modern cosy cafe. I remove my soaking outerwear and shuffle to a table in my socks, cleaning the floor as I go. A good meal and multiple pots of tea later, I feel human again after those eighteen miles in a sensory isolation tank. Conditions improve as I head south and off the ridge into woodland. My ears can take a rest now the rain has stopped. I can refocus on objects with sharp edges and recognisable form. The rain eases for the final few miles to Osmotherly. The Golden Lion is a very welcome sight; the landlord is sitting outside with a cup of tea.

'Ah, we are expecting you,' he says. 'Glad you found your way across the moors in these conditions.'

The room is a delight; I have time for a nap, and a shower in a stylish room dedicated to that function, its floor tapering to a drain. The evening meal is sublime, served in the bar, in which artificial light has been purposely replaced by candles. The light flatters diners and drinkers and creates a romantic atmosphere; I must return with my wife.

'Those candles cost £200 a month, but they're worth it.'

'I heartily agree, worth every penny. I felt transported back in time.'

I'm chatting to the landlord again after paying the bill, which is surprisingly modest for full board; perhaps this is low season.

'It's a wonderful pub,' I add. 'I'll come back soon.'

I walk back into the cloud again, but it soon clears. The path follows the moor edge, and I can see what I missed the previous day. The rain has flushed the skies clean, and I can see for miles across a patchwork quilt of arable and pastoral land. It makes for a pleasant meditative walk where hours pass without effort. I reach the gliding club fields at Roulston Scar and sit for lunch above Kilburn White Horse, a structure carved into the grass escarpment by a local schoolmaster and his pupils in 1857. I can barely see its shape, but I later look for it as I travel north on the Virgin east-coast line. I munch my sandwiches and watch the gliders approach the runway, judging their approach correctly (with dramatic consequences otherwise). I double-back along the same path to cross the main road again, heading east towards Helmsley, my final destination.

The village of Cold Kirby seems stuck in a time warp: old tractors puff up the broad street; there are no cars. Greystone cottages sit back from the road with tidy front gardens. Washing hangs from lines. Hardly any object of modern life can be discerned. The path enters Nettle Dale and skirts the grounds of Rievaulx Abbey, surrounded by impossibly pretty cottages with gardens full of spring flowers. In a valley peppered with natural springs, the ruins lie in quiet contemplation – another religious relic of the dissolution in the sixteenth century.

I approach Helmsley, its castle lit with a beam of sunshine. Within a few moments, I am touching the pyramid stone that marks the end of my journey. The town is busy with shoppers, and there are numerous options for refreshment. I plod along to the youth hostel and check in. Even though I am the only guest, the warden serves a wholesome meal, which he is no doubt enjoying in his private room too.

I take a bus to York in the morning, in the company of three Yorkshiremen who remind me of the characters from *Last of the Summer Wine*. The alpha male talks non-stop for a whole hour about the *Flying Scotsman*, quoting timetables, history, refurbishment details and that most precious of considerations: price. We reach York; his companions have barely said one word, but roll their eyes at me as we disembark.

14

PENNINE BRIDLEWAY

Distance: 205 miles
Days to complete: 9 days
Mileage so far: 2,260 miles

UNFINISHED BUSINESS

Now, shall I walk or shall I ride?
'Ride,' Pleasure said; 'Walk,' Joy replied.

– W.H. Davies

Anyone with an ambition to walk all the National Trails will have to complete the Pennine Bridleway. The northern section was opened in 2012 by the actor and president of the British Horse Society, Martin Clunes. There are plans to extend it even further north, but for now you can walk, cycle or ride 205 miles between Kirkby Stephen and Middleton Top, including the optional Settle and Mary Towneley loops. It is fair to say this is not at the top of most lists of excellent walks in Britain, but with hindsight, I thoroughly enjoyed the experience; it exceeded my expectations.

I decide to walk north to south on the flip of a coin, but find there are no public bus services along the A683 between Sedbergh and Kirkby Stephen that run to a sensible schedule. The advanced first-class ticket from Euston to Oxenholme is cheaper than the taxi to the start point, a remote lay-by twenty miles east of the station. I look at the Met Office forecast as I depart from London

– a glorious day in the Lakes. By the time I reach Preston, it has changed to heavy rain! So much for accurate five-day forecasts from those government supercomputers in Exeter.

The taxi driver has his windscreen wipers on for the journey. I dread leaving the warm comfort of the passenger seat for the moors.

'Looks like you're going to get a bit wet,' he says, stating the obvious.

'At least I only have a half-day. I'm planning to camp on the moors tonight,' I reply glumly, 'unless something else turns up.'

'That'll be £45, please,' he says, pulling up the handbrake to park.

I can't unpack and put on my waterproof quickly enough to prevent water from running down my neck, always dispiriting, but at least I am warm as I set out south towards Garsdale. I pass through a farm and see a red squirrel dart across the track and up a tree. He is not wearing Gore-Tex outer layers but seems happy enough underneath a huge bushy umbrella-tail that he flicks at intervals to remove water droplets. I now commence marching through the flooded ground, frequently crossing streams that have replaced the network of sheep tracks and paths. I ascend to a moorland ridge named High Dolphinsty (how appropriate) at 582 metres before a descent to the River Eden. I'd make better progress in a slalom kayak, such is the volume of water streaming off the moors, finding the shortest path to the river below. I splash through another farmyard before ascending south along twin-channelled Land Rover tracks towards an isolated sculpture that looks like a cracked egg. The trail crosses Hell Gill Bridge; Hell Gill Beck is in full spate and only just passable. Along the route, pretty tiles, vignettes of bygone days, are nailed on the direction posts. They depict scenes along this ancient drove road: highwaymen holding pistols and maidens looking anxiously out of their horse-drawn coaches.

The Moorcock Inn is only a few miles now. I had planned to camp nearby, but the ground is so saturated that I explore the possibility of a bed. The landlady doesn't blink an eye at a soaked and expectant walker. It is not the cosiest room, but it is dry, and I can get out of my wet clothes. The beer and wholesome food trump the rooibos and freeze-dried meal I have in my pack.

A huge Cumbrian breakfast should keep me going for a while. I have spent a fortune on trains, taxis and accommodation getting to this point. My next destination is a youth hostel in Clapham. I pace slowly up a tarmac ascent on to the misty moorlands. Signs say the road is closed, but I ignore them. I can hear the workmen and machinery ahead. They look at me puzzled as I emerge ghost-like from the landscape; even though they must work in these conditions, they cannot comprehend why someone would walk here for pleasure in this weather.

The sun is doing its best to break through as I meet groups of army cadets learning the basics of outdoor survival. Their heavy backpacks are full of regulation-issue equipment, all a drab olive-green colour and covered in Molle strips for attaching even more gear (or camouflage) if needed. The area is popular with cadets and school groups – a managed National Park environment with defined areas for wild camping. They study their map and take compass bearings before marching off across pathless heathland. Soon afterwards, a Duke of Edinburgh team emerges from the mist, led by two teachers.

'Everything OK?' I ask.

'Yes, they had a good first night in their tents and are raring to go.'

The expressions on some of the faces read otherwise. They are doing a gold-level award; their leaders will soon leave them to fend for themselves – a real test yet to come. Their school is just a few miles from my home, a surprising coincidence. I usually see packs of DofE candidates bedraggled and lost, walking along my local roads, seemingly unable to navigate through woodland or footpaths.

The Pennine Bridleway signposts (PBW) join briefly with the Pennine Way markers as I skirt to the north of Horton-in-Ribblesdale to cross the River Ribble. Curlews are nesting in the fields and make their presence known – a loud 'chew-wuh-wuh' call as

I enter their territory. They are imposing: Europe's largest wading bird. I initially mistake them for a bird of prey, before I see their long curved beaks.

> O curlew, cry no more in the air,
> Or only to the water in the west;
> Because your crying brings to my mind
> passion-dimmed eyes and long heavy hair
> That was shaken out over my breast:
> There is enough evil in the crying of wind.
>
> — W.B. Yeats, 'He Reproves the Curlew' (1896)

I ascend again into the Three Peaks landscape under Ingleborough (the second of the three) and walk through a fantastical world. I stop to rest, unlatching a simple gate in the wall to sit above a cliff face overlooking Crummack Dale and the Moughton Scars – immense limestone pavements and Ice Age geology overlaid with a grid of drystone walls. It is a unique view in England and one you might miss on the Pennine Way. I can lean against the wall in the lee of the wind, and munch through a pie so dry it cannot be wolfed down without a flask of tea. It will take a moment to absorb the vista; the details crystallise slowly in front of my eyes.

The descent into Clapham is agony, walking along a stony track covered in ankle-twisting rocks, too large to kick away, too small to avoid easily. I am happy to reach an excellent combination pub, hostel and cafe which has a cosy dorm, functional kitchen and warm welcome. I eat the freeze-dried food I should have eaten yesterday to save weight; it is surprisingly tasty when mixed with bits of food left by other hostellers. My ability to rustle up a half-decent meal is developing nicely, a core backpacking skill.

The bar is the headquarters of the local mountain and cave rescue team; the yearbook makes sober reading. It is a litany of accidents: poorly dressed, ill-prepared walkers and tourists suffering bad falls. An occasional heroic cave rescue features less frequently, where the team might spend days deep in the vast underground network of passages and caves which permeate the landscape. There is an underworld beneath the moors, more complex and extensive than the footpaths and roads above. Much of it is yet to be explored.

I stock up for lunch at the friendly village store nearby, which has a range of homemade pies and cakes. I only have a few miles to reach Settle across fields full of army soldiers and lambs. The lads are demolishing energy bars as the lambs gambol around their mothers, making mischief – two tribes in the spring of their youth. The soldiers hunker down in the lane while radio operators relay orders for a rendezvous. These guys are professionals, not like the cadets I saw earlier. Their packs are supplemented with ammunition (fake, I hope) and full battle gear. Every soldier carries a rifle. I overtake the group as they walk purposefully forward carrying maybe forty kilograms each, compared to my ten-kilo pack.

It is a pleasant day to divert on to the Settle loop after lunch. This optional section is a ten-mile circuit towards Malham and an ideal day trip for mountain bikers, horse riders and walkers alike. I meet a Yorkshireman with a Rhodesian ridgeback, both marching happily along. He starts talking and doesn't stop until we reach Settle. His chosen subject: outdoor gadgets. I am now an expert in digital navigation, global positioning systems and emergency beacon devices. He has a collection which he is keen to show me, but he dare not press the SOS button, hidden under a protective plastic hood, like the switch to launch a nuclear attack.

'Just press this, and a coded message beams to the control room. They phone the emergency services with your GPS location and come and rescue you!' he declares enthusiastically. I can see the value for very remote areas, but this route is busy. His watch is the size of a dinner plate, showing a compass overlaid on an OS map, with a predefined route to follow and a tracker to record progress.

'Today I have walked 10.52 kilometres and ascended 547 metres, marking three trig pillars as waypoints,' he says, smiling. Even his dog has a tracking device on his harness, but I bet he knows the way home without any of these technological marvels. I haven't used a compass for a few days, and the map has been in my pack since breakfast. I follow the PBW acorn signposts and apparent paths. Are these devices a means to an end, or an end in themselves, I wonder.

Trig pillars are a regular feature on all of my walks. They are nodes, or triangulation points, that link together to form a framework to build accurate Ordnance Survey maps. There are over 6,000 of them, enough to occupy fourteen years of Rob Woodall's life, during which he visited all 6,190 remaining trig pillars, thereby perhaps leading him to claim he has seen all of Britain (although I expect he was lost in the clouds more than once). No one knew of this eccentric attempt until he featured in the book *Dull Men of Britain*, which also features roundabout enthusiasts and experts who get paid to watch paint dry. Even I lovingly touch every brass trig plate, which sits on top of the concrete or stone structures. Now I realise I might catch an infectious condition that displays symptoms such as list-making, map collecting and research into the esoteric nature of such objects.

The room at the B&B in Settle has a Theakston Old Peculiar pump clip on the door – a hint to visit the local. I choose the mysteriously named Ye Olde Naked Man cafe in town instead; it used to be an undertaker's residence. Legend has it a naked man lies buried in the foundations. I need to go no further for a great meal and to stock up for lunch the next day. I'm going to need it, as it is a long walk tomorrow.

I reluctantly leave Settle to ascend on to the moors in the direction of Long Preston. The strip-lynchet field patterns are beautifully textured in the early morning light. Any human movement at this time of day sends fields of lambs into a frenzy as they wait to be fed by the farmers riding their quad bikes. The sheepdog balanced in a box strapped to the rear carrier seems to be in charge of affairs. Daffodils are out, and spring is in full swing. PBW signposts guide me through working farms, with the usual detritus of machinery and materials. As I walk further, they change into hobby farms, with brand new Range Rovers and BMWs parked outside manicured lawns. Signs warn poachers of the consequences; this is a rich man's playground more concerned with what you might read in *Horse & Hound* than *Farmers Weekly*.

I walk through Gisburne Park and into Barnoldswick, collecting an evening meal before reaching Earby youth hostel; I stayed here on my Pennine Way journey. The cottage was donated to the YHA by the socialist politician and novelist Katherine Glasier in the 1950s. It is a gem, with a quirky bunch of fellow travellers, although one gentleman has had too many beers and snores through the night like a trooper (just as it was a few years ago). Perhaps he is a permanent resident.

I wake early to the music of the dawn chorus, underpinned by a snoring tenor and bass. I leave early into a dewy, misty morning, with the prospect of a sunny day ahead. It is cold, and I can see the hills to the south covered in a dusting of snow and frost. My boots get soaked in the wet grass as I skirt through the fields, chased by hungry lambs who think I am the farmer, to rejoin the PBW. I try to capture a picture of a white and a black lamb snuggled neck in shoulder together, but they will not stay still for a moment. I cross the Pendle Way, signposted with opposing black witch symbols, each riding a broomstick. 'Which way do I go?' I snigger, as I zigzag through the field boundaries. This area has many witch trails, routes the accused would travel to their execution in Lancaster. The way remains for others to follow – for more pleasurable reasons.

The mist has cleared as I descend into Wycoller, a tenth-century hamlet with a fascinating history: Wycoller Hall is the rumoured setting of Ferndean Manor in Charlotte Brontë's *Jane Eyre*. It is a quaint village, untroubled by motor vehicles. The Wycoller beck flows gently, crossed by a sequence of ancient stone bridges, some rumoured to be 1,000 years old.

I follow the beck uphill to join the Brontë Way which runs with the PBW under the shadow of Boulsworth Hill, still covered in a dusting of snow. I have now reached Mary Towneley Loop and have to decide to turn east or west – a problem of public transport and accommodation that has perplexed me for a few days. I choose west and skirt through a complicated route around Holme Chapel. I come across a monument to Mary Towneley MBE, which reads:

*The air of heaven is that which bLows between a horse's ears.
Pause awhiLe beside this monument and remember Mary whose
vision opened up once more these ancient routes so that you can
refresh your spirit as the wiLd and romantic terrain of the
Pennines BridLeway unfoLds before you.*

Someone has an aversion to lower-case Ls; I can't for a moment
fathom why.

The route crosses the busy A671 into Burnley before following a
proper cycle track into Lumb. I phone ahead to secure a B&B,
strangely named the 678. The owner recommends the Hargreaves
Arms, which serves an excellent foaming pint, steak and chips – all
next to a coke fire, burning gently as the locals chat away. The
combination returns my physiology to its normal state, the twenty-
five-mile day having exhausted my fuel tank and chilled my bones.

The B&B is very cosy, better suited to tradespeople working in
the area, with all of the comforts they like: a big breakfast and a
widescreen TV with sports channels. I depart to empty Sunday
streets and closed shops towards Rossendale Valley before ascending on to the moors to reach Black Hill at 424 metres. Only
the farmers are working and the day is bright and sunny. The
snows have melted as I reach the top to find a signpost with so
many walking labels that it takes a moment to see the PBW acorn
symbol. I turn west to follow a ridge through a network of quarries
and extensive views over the moors to Rochdale and Bolton. The
air is still, and the wind turbines rotate gently. I pass through
Whitworth to enter a remote moorland which navigates around
reservoirs and golf courses to reach the Rochdale canal at Summit.

Crossing the canal after lunch, I am accosted by a rhea, keen to
explore the contents of my backpack. Although I initially believed
it to be an emu, this flightless bird is an unusual resident of the
area. I am glad it is behind a wire fence as it follows me along the
field boundary. The path now points towards Stoodley Pike, and
the going is easy along a flagstone path. The monument was
erected in 1815. Its purpose is embossed above the doorway to a
dark stairwell which leads to an observation balcony:

A BEACON MONUMENT
ERECTED BY PUBLIC SUBSCRIPTION
COMMENCED IN 1814 TO COMMEMORATE
THE SURRENDER OF PARIS TO THE ALLIES
AND FINISHED AFTER THE BATTLE OF
WATERLOO WHEN PEACE WAS ESTABLISHED
IN 1815. BY A STRANGE COINCIDENCE
THE PIKE FELL ON THE DAY THE RUSSIAN
AMBASSADOR LEFT LONDON BEFORE THE
DECLARATION OF WAR WITH RUSSIA IN 1854.
WAS REBUILT WHEN PEACE WAS RESTORED IN 1856
RESTORED AND LIGHTNING CONDUCTOR FIXED 1889

I climb the dark steps to the gallery and drink in the extensive views. Mankinholes youth hostel nestles in the valley below but is closed. Top Brink Inn is fully booked, with a Sunday crowd. I remember both fondly when I walked the Pennine Way, which the route now joins. I head for Hebden Bridge and the independent hostel above the town. It's a wacky place, but a real gem: cosy, friendly and full of Pennine Way memorabilia and postcards. Kipper the cat snuggles up to me as I wait for the warden and follows me around for the rest of the evening, expecting food. David turns up to book me in. We chat a while about the terrible floods on Boxing Day 2015. He is from Brighton.

'A town that suppresses ambition,' he says.

Somehow I imagine Brighton twinned with Hebden Bridge; it has a similar vibe.

'Ignore Kipper, he only wants food.'

Ambition doesn't seem necessary to David; he is a chilled-out perma-festival type, more than happy to be running the hostel and living in the town at a relaxed pace.

Town with a tissue that's quite unique;
Town where history's strata show
Alternative visions cheek to cheek,
Different plants allowed to grow.

In a world where towns are pallid clones
Hebden Bridge stands out a mile,
As the sun lights up West Yorkshire stones
And the sky is as bright as a smile;
You walk through the street and the voices rise
Like steam from a coffee emporium
And very quickly you realise
The whole town's an auditorium!
Hebden Bridge is theatre, so let's all clap
The wizard's cloak behind the new flat cap!

– © Ian McMillan @IMcMillan[14]

After breakfast with Kipper (who is keen to lap up the leftover milk in my cereal bowl), I depart. The Market Street shops show telltale tide marks bisecting their letterboxes; the floodwater was several metres above the river level today. The impact on local business is devastating, with sad notices on independent shops struggling to recover, many uninsured.

It's a cold, windy day as I stroll north alongside Colden Water, a tranquil wooded gully that protects me from the strong westerly I know I will face soon. I ponder diverting to May's shop, a pleasant memory from the Pennine Way, but I picked up a boring triangular sandwich pack from the Co-op in Hebden, so I follow the PBW, climbing further on to the moorland to face biting sleet, driven hard by the gale. It's hard going; my face is red raw with pain. My buff neck tube is pulled up around my nose to compensate. I stub my toes on rocks and ping my face with the waterproof hood pull cord, which slips from my grip as I tighten it. Ouch! My toes, my nose, my cheeks sting. I am close to tears from the pain.

I switch to marching mode, driven by self-anger and adrenaline, and arrive at the signpost I touched two days ago. I have completed the MT Loop and now need to find public transport back to the southern PBW section egress point. I march into Worsthorne and divert to the lane, which should have a bus stop. I shiver as I wait for thirty minutes before boarding a double-decker that will take me to Summit. The bus is warm, but I add to the humidity that condenses on the windows, preventing views from the top deck. I'm soon walking a short distance to the Moorcock Inn (a popular pub name on the PBW), where I secure a basic room. The landlord makes me welcome – a gregarious man who recommends the paella served with a pint of Old Peculiar, while he looks at the TV above the bar. Manchester City are playing.

'Go on, son, pass the ball,' he shouts. 'Arggghhhh, no!' The player fluffs a shot. Other customers groan as they gawp at the screen, pints in hand.

'Refereeeee!'

In the morning, I cross the A58 and head for the even busier M62 on a still, bright, cloudless morning. The traffic noise eases until I am on peaceful, still moorland. A reservoir occupies almost every valley, storing water for the thirsty cities below. Carp fishermen are asleep by their expensive carbon-fibre rods; they snooze with half an eye open, watching their floats. It is a day to relax and enjoy the sunshine.

For the first time on the bridleway, I come across horse riders from the nearby stables. It is challenging to keep pace with them, but they frequently stop to rest; we often overtake each other, politely letting the other pass. I stop for lunch to break the traffic overlap dance by the River Tame and continue on a disused railway line through an urban landscape, before ascending again on to the moorland and yet more reservoirs. There is an insatiable demand by the population of Manchester, and other cities to the west, for both industry and domestic requirements. The waterworks at Tintwistle are a marvel of Victorian engineering helping to control the flow from a network of reservoirs upstream, before processing and delivery downhill.

Padfield has a great B&B, and more importantly, a great pub, the Peels Arms, which I recall from my Pennine Way walk. Unfortunately, the landlord is on a cruise holiday, and his daughter is struggling to cope with a sudden influx on a beautiful day. I share a table with fellow walkers for a natter; they are on the PW – day two – and are keen to know what to expect further north. They all ask questions at the same time.

'Can you stay at the Tan Hill Inn?'

'What are the youth hostels like?'

'Fancy another pint before our meal arrives?'

They are staying at the same B&B I once used, but tonight I sleep in the village. I recognise the driver when he collects them an hour later.

The landlady serves a great breakfast and asks me to sign the visitors' book. It records ten years of guests' comments.

'That's a long time to be running a B&B,' I say. She then brings out three more books. She has been here for over forty years!

'I've been thinking of retiring for twenty,' she says, 'but never got around to it.'

We chat for a while; it is great to see she enjoys social contact and can endure an increasingly demanding public over such a period of service. My father always told me to avoid any work where you deal directly with the public. He should know after thirty-five years running a pub in Berkshire.

I mix in with the local school run into Charlesworth before a steep ascent along Coombes Edge and on to a spectacular horse-shoe ridge, with unbroken views to the skyscrapers in Manchester city centre. It's a beautiful walk, descending gracefully into Hayfield along a converted railway line. I sit and listen to *Trail Tales*, an audio-visual art installation spoken by local primary schoolkids. This place was a hive of activity a hundred years ago: an industrial railway line and marshalling yards. The village has a perfect shop to gather lunch before I disappear again from civilisation along the River Kimber and on to the moors.

It's another beautiful day – still crisp air and blue skies. I take a relaxed pace, drinking in the atmosphere, when suddenly I am startled by a loud swoosh past my ear. A merlin, or maybe a peregrine, has used my body to blindside a defenceless lark that only moments before had been serenading me with a song. It explodes into a ball of feathers. This attack happens so fast I am aghast; it is over in less than a second. I struggle to positively identify the villain as it flaps away with its prey in its talons.

Warily, and with my senses on full alert, I continue down the rocky trail to the road, still digesting the violence and shock of the experience. I see a sign saying, 'No Car Cafe – Welcomes Walkers, Cyclists and Riders'. I have to visit. A perfect cup of Yorkshire tea and a calorific cake calm my nerves as I excitedly tell my story.

Refreshed, I wander into Tideswell along dull lanes to my accommodation at the Horse & Jockey. It seems expensive, but it has a sumptuous four-poster bed, serves Real Ale and Real Food, and has a Real Fire, a Real Welcome and is a Real Pub (according to the sign outside). It scores ten out of ten on all counts; the advertisement is for once correct. I tuck into faggots, peas and mash, washed down by a pint of Tetley's (or two) as I open a conversation with weekday walkers, also staying upstairs. They have a few days in the Peak District National Park.

'What's your plan for tomorrow?' they ask, picking up my map.

'I'm walking the Pennine Bridleway.'

'It's all cycle track after Monyash, a bit boring if you don't have a bike.'

'Well, I have walked from Kirkby Stephen. I have to finish it now.'

'Wow, that is a long way. Sure you haven't got a bike out back?'

The bed is too comfortable; the convex mattress absorbs my tired body, locking it in place for the night. I oversleep, which is an uncommon event for me. At breakfast, the banter continues as we fuel up for the day ahead. The total bill comes to £50, for food, bed, breakfast and several beers. I ask the host to check, but she says it is correct.

They were right about the route; a gravel pavement opens up. Initially, it is pleasing to walk on, in contrast to the rocky tracks I have seen for the past few days. It is now perfect for cycling: a fifteen-mile trail on a former railway line, bridges and tunnels still intact. It is a boring walk, so I make it exciting by maximising my pace – speed walking, arms swinging hard, walking poles packed away. I know I can go home today if I reach the finish at Middleton Top sooner. Averaging 3.8 miles per hour (calculated by dividing the distance on marker posts by time) I am almost jogging, stretching out my gait and increasing my step frequency, as fast as I can without getting breathless. I can rest aches and pains on the train home.

This is National Cycle Network Route 68, leading to Route 54, part of the Sustrans network of cycleways that cover the UK. Sustrans is the custodian of over 16,500 miles of cycle routes (over 5,000 miles are traffic-free). Their beginnings were humble: following the 1970s oil crisis, a group of environmentalists formed Cyclebag (**C**hannel **y**our **c**alf and **l**eg **e**nergy **B**ristol **a**ction **g**roup) to pioneer the conversion of disused railway lines to cycle tracks. Starting with the Bristol–Bath cycleway (which now carries more people on bicycles than the railway it replaced), they expanded nationally after winning £42 million (that number again), one of the first grants from the newly created National Lottery. The network uses a numbering system similar to the road network; you can take National Cycle Network Route 4 from London to Fishguard, like using the A4 trunk route or M4 motorway. Main routes use a single-digit number, national cycle routes use two-digit numbers and regional routes three digits. These cycleways frequently coincide with the National Trails, triggering thoughts to start cycle touring.

The PBW endpoint is uninspiring; there is a cafe/shop, but nothing to mark the end of a 205-mile walk. I catch a bus into Matlock Bath as my legs seize solid. I am happy now to be on a train to London and relax and reflect on the past nine days. The PBW has far exceeded my expectations and has much to recommend it. It navigates through an urban landscape, never more than a few miles from city life, yet is remote and relaxing in a way that will surprise you – on a bike, on a horse or on foot.

15

SOUTHERN UPLAND WAY

Distance: 212 miles
Days to complete: 10 days
Mileage so far: 2,465 miles

SCOTLAND'S COAST TO COAST

It is good to collect things, but it is better to go on walks.
— Anatole France

I have been looking forward to walking the four designated long-distance trails in Scotland for years, leaving them until the end, almost like a reward for completing the paths in England and Wales. They are now part of a network of Scotland's Great Trails – just a small sample of a limitless range of superb walking routes north of the border. Now I will follow a thistle symbol for 465 miles, instead of the familiar acorn.

The mad plan is to walk all four paths in one continuous journey, starting with the Southern Upland Way (SUW) and proceeding north via the West Highland Way and Great Glen Way to the Speyside Way. This adventure will take three to four weeks, but when? Scotland, for me, is at its best in April/May and September/October. Midsummer means doing battle with midges, together with the possibility of ticks and cleggies (horseflies). Midges need no introduction for anyone who has travelled in Scotland and can be a real pain for those who plan to camp. Ticks (carrying Lyme disease) are an increasing concern and more prevalent when the ferns and grasses grow; I like to wear shorts as much as possible. In summer, cleggies can appear as you stop for lunch to completely spoil your day, with a vicious bite on the neck as you eat your sandwich, usually drawing blood. Winter is for the experts, masochists, or students in Doc Martens, as I later learn.

A break in my freelance work appears in the spring – ideal for a three- or four-week expedition. My wife thought I might think about some gardening and loft clearance, but I manage to negotiate a pass for a month with a promise I'll take her to Scotland later in the year to see the best bits.

The SUW is Scotland's coast-to-coast path through the Scottish Borders connecting Cockburnspath, near Dunbar, in the east, with Portpatrick, near Stranraer, in the west. Most people walk from west to east to take advantage of the prevailing southwesterly winds. I choose to walk from east to west as I like breaking the rules, and the logistics are easier for onward connection to Glasgow for the West Highland Way.

The area is remote, like a no man's land between England and Scotland, once the province of nationless reivers and mercenaries, who would raid the wealth of the lowlands irrespective of nationality. The Southern Uplands are not only a political boundary, but a geological boundary, formed some 500 million years ago when Scotland met England for the first time, with Scotland coming out on top as England folded beneath the continental crust, scraping a seabed to form the uplands. This upheaval built a string of volcanoes like a row of facial spots, now polished by an ice age or two, creating the landscape we see today. The path is Scotland's longest official trail at 212 miles and follows this geological boundary. Except for the market towns and a few villages, you will only meet local farmers and forestry workers and, if you are lucky, some fellow SUW walkers – more if you walk east to west (you count more people on the opposite escalator). Had the prospect of total isolation and loneliness influenced my decision to walk the wrong way?

Different accommodation itineraries suit each trail. So I study the entire Scotland trip to see what I should do. With several long remote sections, it seems sensible to take a tent and use as many bothies as practical, using inns and B&Bs to meet the locals for conversation, insight and guidance. A quick scan of the excellent accommodation guide maintained by the SUW Association indicates a ten-day itinerary is possible, but this means an ambitious twenty-mile daily average. The West Highland and Great Glen ways have good camping options too.

Having a tent, and carrying evening meals, means I have a contingency plan, so I will only book ahead if necessary. I prefer this flexibility so I can adjust for conditions and fitness. If I were to book a full Scottish three-week expedition, I would be a slave to that schedule, and I like the serendipitous nature of adventure. The Scottish government also has an enlightened policy towards wild camping, and it seems a shame not to maximise nights under the stars and the prospect of seeing the northern lights.

So, with my usual pre-expedition anxiety butterflies, I set off again from my local railway station, taking perverse pleasure from joining the glum commuters into London to connect with the east coast service to Edinburgh. The carriage lights fail just after departure, creating an eerie smartphone glow lighting up each weary face, glued to their daily news and social feeds. I was looking forward to the pleasure of a long-distance off-peak *Flying Scotsman* service from King's Cross, complete with Yorkshire tea, a decent breakfast and a read of the broadsheets. All very civilised.

I am sitting on the right-hand side, drawing a curtain to protect my eyes from the early morning sun. Yet I can trace my previous adventures in Yorkshire as I recognise the hills and rivers, the colossal power stations belching out clouds of water vapour from their cooling towers. Another recognisable feature is the white horse on Sutton Bank, below the gliding club airfield – a turning point on the Cleveland Way into Helmsley. If I had not walked that trail earlier in the year, the landscape would be meaningless, but now I see more. I reflect on the distances I have walked, compressed into minutes on an inter-city train.

Another cup of tea as we progress northwards and then a

schoolboy thrill to cross the River Tyne at Newcastle, with all those beautiful bridges. Likewise the River Tweed at Berwick, with superb views of the harbour, as the train coaches peel around the docks.

Welcome to Scotland, my home for a month.

Unfortunately, the train does not stop at Dunbar, passing within a few metres of the starting point at Cockburnspath; I can see it out of the window. How annoying. It will take me another four hours to reach that point, doubling back to Dunbar by train and then catching the Perryman bus service to Berwick. Never mind, at least I can enjoy the views across the Firth of Forth to Bass Rock, a black volcanic plug covered in white guano. A strong easterly and you can smell it too; this island is one of the largest gannet colonies in the world. White snow covers the hills to the south and north. I hope this does not mean winter conditions ahead as I ascend into the Lammermuir Hills; I do not have crampons.

At Dunbar, I wait at the bus stop, snacking on a Co-op pasty, drawing the attention of a bold seagull. Judging by his cockiness, I can only assume he had served an apprenticeship in the seedier parts of Edinburgh and spotted an unguarded Englishman. It seems sensible to retire to the bus shelter for protection but at the expense of an aural assault from a pair of teenage girls. The high-speed gabbling is incomprehensible to me, fresh off the train from London. I think they are talking about which flavour vaping oil they like to smoke; the sweetie shop nearby offers a variety of choices. They sound like Vicky Pollard's northern cousins. I quickly finish the pasty as my bus arrives; they catch another.

'Single to Co'burnspath, please,' I ask in the hope the bus will stop there.

'£1.80, please.'

The driver forgets to stop at my destination, but a quick guttural exchange of dialogue saves the day.

'You f'got to drop off the walker at Co'path, Jim!' a fellow passenger shouts. Emergency brakes are applied.

'Thank you.' I am grateful for the intervention, not knowing where to alight.

'Cheerie bye,' comes a friendly reply and smile. The bus driver groans.

I am now in an oasis of peace and tranquillity in the village of Cockburnspath. Population? Seems to be declining. I ask for a room (speculatively) at a house with a B&B sign, but the business has ceased to trade despite a clear sign marked 'Vacancy'. My tent will be put to good use tonight.

The Mercat Cross marks the start of the path, I assume, as I cannot find any official marker. This cross, erected in 1503, commemorates the marriage of King James IV of Scotland to Margaret Tudor, sister of King Henry VIII of England. The rose and the thistle are carved into the cross to symbolise the proposed union between the two countries. I take a look at my watch and take my first step on the Southern Upland Way.

The first task is to find a campsite and water. I see a tap at a commercial camping farm at Pease Bay but no accommodation, even for a wee tent. There are no discreet areas to pitch on the coast path, so I progress inland to enter thick woodland and pick a sheltered spot. No sunrise across the North Sea for me this time. A pity, as the limitless seascape will transform in twelve hours into a shimmering dawn. The pitch is pleasant enough – quiet and sheltered. I sleep well after a full day of travelling, sometimes more exhausting than actually walking.

The sight of a kingfisher on an undulating flight path down the stream is a reward for an early departure. The winter rains and snows have left the ground boot-suckingly muddy, stirred up with cattle hooves and tractors and blended with slurry. The earth is firmer into Abbey St Bathans, crossing a river via the footbridge instead of the ford in flood – a challenge for the gnarliest 4x4.

I meet my first SUW walker, a Dutchman on holiday, with suspiciously mud-free boots.

'Walking the Southern Upland?' I ask.

'Yes, only one more day to go,' he replies. 'Conditions are good ahead, but the weather has been difficult.'

'It's a bit muddy in this direction, I'm afraid.'

Either he has walked through a car wash or the path ahead is dry;

he is spotlessly clean. We stop and chat for a while to exchange knowledge of the path conditions in my direction. I suggest he continues on the farm track to avoid the cattle-hoof mud pond.

'Are you not walking the wrong way?' he asks.

'There is no wrong way.' I go on to explain my plan, before asking, 'Why do you like Scotland so much? I meet a lot of people from the Netherlands.'

'I like the hills and mountains. Holland is flat.'

The village has the first of many information boards along the way, which reminds me to look for buried treasure. There are thirteen *kists* along the route which each contain a *weymerk* coin, each designed by a local school. You can collect all thirteen, or 'the hoard', on the SUW. It is such a fantastic idea; I am surprised other trails have not copied it. On reflection, I am sure this can only work on the remoter paths. Each *kist* is in a very remote area, taking an effort to reach. I have missed the first coin, but I am not concerned about collecting all thirteen; otherwise I will spend a month in the Borders looking for the damn things. Little metal plaques saying '*Ultreia*' appear on waymark posts; the *kists* are found near them. All very Middle Earth. On with my quest!

The path out of Abbey St Bathans continues on farm tracks until you reach Longformacus. The village is tranquil, if not closed for the season – perhaps a holiday home ghetto. I find a wild campsite near Twin Law, behind a wall. I filter water for the evening and reflect on the inscription written on one cairn:

> And they biggit twa cairns on the heather
> They biggit them roond and high
> On the top of Twinlaw Hill
> Where they twa brithers lie

The story goes that two brothers, separated at birth, fought with opposing Saxon and Scots armies and were killed in battle. When the lairds discovered the family connection, they built the twin cairns in their memory. As if to continue the tradition, one cairn contained a visitors' book in a tin, alongside a half-full bottle of single malt, inviting you to take a dram in their memory. Ironically, the original cairns were destroyed in the Second World War, as target practice on tank manoeuvres, to be rebuilt later. After pitching, I cook the evening meal, a freeze-dried favourite of spaghetti bolognese. Something about that meal is not quite right, but I am starving.

I wake early, feeling very ill. My body rejects the meal from both orifices; it was rancid. I pack up, anxious about my condition, and depart. I find my walking poles useful to hold me upright as I retch. I have no choice now but to walk into the next town and rest, even taking a day off. I cannot contemplate eating breakfast or even drinking, but my legs are working.

After a while, I reach Lauder. The local shop sells Lucozade, which seems to have a remarkable effect on my energy levels. I decide to keep going and shortly cross the River Tweed at Montrose. The river has recovered after the severe winter floods, evident from the detritus hanging five metres above, in the trees. I take another sip of the sugary liquid.

After crossing a suspension bridge, I follow the river until I reach a cycle path and a railway line. In 2015, Britain opened a new domestic service, the longest in a hundred years, connecting Tweedbank and Galashiels to Edinburgh. The Queen officially opened the line on 9 September and the Borders community made an occasion of the day. Arriving in the town centre, I have completed a full twenty-mile day, across the Lammermuir Hills, without food and feeling ill – a significant achievement. I will never complain about sugary drinks again. Perhaps the freeze-dried package split, compromising the contents. I'll take great care in future. I find a cosy B&B, with a delightful landlady who shows me to a comfortable room. I rest well, but still eat nothing until the morning, where I have no option but to demolish an FSB (full Scottish breakfast) and sod the consequences. I have made a full recovery, but take the precaution of booking into a hotel in Innerleithen, sixteen miles away.

Galashiels has an M&S, so I stock up with some healthy goodies and stroll to the River Tweed. I then open the throttle and ascend to the Three Brethren at 465 metres. No, not triplet brothers separated at birth, but a boundary meeting point of three estates: Buccleuch, Yair and Selkirk Burgh. Each territory is marked with a massive stone cairn, where they should have built one. The Selkirk fence post holds a brass plaque listing names going back to 1960, each new person an annual standard-bearer for the Burgh.

The views are extensive across the uplands and moorland. You can see for fifty miles in all directions, but more clearly to the north. The rolling mountains lie coloured with a chequerboard of brown heather, green grassland and white snow. Three volcanic cones (the Eildon Hills) protect Galashiels, like chess pieces defending their king.

A more recent scenic interruption is not so welcome: vast tracts of wind turbine farms litter the hills. Some are idle, even with a fresh wind blowing. I am sure it has to do with supply and demand; the wind doesn't necessarily blow when the grid needs energy. Another feature is the Roman and drove roads which criss-cross the upland landscape – predecessors of the A74(M) and A7 trunk roads that connect Scotland and England. Instead of an articulated lorry full of sheep en route to the abattoir, drovers would have driven the flocks many miles to the markets.

The first of many art installations gives me an excuse to pause before I enter Innerleithen. Patterns cut into the heather form art seen through a stone lens. It has a practical use too: the maintained crop provides food for black grouse (less common than red grouse). These wild birds are encouraged to breed for shooting later. It is a significant source of income for the community. I meet a Dutch couple as I stop for lunch at Brown Knowe, 523 metres above sea level. They are cheery and suspiciously mud-free too. With the wind behind them and glorious views ahead, they have every right to be joyful. Their experience is perhaps more intense than walking along a polder or dyke in their home country.

The Minch Moor bothy, planned initially as a stopping point, has been demolished for safety reasons, so I do not feel guilty staying at the Traquair Arms Hotel, even though I have a two-mile road walk to reach it. I pass Traquair House, dating back to 1107, the oldest continually occupied house in Scotland, strategically placed at a crossing point for the River Tweed. It has a brewery, so I make a note to visit when I come back to the Borders with my wife. The hotel owner meets me with a broad Welsh accent, which throws me for a second.

'All right, lad?' he asks, before showing me to my room. 'Restaurant's closed tonight, I am afraid. Chef has called in sick, but you'll find plenty of options in town.' I am made very welcome and find a good meal at the Whistle Stop cafe, with dessert at Caldwell's, the famous ice cream shop. I sleep well, relieved that my illness is behind me.

Breakfast comes with a Welsh natter and gossip (and mandatory exchange of life stories). He tells me the crime rate is non-existent and the town is popular with cyclists when the weather is good.

'No, I'd never go back to Wales, love it here, see,' he says as I put on my boots. I can't blame him.

Back in the hills, I discover my first *kist* and collect one shiny coin; the container is disguised as a drove road marker. As you touch a symbol on the side, it opens up to reveal several hundred coins in a bowl. I take one and store it safely in my pocket.

I reach St Mary's Loch at Dryhope Tower, a ruined building formerly used by locals when the marauding armies passed through. It provided enough defence against attack in an area too remote to lay siege. The path follows the shoreline until I walk into a Guy Martin-themed cafe. They serve a welcome lunch in the company of twenty identikit American tourists on a Rabbie's tourist bus.

'You've walked from Dunbar!' they exclaim. 'In this weather!'

'You're mad.'

'Who's this Guy Martin fella, anyway? He looks a nutter too. Is he from Scotland?' they ask.

I try my best to explain the meaning of a 'proper bloke' who likes mugs of tea, but it does not translate. They are jetlagged and more attentive to the bus driver's commands. He is dressed in a regulation kilt, and spurts forth a pre-recorded stream of historical facts, without a pause or rewind button: 'St Mary's Loch is the largest natural loch in Southern Scotland ... three miles long ... created by glacial action ... ' and so on for a few minutes.

I sit with a competitive cyclist, out on a long-distance training session for the day. We exchange stories, and he gives me further insight into cycling in the area, a subject which is beginning to trigger some thoughts in my mind about what I will do after I have finished my quest.

'The headwinds are murder,' we agree.

'But at least I'll have a tailwind to Galashiels,' he is pleased to say. I have another ten miles over rough moorland ahead, to Over Phawhope bothy, into a freshening breeze.

As I go to pay, I realise I have lost my *weymerk* coin. I wonder what value a coin has to be for me to turn back. 'Damn,' I mutter as I make a brief foray back to the sailing club to see if it fell from my pocket when I checked my map.

Another ascent into the hills to meet another Dutchman! I have to stop and ask, 'Why so many Dutchmen in the Southern Uplands?' He repeats the logical answer I heard before: 'Because the Netherlands is flat!' He is unaware of the *kists*, so I ask him to look out for the *Ultreia* signposts and collect a memento of the trip. Unfortunately, I do not have a coin to show him.

'On with your quest,' I say as we walk apart.

After a long boring road walk, I reach Over Phawhope bothy – what a delight. It has unheard-of levels of luxury: a sofa and a new green watertight roof. I light the cast iron stove, make tea and prepare a meal. Afterwards, I try my best not to fall asleep as the stove crackles and the calories soak into my tired legs. I make an effort to replenish the kindling and logs by attacking a tree left by the forestry workers. Knowing the pleasure of arriving at a bothy with dry wood and a fire ready to be lit, it is a social duty. Phawhope means a valley of different colours. But today that variegation is now a dark green monoculture of Sitka spruce. While many praise its commercial value as timber, I welcome the protection from the wind and rain showers. In the early morning mist, the sun shines down the orderly corridors, an ethereal light, like walking in a smoky cathedral. The forest is peaceful and quiet, a sanctuary from the relentless rage of the southwesterlies.

The Sitka spruce was introduced by David Douglas (of Douglas fir fame) in 1831 from the west coast of America. It was planted extensively, and provided construction material during the two world wars. This variety has durable fibres and an excellent strength-to-weight ratio. The fastest aircraft in the Second World War, the Mosquito, is almost entirely made of this wood. Today, it is praised as a top-performing asset class and a vehicle for inheritance tax avoidance.

The Roman roads and drove tracks continue through the Eskdalemuir Forest to Ettrick Head en route to Moffat, a significant town on the A74(M) and an opportunity for a decent lunch and to resupply. I need a few items from the outdoor shop, but it is closed. The owner sees me waiting on the steps and runs across the road.

'I'll open up for you,' he says, carrying his lunch. 'How can I help?'

This shop is not high-street fashion and is full of precisely what a SUW walker might need. I buy gloves and volume adjusters for my new boots: gloves in case the weather turns, and the adjusters to fit underneath the insole to compensate for the fact I have gone up a boot size. I have noticed that my feet grow as I age and walk more frequently.

I spend a while chatting about the route ahead.

'One student from Edinburgh walked the SUW in winter in Doc Martens, and he seemed none the worse for wear,' he says.

'Did he make it?'

'I don't know, no reports from mountain rescue; the conditions in winter can be very severe.'

The Italian-style Cafe Ariete on the high street offers an excellent FSB and Scottish high-calorie cake and pastries with indecipherable names. Refreshed and resupplied I set off to pass under the drone of the A74(M) motorway into the Lowther Hills and to Brattleburn bothy. I am back on the drove roads again.

When we first rade down Ettrick
Our bridles were ringing, our hearts were dancing,
The waters were singing, The sun was glancing,
An' blithely our voices rang out thegither,

As we brushed the dew frae the blooming heather,
When we first rade down Ettrick.

When we next rade down Ettrick,
The day was dying, the wild birds calling,
The wind was sighing, the leaves were falling,
An' silent an' weary, but closer thegither,
We urged our steeds thro' the faded heather,
When we next rade down Ettrick.

When I last rade down Ettrick,
The winds were shifting, the storm was waking,
The snow was drifting, my heart was breaking,
For we never again were to ride thegither,
In sun or storm on the mountain heather,
When I last rade down Ettrick.

– Lady John Scott (1810–1900), 'Ettrick'

A concerned gentleman stops his car.

'Fancy a lift to the top of the hill?' he asks – one of many offers I have received in remote areas. I have to explain what I am doing and regret the opportunity for a chat when I refuse the offer.

'I'd love to, but I'm walking the Southern Upland Way.'

'Good luck,' he says as he struggles with a hill start in a car that has seen better days. White smoke billows from the exhaust; his piston rings are on the way out.

I am early, and the bothy is empty, so I set about making myself comfortable. Starting the fire in the stove is almost impossible as the wood is very wet, but after some persistence, I can make tea, warm up and settle down. I cut more wood and bring it indoors to dry, also cutting more kindling for the next guests. There are enough axes, saws and billhooks to build a small town, so there is no excuse not to gather wood.

This bothy is covered in humorous graffiti and friendly Scottish banter as if a party of Edinburgh Fringe comedians were stranded here for weeks with nothing else to do. Mel Gibson doesn't fare too well for his portrayal of William Wallace in the film *Braveheart*. Neither do Englishmen, particularly from London. A half bottle of whisky has been left, with a note saying, 'Enjoy!' An ideal nightcap; I make a toast to all the good people in the world. No other walkers turn up, so I drift off to sleep, expecting the last-minute sound of a lifting door catch and a late arrival. It doesn't happen.

I sleep well until woken by the sounds of mice scratching around the bed, and turn on my head torch to see a pair of the wee devils eating the remains of the paper bag that contained my Danish pastry. The utter peace and silence of this remote bothy amplify any strange noises, so I watch the entertainment in the light of my head torch as they search for a juicy morsel until my eyelids close. I depart early, leaving thanks to the Mountain Bothy Association for another gem.

I pass one of two memorial stones to shepherds who lost their lives on these moorlands – a healthy reminder of how exposed the moors can be and the precious shelter that is offered by a bothy. The stones mark the exact spots where the bodies were found as they sought to protect their flocks. The usual pattern of an early morning ascent brings me over Hods Hill to the Daer Reservoir and then a crossing of the A702 and the River Clyde. A newborn lamb, maybe a day old, follows me over the boggy moorland, bleating for its mother. I climb a fence and leave it to its fate.

Next up is a long, arduous ascent to the summit of Lowther Hill near the golf ball radar station on Green Lowther. I collect another coin and get into 4x4 mode as a never-ending summit eludes me for an hour. Eventually, I reach Lowther Hill and the highest point on the way at 725 metres. Clear skies, light winds and extensive views over Dumfries and Galloway greet me; I'm a lucky man. The silence is absolute, save for the background tinnitus in my ear. If it were not for the wind turbines, there would be little evidence of man. I find an ideal spot for lunch near a rusted hut wearing camouflaged steel panels that hide it in the heather. I couldn't be further from city life.

I descend into Wanlockhead, taking shortcuts across the hairpin maintenance road. I catch glimpses of several mountain hares, yet to lose their white winter camouflage and easily seen against the brown heather terrain. Feeling elated after crossing this section, I fall into the museum cafe and demolish a toastie and several slices of cake.

My legs have seized up after the unexpected afternoon break. They slowly recover as I dawdle through the disused workings of Wanlockhead, the highest village in Scotland, where they once mined lead, copper, zinc, silver and gold. The gold is some of the purest found, at 22.8 carats, and was used to make the Scottish Crown. Judging by the incredible landscape and presence of beam engines and sluice gates, that must have taken some effort to find. I wonder where that crown is today. I suspect it is in the Tower of London.

I ascend again into the last remains of the Lowther Hills and descend into Sanquhar, after negotiating some very treacherous undrained cattle fields. I'm covered in mud and it is time to find accommodation.

'Sorry, lad, we're fully booked. It's the wind farms, you know,' is my first response.

'Try down the road, opposite the shop,' is another.

'Sorry, fully booked. You'll be lucky to find anywhere during the week.'

I am concerned. I sit on a bench and get my smartphone out, and find a delightful farm B&B nearby, with my first call.

'We don't do evening meals, so eat in town before walking to us.'

I eat a decent stew at a restaurant and walk towards the manor farm to meet a wonderful landlady and her enormous Great Dane. She cannot be more accommodating.

'If you need a hot-water bottle, let me know,' she offers. 'We only have a bath; use as much hot water as you like,' she adds. 'I'll get the kettle on.'

A china tea set appears, with homemade cake, while I browse a small library of local books in the hallway. The house is delightful, stuck in a Victorian time warp, and has remained in the family for four generations. The bed is a mound of blankets and sheets, not the usual continental duvet. I switch on the electric blanket – what a guilty pleasure. It must have been half a century since I last experienced such luxury. I should have asked for the hot-water bottle too.

I sleep deeply, to awake to a huge FSB served with Victorian cutlery and crockery and a silver teapot of similar age. It is more than I can eat and I have to ask for some silver foil to build a lunchtime feast from the remains. She has no problems with any leftovers, with that hungry dog around. The abundance of calories is no bad thing, as I have a twenty-six-mile day ahead into St John's Town of Dalry – a remote, rugged section. I thank the landlady for her hospitality. She refuses to let me round up the bill and places coins carefully in my hand as she counts from her purse. I make a note to return to Sanquhar and its many attractions, as I head up into the hills across the River Nith.

The Sanquhar to Dalry section is the longest stretch of the SUW, with no facilities or accommodation en route, save for a bothy, which I could not find, at Polskeoch. The sense of isolation and remoteness is terrific yet humbling, and it is a welcome sight to meet any other walkers. The ascent to Allan's Cairn is tough, as many trees have fallen, blocking the path. I meet a party of organised walkers who want to keep themselves to themselves, somehow troubled by a lone walker. They are on a day trip to see the red sandstone arch sculptures, by artist Andy Goldsworthy, that stand on Colt Hill and Benbrack nearby. They are visible for miles and yet change in shape and form as you approach them, enough to question their permanence. I ascend to Benbrack and linger, studying the landscape for more artwork. Standing underneath the considerable arch structure, I can see one more sculpture in the distance.

We are now in the land of the Covenanters, the Scottish Presbyterians who objected to English Episcopalian interference in their worship. Their opposition was countered with force in the seventeenth century. Many of them were killed as they conducted their open-air gatherings (conventicles) – a religious division to add to the geological and political boundaries between England and Scotland. Allan's Cairn is the first evidence that draws my attention to the Killing Time, as it is locally known. In this case, the cairn is a monument to George Allan and Margaret Gracie. They were shot nearby on the Fawns of Altry.

I see more deer, a common sight in the moorlands and forests, but this time a sizeable herd in transit. The effortless manner in which they cross the landscape is a marvel to behold. Two-metre fences are no obstacle as they move – a fluid pouring down the crags. The motion is unreal, like a poor-quality CGI animation in a Disney film. I wish I could traverse a pathless landscape like that; they must cover three or four times my distance in a day.

A long descent leads me into St John's Town of Dalry, after meeting another Dutchman and a group from the Long Distance Walkers Association called the Irregulars. Similar in a way to the Covenanters in defying convention, they usually walk on a Wednesday, instead of the traditional Sunday. This action was deemed 'irregular' by the organisation's executive, hence the name stuck and became a movement.

'Where are you staying tonight?' they ask.

'The Clachan Inn, about eight miles ahead, I hope.'

'We're catching a bus later, so we'll see you this evening.'

I arrive late afternoon, to a public bar packed with locals a few pints ahead of me. The atmosphere is buzzing, so after a shower, I return to have a pint or two to wash down an excellent meal of Cullen skink (smoked-fish soup) and black pudding pork belly for the main course. What a fantastic place, full of character. Each room has a gun cabinet ready for the Glorious Twelfth. This pub is the sort I'd love to live next to, for the buzz, sense of community and delicious beer and food.

Early morning, I rejoin the Irregulars for breakfast, and we exchange notes. They are walking west to east, looking for coins. They are a great team of walkers who also venture abroad. I welcome their chat and banter after having spent a week in the wilds. It does get lonely in the hills, but you find plenty of people to talk to in the villages.

I start the day, crossing a recently repaired suspension bridge to reach the SUW. I see an enormous buzzard hiding in a tree. It watches me for a second before lifting to blue skies above the mist. Open views of the Rhinns of Kells are followed by a very long forestry track, merging with National Cycle Network Route 7 at Loch Dee. I'd love a bicycle at times like these when the trail becomes monotonous.

'*Bonjour*,' a French couple announce as they cycle past me. I am too envious to reply immediately.

'*Au revoir*,' I mutter, out of earshot.

Loch Dee has some fascinating art installations and panoramas to please any landscape photographer. A stone carved with ancient runes is particularly striking and fits well into the scene, as do a pair of stone surfboards. I can hear cuckoos at regular intervals, and mountain goats, high above and difficult to see unless you stop, young kids bleating to their mothers and progressing across seemingly impassable rock faces with ease. Walking offers an opportunity to study such flora and fauna, although I'd still like to be riding a mountain bike today.

Forestry operations close the path at Loch Trool. A 'Listen to the Hand' stop sign leaves you in no doubt that the diversion is mandatory. At least I get to see Bruce's Stone, overlooking the loch, commemorating Robert the Bruce's first victory over the English in 1307. Behind me is Merrick, the highest point in southern Scotland at 843 metres. The cycle track turns into a road until I reach the Water of Minnoch, where evidence of severe flooding is quite frightening. At least the grass path is a welcome change from hard trails as I turn towards Bargrennan, and my hotel for the evening, through some pleasant woodland. It has been a long day, and the terrain has made my legs tired, even though the map suggests less climbing and distance than the previous day.

I wish I had stayed at the campsite nearby, but the hotel is comfy enough and eating in the restaurant is an opportunity to meet some fellow walkers who are a few days into their west-to-east walk.

'Are you walking the Southern Upland?' I ask, a rhetorical question as I can see the guides and maps on the table.

'Yes, and you too?' they reply, seeing my identical map on the table.

One woman, in her seventies, is quite inspirational; she has completed many long-distance routes, always camping. 'Oooh! You'll love the West Highland Way,' she says. 'I've completed it four times.'

We have a long geeky chat about boots, lightweight tents and walking poles. The other couple are making slower progress, accompanied by a manic springer spaniel, which I would have happily abducted for company.

The Galloway Forest, a dark sky reserve, is now behind me and I can sense the sea, two days away. I am sure I would be able to smell it, but for strong easterly winds. This is a much shorter day, so I take it easy and settle into a meditative pace over a gentler landscape, peppered with new wind farms. I meet a Californian woman, exhausted, with boots off, relaxing under a tree.

'Are you OK?' I ask.

She is fine, but it doesn't explain why her Scottish guide is a few miles behind her, and asks if I have seen her guest ahead.

I need to start learning Dutch as the half-expected Dutchman appears later. They are becoming part of the community in a big way.

'What is Dutch for good morning?' I ask, committing *Goedemorgen* to memory.

I explore the bothy at Laggangarn, which has no stove (being of wooden construction) and is shaped like a beehive, not dissimilar to the glamping units found now at many campsites. It is cosy and next to a good water source and sits alongside two ancient prehistoric standing stones. Once part of a stone circle, they still serve as sentinels that mark the route over the moors. The stones are estimated to have been in place for some 4,000 years, later vandalised with Christian crosses in the eighth century. Those who interfere with them will bear a curse. It happened to a farmer who tried to remove one to build a barn and died of a rabid dog bite the next day. Spookily, a small gravestone lies a few metres away – dog or farmer or both, I am not sure.

I can see a walker approaching, who I judge to be from Europe (brand names give the game away).

'*Goedemorgen,*' I say, careful to get the pronunciation correct.

'*Guten Morgen,*' comes a reply.

Oh, well, I can practise my limited German at least. We exchange path news, and I point out the bothies ahead, which she is keen to use.

The descent into New Luce is through fields of young lambs and calves until I reach their home farm and follow a road into the village. I was hoping to camp at the pub and spend my money in the bar, but it is closed. 'Damn,' I grumble. Fortunately, a B&B is open a few hundred yards away, and I take that option rather than search for a wild campsite. It is early enough for an afternoon nap and a cup of tea. The weather forecast for Scotland a week ahead is glorious, temperatures approaching 20 °C with strengthening easterlies. A decision to walk east to west is now paying dividends.

My host makes a bowl of porridge, and I instinctively reach for the sugar bowl.

'Try using salt, not sugar,' he says. 'It will taste just as sweet.'

'You're kidding?' I answer, but he is right, and it is good to know I am replacing this vital mineral you lose through sweating. The toast and homemade marmalade please my sweet tooth, washed down with a bitter mug of coffee; all my taste receptors are triggered to happy.

I am back in the hills after getting lost, the typical outcome of being too relaxed about navigation. I come across a *kist* with the theme of 'mid-life crisis' and ponder the symbolism of the ivy and iron construction. If my age is suffocating my freedom, I don't feel it. It is not a day for contemplation, but to enjoy the weather and the relaxed wind-assisted walking towards Stranraer. I grab lunch at a petrol station, crossing paths with high-speed travellers topping up with diesel and coffee. I treat myself to a Lucozade now that I am addicted to its restorative powers; the shelves are stocked with nothing else.

My first view of the sea is confusing, as it is not to the west! A quick check of the map shows I am on a ridge overlooking Stranraer and Loch Ryan to the east. I can see the Belfast ferry gliding into port. I expected to see it docking in Stranraer, but the ferry terminal is a few miles further north at Cairnryan. I am now back in the modern world, having left the moors, mountains and border folk behind. I know I do not have far to walk until the finish. The next section is easy going but very windy and exposed. A medium-sized wind turbine has self-destructed recently, its blades lying smashed on the ground. The fibrous mess dangling above is evidence of their construction. It is a sorry sight and a place I would not have liked to have been when it happened.

I collect the last *weymerk* coin a little further on – one that the Irregulars could not find, just as I could not find the earlier coins on my route. It's well hidden and only visible in this direction.

Makar's Kist
Unbeknownins Kist amongst stone ocean light
Sky spins glass words are made of air
Sculpted fancy will fettle sides handles lid
Trade grain fish axeheads magic or memories
For a weymerk token   So – the journey opens

– Unknown

I have collected eight tokens now, some rusty, some shiny, but all with a story to tell. If ever I return to the SUW, I will endeavour to collect the remaining five.

The Irish Sea comes into view, as do the Irish coast and mountains some twenty miles away. Black Head lighthouse aids navigation for shipping between Scotland and Ireland. I stop to reflect on the journey I have made from the east coast before turning south towards Portpatrick and an excellent coastal walk. Sunsets here must be as spectacular as sunrise in Cockburnspath. It is lovely to be coastal walking again, but all too briefly, as I soon arrive at Portpatrick, my destination. Descending the concrete steps, I see a direction sign for Cockburnspath: 212 miles to go. I stop to talk to some walkers who recognise a long-distance hiker.

'You must try the Camino de Santiago, in Spain,' they plead. 'It's a wonderful pilgrimage.' They ask questions on the accommodation in the Borders, quite different from their international self-guided pre-booked holiday. My pilgrimage has not yet ended as my mind turns to the West Highland Way.

I want to stop for a coffee and cake, but I can see the bus arriving and make an impulsive decision to jump aboard to return to Stranraer.

'Single to Stranraer station, please,' I puff, having run a few yards to the stop.

A quick check of the timetable shows I can reach Glasgow by late afternoon, so I hatch a plan to stay in Milngavie that night. As I reach the station, I have ten minutes to secure accommodation. If I can make a booking, I will not have to stay in Stranraer and can immediately start the West Highland Way the next day. By some incredible luck, a B&B has a cancellation, so I buy a ticket with seconds to spare and jump aboard the train to Glasgow.

I can see much of landscape I have walked from the window and chat to cyclists using the train about the route they have taken that day. They too recommend the area and this further cements an idea in my head to explore cycling in Scotland. From the west window, I can see Ailsa Crag as we approach Girvan, an impressive volcanic plug, not dissimilar to Bass Rock near North Berwick on the east coast. The start or end points of the walk are extinct volcanoes, I note. What punctuation could be more fitting?

Changing at Ayr to an express service has me in Glasgow in good time, and I grab a meal before joining the homeward-bound commuters to Milngavie. I am pleased a Scottish friend of mine has told me how to pronounce the name ('mul-guy') as I would have never got on the right train.

I am in a strange world now of commuters and city folk. I pass through in my shorts and muddy boots, until I reach the B&B. A wonderful landlord shows me to my room, after ten minutes explaining all the rules about keys, evening meals in town and breakfast. I can reflect on the beauty of the Southern Upland Way and my adventure.

16

WEST HIGHLAND WAY

Distance: 95 miles
Days to complete: 4 days
Mileage so far: 2,677 miles

JOIN THE QUEUE

On every mountain, height is rest.

– Goethe

The B&B breakfast room is packed with an international crowd of eager West Highland Way (WHW) walkers; a national flag is placed at every setting. Today, we have Americans, Canadians, Germans and Swiss, all on package walking holidays. A lonely Union Jack tells me where I should sit.

The canny landlord is running a tight ship, and everything is organised in incredible detail, all to a strict timetable. I had the rules read to me on arrival the previous night; it was made clear (by Scottish tone alone) that there would be trouble if I broke any. It is a great B&B nonetheless, full of character and charm. I'm grateful for the last-minute cancellation, as this place is booked months in advance.

Walking to the start of the West Highland Way, I can see other walkers converging on the town centre. On arrival, there is a crowd and a queue to take photographs at the granite obelisk. I snap a shot for two women with strong Yorkshire accents, who return the favour. They are chatty and excited as they set off north along Scotland's first official long-distance trail. I pop to the ATM for cash, and a local M&S to buy lunch; they have an array of food delights I have not seen for weeks.

Weaving through busloads of walkers sorting through their luggage and fretting about their gear, I set off along Allander Water. It is a mass start, in sharp contrast to the lonely Southern Upland Way, where I could spend a whole day walking and not meet a soul (except Dutchmen). I walk alongside individuals, trying to open a conversation. I sense many are anxious about what lies ahead and are lost in their thoughts. At Craigallian Loch, the mountains appear, still capped by winter snows. The Yorkshire lasses have stripped off for a skinny dip and shriek with pleasure as they enter the cold waters of the loch.

'The water's lovely, come on in,' they scream, as they immerse their entire naked forms into the crystal clear waters. What a plucky pair; I admire their style, reminiscent of a *Calendar Girls* WI photoshoot.

'Aren't you supposed to be walking?' I shout back.

'Whhhooooa, it's soooo coooold,' they can just about answer, their voices taken from them by the freezing water.

The clickety-clack of walking poles diminishes as I join the John Muir Way, named after the famous father of the US National Parks. Our American friends will immediately recognise his name. John of the Mountains, as he was known, made a significant contribution to the protection of North America's stunning wilderness areas. You could not overstate the importance of his work at a time when commerce and industry sought only to plunder natural resources. His legacy led to the creation of Yosemite National Park. He was the co-founder of the Sierra Club, which continues to lobby for the protection of beautiful landscapes and ecosystems.

Coincidentally, I notice a new label sitting underneath the familiar thistle symbol on the signpost: IAT–SIA – the International Appalachian Trail–*Sentier International des Appalaches*. Later research reveals that this trail belongs to a geological family of the Appalachian–Caledonian mountains formed 250 million years ago (when the Earth's tectonic plates collided to form Pangaea). This supercontinent fractured and drifted apart over the next 200 million years to establish North America, Africa and Europe, separated by the new Atlantic Ocean. In 1993, Dick Anderson proposed a new trail along the Appalachians across North America and Canada, and this pioneering route grew to embrace other communities across the Atlantic: Greenland, North Africa, Brittany, Spain, Portugal, Scandinavia and the British Isles, extending an original 1,800-mile trail to over 12,000 miles. This common geo-heritage aims to bring together cultures and to inspire walkers to think beyond boundaries. The WHW joined in 2010, the first European chapter to do so.

I descend into Strathblane and join a former railway line which passes the Beech Tree Inn. Quirky humour announces your arrival: 'Only 200 metres – Rest – Food – Drinks'; 'Hookers' is written underneath. A more thoughtful poem follows:

You've walked about 7 miles
Cum see oor smiles & have a cup o tea
Or try out oor platter it disny matter
There's a warm welcome at the Beech Tree

If the rain starts to piss – gee the garden a miss
Or maybe try out our shelter
In or out you can wear muddy boots
The welcome you'll get is a belter

When you're fully replete & you've had a seat
Thinkin about your next night on the tiles
Keep that smile oan yer face – Fort Bill is the place
It's only anither 87 miles!!!

Not quite to Rabbie Burns' standard of poetry, but amusing none-theless. For the sake of brevity, I have missed a few paragraphs, yet the tourist humour continues as you reach the cafe: a selection of daft WHW T-shirts and other such memorabilia. Just one example: 'I walked the Highland Way, and all I got was this lousy T-shirt'; you get the picture.

The railway line ends as I skirt around Drymen and into the Garadhban Forest, where I stop for lunch. The M&S packaging piles up as I demolish the contents. I'm shocked at how much plastic waste I generate over a simple meal; I'll shop elsewhere in future. The path now follows forestry tracks towards Conic Hill, where I spy a peregrine falcon heading in the same direction. The ascent leads to a stunning panorama of Loch Lomond – a picture-postcard scene. Crowds of walkers have come from the visitor centre to see the view, which I descend to, and add my sighting to the daily birdwatching noticeboard outside the visitor centre.

'A rare sighting,' the ranger says. 'Well done', which makes me doubt what I have seen, but there is no mistaking its wing and tail shape as I check the guide.

'I'm thrilled, what else can I expect to see?'

'Golden eagles maybe, mostly in the mountains above the loch. Keep looking up for their silhouette and thermal soaring.'

Balmaha is bustling with daytrippers on a glorious sunny day. The Oak Tree Inn is packed with customers eating lunch and basking in the sun. There are plenty of tables inside, so over lunch I research campsites. Even though Scotland has progressive wild-camping laws, the lochside has suffered abuse of this privilege. Specific bye-laws prevent camping in this area to avoid carloads of weekend campers leaving an unimaginable mess: bottles, glass, food rubbish and trees cut down for fires; definitely not LNT (leave no trace). A tragedy of the commons.

Another famous Scot, Tom Weir MBE, a pioneering campaigner and TV personality, did a great deal to protect the Scottish land-scape. His bronze statue stands at the edge of the loch; he is dressed in walking gear from the 1970s. He is best known for his red woolly bobble hat, which someone has thoughtfully knitted and placed on top of his head (although a bronze version lies under-neath). He would applaud the work of the Scottish government to open the countryside but would be shocked at how some people treat their natural resource.

Milarrochy campsite looks luxurious; it is time to stop after nineteen miles, and I fancy a mini-nap. There are no midges (a rare event on Loch Lomond), and I can sunbathe on the shore, writing up my diary and planning ahead. The facility block has a laundry, so I can do a deep-clean of my clothing. They have a dryer too, and within the hour I have a pile of neatly folded clothing as I walk back to the tent, naked underneath my waterproofs.

I'm up at dawn, feeling refreshed. My body rhythms are now in tune with daylight. I delight in walking in the early morning as others still sleep. The Rowardennan Lodge is just opening; time for a good bacon butty. Forestry Commission shoreline campsites at Cashel and Sallochy are simple; the latter has firepits and composting toilet blocks in keeping with its semi-wild-camping experience. The location is fantastic; they can only be accessed along a dead-end road.

The path beyond is hard going as it hugs the lochside; the rocks are difficult to navigate. It takes effort and concentration not to fall or twist an ankle. The reward is a sighting of the famous Loch Lomond goats. These long-haired beasts are basking on the shore, safe in the knowledge that they have a king's protection. Robert the Bruce, while a fugitive, hid in a lochside cave which the curious goats surrounded just before a party of soldiers arrived. Discussing if they should search the cave, they concluded the goats would have been scared away if anyone had been occupying it. Upon his ascent to the throne, he forbade anyone to harm them; they remain guardians of the loch today.

I stop at Inversaid Hotel for lunch, along with many others; I share a table and ask about their plans. Strangely, no one is walking to Fort William. A few kilometres north, I meet a thru-hiker who has occupied a bothy. He is hiking the Scottish National Trail between Kirk Yetholm and Cape Wrath (over 500 miles long) and has decided to rest for a few days.

'The Scottish National Trail? I saw a TV programme about that once,' I say. 'It's a very diverse route; the tough bits are coming up.'

'Aye. I take it steady, I have all the time in the world now I lost me job.'

He has gathered a few possessions and borrowed camping gear to complete the toughest route in Britain. Although not one of the official Scottish Great Trails (lacking the thistle waymarks as a minimum), it surely deserves the title.

'Good luck to you.'

'Whatya doin'?' he asks. I explain my plan to walk to Inverness from Dunbar.

'Ah, nae bad,' he replies.

We could quickly become walking companions, but most of his gear is hanging on a line to dry; he won't be leaving anytime soon. I could do with some company.

The campsite at Beinglas is a perfect stop for a WHW walker, with a bar, menu and excellent facilities. The Drovers Inn is a short walk across a bridge to the busy A82 trunk road, but the campsite bar has a friendly crowd of people. Back at my tent, I meet a Glaswegian fireman who is training for an Ironman event and has joined up with a mate for a few beers. He throws me a can of Tennent's, and we share notes on lightweight gear and possible wild-camping sites ahead. He plans to leave at 5 a.m., but you would think otherwise, judging by the number of crumpled cans in front of his tent. Ironman training, he said?

In this weather, it would be criminal to waste the day. I am blessed with a clear, still, blue sky and little wind, which makes packing up a pleasure, apart from the midges, which must have bred in numbers overnight. I'm marching north along good tracks that follow Glen Falloch, towards Crianlarich, where I can see a line of walkers ascending into the woods to join the path for the day. I'm sure I can see the fireman ahead; his tent had gone. I up the pace, but cannot catch him. This could turn into a race; my competitive response triggers, like a dog chasing a ball.

Tyndrum has a well-stocked shop. There are also delightful honesty box stops, with Tupperware containers full of Scottish cookies (calories) and tablet (even more calories) – all home-made. I do not want for food as I head into Rannoch Moor, a vast expanse of remote, loch-peppered moorland, on the way to Glen Coe. The only path now follows an old military road, built by

General Wade's successor, Major Caulfeild, in 1752. This will be my route all the way into Fort William.

> Had you seen these roads before they were made
> You would lift up your hands and bless General Wade.

Cars peep at me from the A82 (the only vehicular route); I return a wave. They recognise a WHW walker entering the moor alone with a common destination. The mass crowd I saw at Milngavie has now spread out. It has been a few hours since I last met anyone. I cross the Bridge of Orchy and ascend into the mountains to reach the Inveroran Hotel, a very cosy looking but fully booked former drovers' inn; it seems welcoming enough. I press on, intending to wild camp near the river, which can be used as an alternative, with a sign encouraging campers to use their facilities. I can feel a few extra miles in my legs, so continue further and deeper into Rannoch Moor.

I wild camp near Bà Bridge. It is cold now, although the sun lights the snow-topped Munros that surround the moor in a crystal-bright light. The River Bà is a deep blue stream cutting through the brown heather bogs. I can see red deer in the distance, only detectable as they move. You spot one, then two, then a dozen as your eyesight tunes to their shape. A curious hind approaches me as I filter water, I suspect looking for food; it doesn't seem afraid of me. I make sure no crumbs are left out after I cook an evening meal.

Sitting with a mug of tea, dressed in all my clothing, I stare across the wilderness. The silence is deafening; only the gentle flow of the river can be heard, the only indication that time is passing until the sun moves lower and the temperature drops. This is the most peaceful, awe-inspiring, humbling place I have been for a while. I feel so insignificant in its vastness. I cannot see another human being anywhere. Aonach Mòr is to the west, and the Grampians are to the east, guarding the desolate exposed moor. I must get into my sleeping bag, fully clothed. It is going to be a cold, cloudless night.

It is fourteen miles to Kinlochleven, another sixteen miles to Fort William. I contemplate the possibility of finishing today as I walk along the track to Kingshouse Hotel. Departing at 5.30 a.m., I am still wearing all my clothing, but slowly shed it as I warm up. The early morning light is sharp and picks out every detail of the landscape. This is a no-filter day; not a jot of cloud, mist or fog to obscure the view to Buachaille Etive Mòr, standing as a sentry to Glen Coe. I meet a climber who has just descended from its peak, having wild camped at 1,000 metres the night before. He is hitching a lift back to Glasgow, with a massive smile on his face, having had a more intense experience of the Scottish Highlands at their finest.

'It's fookin' freezin' up there.' He points to the summit. It must be a warm day for him at this elevation.

'You must have a good sleeping bag, I had all my clothes on last night.'

'Aye, and a good sleeping mat; that makes the difference,' he answers.

The Kingshouse Hotel will serve me breakfast at a reasonable fee, so I join the package holiday walkers in the restaurant. An FSB (full Scottish breakfast) is in order, after a pre-meal of muesli, toast and buckets of tea. I glide my hands over the clean white tablecloths and examine the fine cutlery as if I have never seen such things before. I am going to get my money's worth.

It's time to join more walkers, emerging from the hotel campsite, to reach the Devil's Staircase. I help a Korean woman open a horse gate latch – an unnecessarily complicated mechanism. I strip down to a T-shirt base layer before ascending the steep, zigzag, unrelenting climb. This is still the military road; obviously no Roman influence here, as it reaches a col at 550 metres. I chat with a young couple who will return to their car on the same route.

'What a wonderful day,' they declare, with big smiles on their faces.

'Aye, nae bad,' I am tempted to say, but stick to the English 'Er, it's not too bad,' so as not to make a fool of myself. Am I turning native?

I start my descent, hopping over boulders and rocks with glee. As I reach the final roads into Kinlochleven, I twist my ankle sharply as a section of pavement gives way. I am thankful for a sturdy pair of boots. I curse the pain, but no damage is done. I will walk this off soon, I hope, as I hobble alongside the huge pipes carrying hydroelectric energy to the Rio Tinto aluminium smelting works at Kinlochleven.

Before contemplating another stint, I visit the National Ice Climbing Centre – a twelve-metre-high vertical fridge containing a climbing wall. It is deserted. I ask the instructor why.

'Everyone's out climbing in the mountains,' she says. 'This place only gets busy when the weather's bad.' It seems a pity, but I can understand why.

The day is still young, so Fort 'Billy', here I come. It is an ir-reversible decision as soon as I am in the mountains again. The track is rocky, and progress is difficult; so I stop frequently at the stone bridges to snack and rest. I can bathe my swollen ankle in the stream in an attempt to reduce the swelling. As I turn north, Ben Nevis comes into view, stubbornly occupying the horizon with its snow-capped peak. It is a massive lump of granite, im-pervious to erosion, a remnant of its volcanic past. I come across another pair of boots, hung casually over a WHW fingerpost, apparently abandoned in disgust. It is the second time I have seen this art. An earlier pair of boots had their laces tied together, and copious amounts of duct tape wrapped around the toe box, in a last attempt to waterproof them. It is an odd picture, but one that tells a long story, I am sure.

I have completed my descent along a forestry track into Glen Nevis – midge capital of Scotland. The finish was prematurely marked near the woollen mill, before it was moved, in 2010, to the high street in the centre of town, another mile away. It is worth it, as you are greeted by the 'sore foot' statue of a seated man rubbing his weary right foot. Maybe he too has twisted his ankle descending from the Devil's Staircase.

I have to phone half a dozen B&Bs before finding one with a vacancy. I'm not camping tonight. Eventually, I get a bed; the room is like the jump seat on an aircraft, but it works. I sink three pints in quick succession to wash down the cod and chips I had earlier. Now I cannot move and have to crawl up the stairs to bed. The new English landlord laughs aloud at my efforts (evidently a regular sight for him in Fort William). I am walking too fast and need to slow down, but will take a four-day WHW completion any day. I have no plans to take up ultrarunning, though, as I read an article about the well-known annual event.

In 1985, Duncan Watson challenged the fell runner Bobby Shields to a race from Milngavie to Fort William. After exhausting themselves on Rannoch Moor, they ran together to the finish in seventeen hours and forty-eight minutes (a shorter route than today). With such humble beginnings, the race grew. Now, over 200 ultrarunners attempt the course each year. The time limit for the ninety-five-mile race is thirty-five hours, so walking at my usual three miles per hour, I could conceivably get a finisher's medal. The record is thirteen hours and forty-one minutes, set by Rob Sinclair in 2017, an astonishing achievement. How is it humanly possible to traverse ninety-five miles in that time?

17

GREAT GLEN WAY

Distance: 73 miles
Days to complete: 4 days
Mileage so far: 2,772 miles

SEARCHING FOR NESSIE

One meeting by chance is worth a thousand meetings by appointment.
– Arab saying

With all the excitement of completing the West Highland Way, I had not thought through the approach to walking the Great Glen Way (GGW). I scan the map over breakfast, distracted by the superb view across Loch Linnhe at the dogleg into Loch Eil. The weather is as good as you can get in Fort William. This is not a day to plan, but a day to walk. Wild camping will give me the flexibility to make any schedule work.

I set out to walk one of the most remarkable geological features in Scotland: the Great Glen Fault. It is sixty-five miles in length. There is an ongoing debate to determine if it is a vertical or lateral slip fault. Still, there is no doubt about its presence; fresh water has filled the fissure, gouged out in the Ice Age, to form vast inland lochs, the largest being Loch Ness, the second deepest in Scotland, at 230 metres, after Loch Morar at 310 metres. That is plenty of space for Nessie, the Loch Ness monster, to hide. The fault line divides the Scottish Highlands in two: with the Monadhliath (pronounced 'mona-lee-a') and the Grampian mountains to the south, and the north-west Highlands to the north – each an adventure junkie's paradise, by any measure.

The Great Glen Way is a straight-line sentence: starting with a capital letter (Fort William) and punctuated by a comma (Fort Augustus) before reaching the full stop at Inverness (Fort George). These three forts were constructed in the seventeenth and eighteenth centuries to pacify the rebellious Catholic Jacobites in the Highlands. Much of the GGW follows the shorelines of Loch Lochy, Loch Oich and Loch Ness. Together with the Caledonian Canal waterways (completed in the nineteenth century by Thomas Telford), they form an inshore navigation route, connecting the North Atlantic to the North Sea, avoiding the treacherous northern journey through the tidal races of the Pentland Firth.

You can walk, cycle, ride, kayak, sail or swim from Fort William to Inverness, if so inclined. Had my legs had a vote, they would have selected anything other than another four days in boots. So I take my time, relaxing at a modest pace as I leave the town behind and ascend Neptune's Staircase, a sequence of eight gates forming the longest lock staircase in Britain; even the canals have to climb in Scotland. I have an annoying bruised ankle to nurse, but it won't stop me; I'll walk the pain out.

The canal has occasional river traffic, mostly leisure cruisers captained by chilled-out retirees who are more than happy to take life in the slow lane. Commercial traffic has been replaced by more efficient road juggernauts. The towpath, if that is what it should be called, is a cycleway kept in good order. At Gairlochy, plaques announce the proud winners of the Waterway Length Competition over consecutive years, which I assume to be a gardening contest for canals. They could do with trimming back the yellow gorse, which has run riot on the opposite bank.

I stop at the Moy Swing Bridge, whose sole purpose seems to be to permit a farmer to access his land. As I sit down on a bench, I am harassed by the bridge keeper's collie, who has found someone new to play with; her bright blue eyes plead with me to throw the ball. The bridge keeper sits in the hut, drinking tea, glad of a break from entertaining a bored sheepdog. What else can they do to make life enjoyable, I wonder, other than protecting this listed monument, built in 1820?

The collie wants to follow but is called back. I continue on the track overlooking the River Lochy, which runs a few metres below the canal and is the natural waterway flowing from Loch Lochy, a few miles north-west. The loch entrance is marked with a white pepperpot lighthouse, a perfect foreground interest to the expanse of water ahead or the imposing mass of Ben Nevis to the west. A rough shoreline track turns into a forestry track which hugs the north shore. It is time to find a wild-camping pitch for the night.

I can see a ruin on the map at Glas-dhoire, which is worth a look, so I dive into the woods to find a patch of grass. Nothing presents itself, but as I explore the shoreline, I come across a Trailblazer Rest campsite, ideal for canoeists and kayakers. This unexpected gem has three-sided shelters and open fires; it's perfect, far better than a wild camp. I gather driftwood from the shore and light an open fire, before making the evening meal. I have no need to pitch a tent and can roll out my sleeping mat and bag on a clean wooden floor.

Just as the sun is setting, a couple arrive on backpacking 'fat bikes'. These new bicycles have huge four-inch bright pink and lime green tyres and very lightweight camping gear, taped, bungied or strapped to any open length of the frame; this is a new trend.

'Lovely bikes, what a great idea,' I say. 'Where are you from? I've never seen such set-ups before.'

'We've eloped,' she proudly announces.

' ... from Western Canada and Baffin Island,' he adds.

They are a young couple who have secretly flown across the Atlantic to cycle the beaches and mountain pathways of the Scottish Highlands. They have a rough itinerary to visit as many distilleries as possible (being passionate single-malt fans) and then get married in Talisker Bay on Skye.

'Gosh. That sounds like a plan,' I say. 'Do your parents know?'

'Er ... not yet; we'll tell them when we get back.'

'Fantastic, well done. Congratulations.'

We continue the conversation next to a roaring fire, passing around a hip flask of single malt. They are a delightful, inspiring couple, and we share stories about the remote Canadian north and how they usually ride their bikes in the snow. I tell them what I know about Scotland and the western Highlands. They have travelled extensively in New Zealand, hence their choice of a similar landscape to get married. The bikes have the patina of use: the Brooks saddles are beautifully polished and concave, something that takes a backside several thousand miles to mould. I envy their youthful and carefree existence but remember my crazy courting days before marriage. My future wife and I would walk in the hills of Wales almost every weekend and seize any opportunity to travel.

It is dark and time to lay out my sleeping bag in the shelter. There is no wind. I close down the hood to keep a few midges away, which have found a path past the smoke of the fire. I am woken by a loud hoot from a short-eared owl (later research confirms) sitting in the tree above me. I can just see it, a few metres away, so I remain absolutely still. It drops down near the fire to catch a small rodent sniffing for food scraps or liking the warmth. Returning to the tree, the owl repeats this strategy several times before departing fully satiated. A smart raptor.

I wake and depart early, saying my goodbyes to the engaged couple as they emerge from their tent. A local ranger and trainee inspect the site and point out the donation box. We chat about the fact this is not an advertised stopping point. 'We like to keep it that way,' she says with a wink. I agree. It is nice to be surprised; it is worth a £5 note at least. I place two in the box.

The lovebirds overtake me soon enough at Laggan. The bikes are barely moving above walking pace, their gearing is so low. They could ascend steep, rough ground with ease. I'm envious and wish I was on a bike now, as walking on the cycleway is monotonous and irritates my swollen ankle. At Leitirfearn, on the southern shoreline of Loch Oich, there is another similar campsite, with composting toilets that separate number ones and number twos into different tanks. A scoop is used to add sawdust to the latter. This simple method somehow prevents noxious odours, making a welcome change from some public toilets I can recall. It is a brilliant idea and utter luxury compared to the usual cat hole.

The walk continues along an old railway line to join the towpath once again. A gaggle of middle-aged women are sitting on the benches at Aberchalder. They are on a walking holiday, which I think is a ruse to get away from their husbands and misbehave. I'm offered a hip flask, which I decline before I am trapped; my life story is extracted from me bit by bit, as if they know a secret interrogation technique. They all cackle as I depart. I can't imagine what they will get up to that evening. It is perhaps wise not to know lest I am drawn into alcohol-fuelled behaviour I might regret should I bump into them again.

It is now a level walk along the canal side to Fort Augustus, where I will have to find accommodation or move on to find a wild-camping site. The village is bustling with tourists; there are fleets of Rabbie's tour coaches in the car park. They have come to see an engineering marvel: a sequence of locks to bring the Caledonian Canal down to Loch Ness. No doubt they will take one of the many cruises on the loch too, searching for the mythical sub-aquatic creature. I grab some fast food and ask the cashier if there is a campsite nearby. I'm in luck. The Loch Ness Highland Resort has a field I can use. As I enter the grounds, I am greeted by a surreal sight: over twenty single-man lightweight tents pitched in clusters. I find a spot.

'It's the TGO Challenge, mate,' I am told by my neighbour. 'How many days have you been going?'

'Er … this is day number [I take a moment to count] … er … sixteen, or maybe seventeen,' I answer.

'Bloody hell, which route do you take?' They assume I am a TGO competitor.

'The Southern Upland, West Highland and now the Great Glen Way,' I explain.

'Oh wow, impressive walking.'

'What's the TGO challenge?' I ask as I inspect a priceless collection of tents and sleeping bags, mats and backpacks.

Each item is made of expensive ultra-lightweight materials; the discussion moves to Dyneema composite fabric and titanium cookware. It looks like a trade show, but it is actually a perfect gathering point for the self-supported, west-to-east, coast-to-coast backpacking adventure, with no set route, that finishes in Montrose. The event is sponsored by *The Great Outdoors* magazine. It is not a race and there are no prizes, but I wonder how much of a part the gear plays; the obsession with the kit seems to be an end in itself. Everyone quotes the weight of an item to the nearest gram. I'm perhaps as guilty as these gearheads, and it is good to meet like-minded long-distance walkers. They are impressed by my sixteen-day odyssey. It then dawns on me that I have already done a coast-to-coast Scottish route this month: the Southern Upland Way. That makes me feel good.

A local restaurant is almost empty now that the Rabbie's tours have gone. It is a chance to reset my vitamin and calorie levels as I can feel I have lost a few kilos. I'm up early, way before the TGO crew, who are still snoring. The town is deserted as I wait for the petrol station shop to open, for something to keep me going for a few hours. The route now ascends into the woods, maintaining a respectful distance from the A82 below. Invermoriston has a wee shop, serving home-built sandwiches. The young girl happily fills a roll with scoops and layers of filling, before wrapping it up in clingfilm for me.

I take a high-path optional route to reach a great viewpoint, one marked by *The Viewcatcher* sculpture, a circle of Caledonian pine and local stone, designed to frame the views of a group of Munros north of Loch Clunie, some twenty-five miles away. The Forestry Commission has also built a troll's bridge, decorated by the local children, who have also written a few poems, two of which read:

A big fat troll is what I can see,
He's as big as 6 foot 3,
My goosebumps go Bing!

He's allergic to a bee's sting,
So he will run from a bumblebee!

Here's a sleeping toll,
In a sleeping stroll,
Under a bridge,
He would put you in his fridge,
And stuff you in his bowl.

I must admit I take a peek under the bridge before I cross, even though I am six foot four in my boots. The child in me surfaces from time to time, something that keeps me youthful and curious. I make no excuses for my behaviour, and besides, no one is looking.

Another viewpoint offers a 180-degree panorama of Loch Ness. Does a reptilian beast live in the depths of Scotland's second-deepest loch? It certainly picked a good home, as it holds more fresh water than all the lakes in England and Wales combined – 7.45 cubic kilometres (Windermere is only 0.3 cubic kilometres). I think Nessie has lived happily in the loch since the 1870s, possibly longer, entertaining tourists and researchers for decades. Her story has grown legs (or more likely flippers) from numerous sightings and dubious photographs. The loch formed after the last Ice Age, and perhaps she emerged from her cryogenic state, a remnant of a dinosaur age. No one knows; there are many theories, yet recent DNA analysis of organic sediment suggests just a few slippery eels. But don't tell Steve Feltham (a full-time monster hunter); he has been searching for Nessie for almost thirty years – a model British eccentric following his dream.

I can see the low-level route below, ideal for cyclists and my Canadian friends; it is a shorter journey too. I find myself in Drumnadrochit earlier than expected. A local cafe serves excellent cake and a nice cappuccino; I can relax and research options for tonight. The waitress tells me a hostel may have a spare cabin in their garden, as the usual semi-permanent wind farm engineers are away. I'm in luck. It is clean, welcoming and situated opposite the Fiddler's Highland Restaurant – what a meal, what a pint, what an astonishing collection of whisky. The first glass of Loch Ness Brewery's DarkNess (4.6% ABV) settles gently like a pint of Guinness; it is delicious. I'm transfixed by the food and whisky menu; my purse strings loosen as I salivate over the options. No wonder the place is so popular. I was not expecting a culinary tour of the Great Glen.

The next morning I am woken by workmen, building new Hobbit cabins similar to the one I am using. I join them at the post office, which is doing a grand trade in bacon butties and sandwiches for passing workmen in their lorries and vans. I loiter with a cup of tea before setting out in the rain to Inverness. I've been lucky with the weather, so I cannot complain. The route goes high after leaving a busy A82, fleets of lorries clearly on a mission to move materials to a major construction site nearby. It is cold, so I up the pace. It's a *dreich* day (Gaelic word for gloomy, depressing, persistent rain) walking in featureless forests. There is nothing to recommend it other than a post which marks the highest point of the GGW. I pass two American walkers, in cheap polythene cagoules; they left Drumnadrochit at 6 a.m. and look miserable. We walk together through a ghostly lichen-encrusted wood before I walk on ahead.

Gets in yer neb, lugs,
unner thi oxters tae.
Oan yer heid, in yer een
til ye're drookit, ken?

An it's aye cauld
an gaes sidie-ways.
Whit, warm rain?
Nae here (mebbe in Spain).

Woke up this mornin,
crawled oot o bed,
keeked oot thi windae pane
Aw naw! Rainin again!

— Tom Bryan, 'Scottish Rain' (2006)[15]

271

Civilisation starts to make itself felt as I enter the outskirts of the city, walking through housing estates to the final section of the Caledonian Canal. The River Ness is high, almost submerging an island park. The route terminates at Inverness Castle, and I am now lost without a signpost to follow. It should really continue to Fort George, but there are no easy paths; it is a pity, as you can see bottlenose dolphins feeding just after high tide.

I find the railway station and ask about the sleeper service back to London, before contemplating accommodation and the Speyside Way. My resolve weakens; I'm homesick after three weeks, and I buy a ticket, which gives me a few hours to explore the streets. I browse in a few outdoor shops, inspecting everything on offer, but I am wanting for nothing. Leakey's Bookshop is a superb place to wind down the clock, with its astonishing collection of second-hand books, shelved in a former church. In the centre of the room stands a huge wood-burning stove (can you believe that in such a combustible space?). They kick me out, so I find a good restaurant, where I can loiter further, not wanting to spend too long in the waiting room at the station.

The ScotRail sleeper service is a romantic pleasure, even if you book a £50 seat rather than an expensive sleeper bunk. Several like-minded passengers are returning to London after their hiking or cycling adventures. We chat and consume too many single malts from the bar, sharing magazines and stories. Nobody minds the ingrained odour accumulated over weeks in the outdoors – a sweet peaty aroma that mixes well with the whisky.

The alcohol promotes some rest before we are walking along the platform together at King's Cross at 7 a.m., overtaken by the commuter rush hour. I wonder what planet I have landed on; we all look ridiculous in our gnarly outdoor clothing and backpacks, like a bunch of middle-aged backpackers returning from an interrailing adventure. I arrive home to give my wife a big *cwtch* (a beautiful Welsh word for an affectionate cuddle, pronounced 'cutch'). After a few pints at my local pub, I help her cook a roast dinner, washed down with a bottle of wine. After three weeks, this is an unimaginable pleasure.

My homesickness is cured in a day, yet my wanderlust persists.

18

SPEYSIDE WAY

Distance: 85 miles
Days to complete: 4 days
Mileage so far: 2,845 miles

AN UNCERTAIN START

Not all those who wander are lost.
— J.R.R. Tolkien

It was homesickness that moved me to catch the sleeper service home when I reached Inverness, having walked three of the Scottish long-distance trails. The plan was to continue on the Speyside Way to complete them all. The opportunity to rest was welcome: my ankle would be fixed, the forecast was dreary, and the shop manager at Craigdon Mountain Sports said the route had been extended to Newtonmore. The additional mileage broke my schedule; I had to be home for work. Homesickness and work – valid excuses to bail out?

I can't return until July, when I have a short one-week window to walk from Newtonmore to Buckie on the Moray coast. The Scottish sleeper service is perfect, stopping exactly at the start of the walk at 7 a.m. on a Monday morning. I am the only person to disembark into a bright summer's day. I can't find a thistle mark or any signpost to signify a start. Still, my GPX route puts me on to National Cycle Network Route 7, a section of a cycle track linking

Sunderland on the east coast of England to Inverness (maybe a future expedition over 600 miles long).

No one is around. Toshac's Tuck Shop & Tea Room doesn't open until 1.30 p.m., so nae chance fae breakfast. The path is easy going, past the open-air Highland Folk Museum into Kingussie, and an unusual football field. The local shinty teams (a Gaelic form of hockey) have a fierce rivalry, competing in the Camanachd Cup each year. It is a popular sport, played for several millennia, and similar to hurling in Ireland. The local Co-op is open, so I buy food for the day before walking a short distance to Ruthven Barracks, built in 1719, after the Jacobite rising. It played a role in returning the Catholic James II of England and VII of Scotland to the throne. The site is built on a defensive hillock of strategic importance in the glen, having replaced a succession of structures first constructed in 1229. A farmer's wheeled hay rake has collected freshly cut grass into parallel strips that look like neat lines of soldiers entering the fort – perfect for an abstract photograph.

It is a lovely forest walk into Kincraig through Inshriach Forest, but it is not signposted; I follow my downloaded GPS route. Through the trees I can see the colossal Strath Spey, funnelling rail, road, river and all forms of traffic (natural and mechanical) between the Monadhliath and Cairngorm mountains. There is still snow on their peaks, even at the start of summer. They dominate the skyline, and I feel drawn to their brooding presence, as if by a mesmeric force of planetary gravity. Kincraig has a quaint village shop, open since 1896, that is struggling to survive in a modern world blighted by second homes and a fading local community. It has been orphaned from the A9 trunk road, yet it makes a welcome stopping point for a walker. I can now see official Speyside Way signs indicating Aviemore is six miles further. Perhaps the warden's signpost team only made it this far? I have plenty of time to reach a campsite at Dalraddy. It is a large site, dimensioned to support static homes, caravans and tourers for the summer. The tent section is quiet, and I need a map to find the secluded pitch. By quiet I mean no other campers, but it's very noisy due to roadworks on the A9, which start up at night.

The mandatory reversing 'beep! beep!' warning of the dumper trucks pierces my earplugs, so I wrap my head in clothing to deaden the sound.

The road gang are still working hard as I decamp at 6 a.m., keen to seek quieter space. The high-quality cycle track continues into Aviemore, which is opening for business on a sunny day. It is a hotspot overrun with outdoor fashion shops and tourist traps, catering for the summer hikers and winter ski seasons. I am happy to leave the bustle behind to rejoin National Cycle Network Route 7, which now follows the Strathspey Railway, a heritage branch line supported by 900-plus steam and diesel enthusiasts. Engine 46512, the *Strathspey Clansman*, gives a loud toot as it chuffs backwards on its way along the line, pulling carriages full of happy passengers enjoying refreshments.

I reach Boat of Garten, walking past some very fancy houses with views across the River Spey to the Cairngorms. The excellent village shop is thriving, its small frontage hiding a long corridor that leads deep into a delicatessen serving a delicious array of Scottish food. I take a seat outside for a moment, watching village life unfold.

The cycle track continues. I'm starting to ponder what to do after I finish all of the trails. The answer seems to be cycle touring. Several bikes pass me by, gliding along the path, making smooth progress. A voice inside my head considers the option.

'I can carry more gear.

'Greater flexibility on accommodation and a proper camera.

'NO MORE BLISTERS!' I shout, tempered by the thought of saddle sores.

The list of benefits expands as I continue into the woods. A plan is forming in my mind.

Chicks have just hatched at the osprey centre nearby, according to a New Zealand couple I meet on the path.

'They'll be flying all the way to western Africa soon,' they say, 'a fifty-day journey. Don't miss them.'

I make a note to visit the centre at a later date and keep my eyes peeled for free viewing, rather than a spy-cam video show.

The woods are offering possible sightings of capercaillie and pine martens too, but perhaps it is too late in the day for that now. It is a dream of mine to see a pine marten in the wild. I arrive in Nethy Bridge and grab a sandwich at the store. Before I eat it, I have a text from my brother. I ring him immediately; I can sense something important in those few characters on the screen.

He has some bad news: he has cancer.

My world falls apart. This is entirely unexpected. I knew my brother had been complaining of headaches, but this news comes as a shock. I carry on walking, and the scenery becomes irrelevant; I'm now walking without joy, tearful at times as I process this information. On arrival in Grantown-on-Spey, I can just about function. I grab provisions from the Co-op like a robot before arriving at the campsite. I cannot eat my lunchtime sandwich or make an evening meal, my hunger nulled by other concerns.

After a restless night and several calls home, I set off into the wilderness again, hoping the walk will offer a natural therapy. I see red deer and several stoats dashing across my field of view. My emotions have subsided but re-emerge later, more complicated and difficult to understand. I am confused, angry, sad, angry and confused again. Keep walking, I tell myself.

The route continues along a dismantled railway line passing numerous distilleries. First Cragganmore, then Ballindalloch, followed by Knockando, Tamdhu and Cardhu. Massive bonded warehouses lie silent, protecting their ageing crop of fine single malts. The air is filled with the sweet smell of the 'angels' share', the alcohol that evaporates during storage. I breathe deeply, to calm my thoughts and drink in the aromas; smooth, sweet Speyside single malts are sublime, a superb introduction to Scottish whisky. The catchment area of the River Spey accounts for roughly fifty per cent of Scottish whisky production. The quartz bedrock keeps the mineral content of the liquor (water) to a minimum, and the distilleries are near to the barley fields of the eastern Highlands. These ingredients, with yeast, make a sweet, fruity, honey and vanilla malt whisky, a softer introduction to the palate, before moving on to the distinctly peatier west-coast malts of Islay.

Oak barrels hold the distilled spirit for a minimum of three years. Sherry barrels impart a deep-bodied flavour; sometimes two or three barrels are used to create 'double-wood' or even 'triple-wood' whisky. Glenlivet, Glenfiddich, Aberlour, Glenfarclas and Balvenie are leading sales around the world. These brands, and others, developed after King George IV took a wee dram or two of an illicit Glenlivet during a tour in 1822.

The railway bridges and stations have been preserved. The route has been maintained for cyclists and walkers. Some stations are now private residences, with a rail coach restored and converted into a camping barn at Cromdale. Foxgloves are prolific along the line. This route is perfect for the Canadian friends I met on the Great Glen Way. They must be blissfully married now and mending family ties after their elopement, drinking a bottle of Talisker to remember their ceremony.

I would do anything for a bike now. The midges and flies are swarming out of the overgrowth in the still air. They follow me incessantly. I'm like the Peanuts character Pig-Pen, surrounded by a cloud of bugs, but sweating, not dirty or smelly. I can just about build up enough speed to lose them, but they attack again when I slow down through a sequence of hopelessly complicated gates. Once they smell blood, there is no escaping them.

I pass a few female walkers, one struggling with a heavy pack but making progress. It is not far now to Charlestown of Aberlour, home of Walker's Shortbread, and of course another distillery (Aberlour). I stop to shop and rest on a bench dedicated to the memory of Joey Dunlop, the motorcycle road-racing legend. Thoughts of his passing make me call my brother again. He is in bits and crying uncontrollably, confirming he has brain cancer, the cause of the headaches. Worse follows: it is stage 4 and has spread throughout his body. It is devastating news; I have already lost my parents to cancer and will shortly lose my younger brother too. I stare into space after the call ends, my senses numbed by pain.

I contemplate finding the fastest route home, but resolve to walk for one more day to Buckie. I'll save the Tomintoul optional spur for another time. It is a fifteen-mile path into the mountains, with intricate public transport connections. It would add two days to the walk, a delay I cannot afford. Time seems so precious now.

I walk past the swanky Walker's Shortbread head office to an excellent campsite. I pitch my tent, and shower. As I write up notes and phone home again, the weary walker I met earlier arrives. Later another backpacker arrives, a software engineer from *amazon.com*. We share a bench and swap stories: she is walking the Speyside Way, and he is touring Scotland by public transport alone, not owning a driving licence. We talk about walks and scalable cloud computing for hours. A local fish van arrives. I see no reason not to have another dinner: piping hot cod and chips washed down with one last beer. My spirits are lifted briefly until my thoughts return to home. The alcohol intensifies my emotions.

I'm up early for a long day. Online research and consultation with my new-found public transport expert has confirmed it is possible to catch the sleeper home tonight. I'm now on a mission, wanting to get home to see my family. The forestry tracks and woodland are packed with wildlife: deer, buzzards and plenty of red squirrels. The views north-east give a glimpse of Spey Bay as the river reaches its destination, much broader and more potent than before.

I buy lunch at Fochabers, with a plan to find a stop along the river. The river is hidden behind overgrowth; giant hogweeds stand twice my height along the path. Frequent notices warn about this invasive non-native monster, whose sap can give very nasty burns. I cross National Cycle Network Route 1, the longest of the Sustrans cycleways, linking Dover to Shetland. It is not the first time my walk has coincided with this long-distance route. I read that you can circumnavigate the North Sea by bicycle. This thought lodges in my mind and will not go away.

I reach the Scottish Dolphin Centre in Spey Bay. Salmon loiter near the river mouth to change their physiology from saltwater to freshwater, a process known as osmoregulation. The tide is not right, and the bottlenose dolphins are off playing somewhere, but when conditions allow, it is quite a sight to see them feeding.

Some of them grow to 400 kilos, much larger than their contemporaries. Something to do with the cold water and abundance of food.

A small pod of dolphins
Working in unison
Six slick dorsals
Rising and falling
In a closing loop
Herding the red fish
To a cradling shallow
Where the surface breaks
Then, mercurial, boils
With a panic
Of salmon
Leaping to nothing –
No breaking loose
From the leisurely beaks
Of the bottle-nosed noose

– John Máckie, 'Speymouth Dawn'[16]

I do not have far to go now. I catch up with another walker. She has spent eight months and over 4,000 miles running around Britain, and she slows down for a chat, getting on to the subject of why we do long-distance routes.

'It makes me happy,' is her reply, so simple, and almost too obvious. I am heartened by what she says; it is a counterbalance to recent news.

'Oh, and I also need an excuse to eat lots of cake!' she adds.

I'll endorse that.

We walk and talk into Buckie, where she continues along the coast to London. I want to ask her about the England Coast Path, but this is the end of my walk and the Speyside Way. She is a brave woman, resolute and focused on an incredible challenge to walk (and run) around the coast of Britain. I have now completed all of Scotland's official long-distance thistle routes, but my mind is elsewhere. Scotland has so much to offer for the outdoor enthusiast, and I vow to return, on bicycle and foot.

A bus takes me to Elgin, and another to Inverness, and a familiar routine, waiting for the sleeper service to King's Cross. I reflect on the day as the train enters England, watching the sea pass by. A symbol of another world, of the afterlife, of death, I realise, but also representing an invigorating eternity, for me at least. I need a couple of single malts from the buffet: one for the walk and one for my brother. The carriage is almost empty; I sleep well.

I shall leave tonight from Euston
By the seven-thirty train
And from Perth in early morning
I shall see the hills again.

From the top of Ben Macdhui
I shall watch the gathering storm,
And see the crisp snow lying
At the back of Cairngorm.

I shall feel the mist from Bhrotain
And pass by the Lairig Ghru
To look down on dark Loch Einich
From the heights of Sgoran Dubh.

From the broken Barns of Bynack
I shall see the sunrise gleam
On the foreheads of Ben Rinnes,
And Strathspey awake from dream.

And again in the dusk of evening
I shall find once more alone
The dark waters of the Green Loch
And the pass beyond Ryvoan.

For tonight I leave from Euston
And leave the world behind
Who has the hills as a lover
Will find them wondrous kind.

– A poem found in Ryvoan bothy
during the Second World War

19

PEDDARS WAY
AND NORFOLK COAST PATH

Distance: 93 miles
Days to complete: 5 days
Mileage so far: 2,930 miles

JOURNEY'S END?

But the beauty is in the walking; we are betrayed by destinations.
— Gwyn Thomas

I am not sure why the Peddars Way and Norfolk Coast Path was to be my last National Trail; it is an ideal introduction to long-distance walking. There is barely any ascent, and the paths are easy going, with plenty of options for accommodation and refreshment.

The route will take me past a village where several generations of my ancestors worked in the fields. In a sense, I am walking home, back through time, through a landscape they helped to shape. Perhaps I will learn something about myself and reflect on the journey I have taken to reach this point. The flat sandy paths and clear signposts will encourage a relaxing meditative walk.

My immediate family have been foremost in my thoughts recently after I learnt of my younger brother's cancer diagnosis. I have lost both of my parents to cancer in the past ten years, prematurely. My father served on Christmas Island in 1957 for the Nuclear Test Programme; he guarded the aircraft that dropped the Grapple X and Grapple Y thermonuclear devices. Many of his friends had succumbed to cancer before old age, quite possibly due to the radiation fallout those men experienced. My mother died shortly after my father, eleven weeks after her first diagnosis of cervical cancer. Feelings of my mortality perhaps triggered my decision to quit full-time employment and follow my passion for walking. Now my initial plan to complete my quest draws to a conclusion. I need time to reflect and to move on and think of another venture to sustain me.

By chance, I meet my cousin at Baker Street Tube station on my way to King's Cross.

'Where you off to, then?' he asks, seeing me wearing shorts and carrying a backpack.

'Off to walk in Norfolk.'

'Sorry to hear about your brother. How is he at the moment?'

'He's coping, but bedridden and as comfortable as can be expected.'

'Send him our love when you see him next.'

Lost in my thoughts, it takes no time to reach Thetford station to grab the last taxi in the rank to the start point a few miles further east. It is 10.15 a.m. by my watch as I take the first step north along Peddars Way. The same signpost points south to Icknield Way, which fittingly can take me directly home in a day or two, as far as Princes Risborough and The Ridgeway.

The path is sandy through the woodland. Bright dark flintstones, common in the area, can be seen in building materials. Peddars Way follows the Roman road to Hunstanton, arrow-straight, passing a noisy military training ground to my left. Strongly worded warnings advise you not to enter, and you can perceive, but not see, patrols that might pounce on you should you try. I stop at a marker stone. As I read the words, a strange sense of synchronicity stirs deeper emotions. I am in the right place at the right time:

The footprint of our ancestors
Familiar as our own faces
Remote as fossils
Written on clay

And washed away
Over & over
Over and over

– Hugh Lupton, from *A Norfolk Songline*[17]

'Wow!' I say to myself. 'Spooky.' My curiosity leads to later research. The storyteller goes on to say:

But remember that you, walking in your time, are as much a part of everything that surrounds you as any other traveller has been. All the past that has led to your moment in time is held like a great secret in the landscape that surrounds you.

I can relate to that; it brings a sense of contentment and belonging that persists across generations.

I am happy enough to forage for blackberries to bring some sweetness to my lunch of dried-up cheese sandwiches and tea. The apples needed another month to ripen; a test bite draws the inevitable sharp outbreath to dispose of the sour flesh into the bushes. The campsite near Ashill is quiet now that the summer holidaymakers and their motorhomes and caravans have departed. A notice says the owner will pop by later and to choose any pitch. I shower to remove the sweat of a hot day before setting up a new experimental tarp and bivouac combination. As I make my evening meal, the owner, a lovely woman, pops across to talk to me as she walks her dogs.

'Nice quiet site,' I say.

'We were full just last week, but the schools are back, and we have time to cut the grass now.'

'Do I need to move?'

'Oh no, you're fine where you are.'

She is relaxing now the busy part of the season is over and only charges me £5 for the night after I tell her my story of walking my final National Trail. Her Labrador is perplexed by the sight of a tent with no walls, sniffing inside and considering lying down on my sleeping bag.

I settle down for an early night. The sun sets just as caw-cawing flocks of crows come in to roost. The noise is deafening as they find their branches in the woodland. No sooner do they settle than the Royal Air Force commences its night operations. Jets are taking off from nearby RAF Marham, flying low. As I drift into sleep, another plane flies overhead – irritating, but at least the usual tranquillity of this remote heathland location resumes before my core sleeping hours. The night is balmy and warm; I am sleeping almost naked outside my bivvy bag, popping my head outside the tarp to see the night sky. It is not a night for shooting stars.

I rejoin Peddars Way as the early morning mist clears. It is going to be another hot day on the path, so I drink deeply from the campsite tap and fill my bottle. I regret buying a soggy sandwich at a BP garage for breakfast, for as I enter Castle Acre an excellent cafe has just opened. The owner is placing chairs outside, as if in a French village. The tables will soon fill up with visitors to the priory and castle, but I pass by, regretting my shopping choices. The village is one of the most exceptional planned Norman settlements in England, worthy of a visit at a later date when time allows you to linger alongside the beautiful chalk streams which meander around the ancient ruins.

The Roman road heads towards Ringstead. My feet are developing annoying blisters, and I rue the decision to wear lighter, untested walking shoes. I hate walking on the road. I wonder what footwear the Roman soldiers would have used. I daydream about cycling and buying a bike to tour Europe. The lanes in the area would be perfect for exploring the area. After twenty-two miles, I arrive at Bircham Windmill, just in time to catch a last meal at the on-site cafe before pitching in their beautiful campsite.

As the sun sets, the working windmill stirs, adjusting its direction to face a changing evening wind. The mainsails are idle, held firm without grain to mill for the working bakery below. The attendant sparrows twitter their last song as I fall asleep, just a few miles from my ancestors' village at Tattersett, their flint cottages still preserved, the date of construction written in brick: 1694. My surname is derived from the Nordic word *haugr*, meaning cairn or mound. The nearby Houghton Hall coincidently has a similar-sounding name, and my great-great-grandfather lies buried nearby. There are unexplored clues to follow still. I think of my brother again; this is his homeland too.

I wake early, startling a huge hare that is munching quietly in the adjacent field. It runs away at an astonishing pace. The dawn chorus is loud, crowding around the bakery for any loose grain. My blisters are raw, so I tape them up before setting off. I soon reach another Norfolk Songline stone. Again, the poetry resonates with a sense of time and place:

> And I being here have been part of all this
> Caught & thrown like sun on water
> Have entered into all around me
>
> — Hugh Lupton, from A Norfolk Songline[18]

My elder daughter will join me for the last stage of the walk, and we have agreed to meet at a car park near Holme-next-the-Sea. She arrives on time, and we embrace. She has brought a tent and backpack to walk and camp with me as far as Cromer. We have now reached the sea and must turn right to enter the new landscape of the Norfolk Coast Path. Peddars Way terminates here, at what must have been a busy Roman port, quite possibly now reclaimed by the sea. We could turn around now and walk to Lyme Regis on the Dorset coast, following the Greater Icknield Way along the chalk ridgeways that slice diagonally across England.

It is a pleasure to have her company and emotional support. We drift easily into long conversations when we can walk side by side. Walking line astern is more of a challenge; you lose important body language if you cannot see each other – Italians would find conversation impossible. I am talking to a fully fledged adult about the usual stresses of life and the thoughts I have had along Peddars Way. My blisters are not good and are getting angry now, so I struggle to maintain the pace. We stop at Brancaster Staithe to camp and walk to a local seafood restaurant for lovely *fruits de mer*, a platter full of local seafood: crab, oysters, mussels and clams, all washed down with a chilled bottle of rosé. It is a pleasant evening on the balcony, watching flocks of birds settling for the evening. I reach into my pocket to pay.

'That's all right, Dad. I've got this,' she says, smiling.

It is a sweet moment, a milestone, a confirmation that she is fully independent and can make her own way. She has flown the nest. It is a gesture I shall treasure.

We wander back to the tent, and I perform major surgery on my blisters, cleaning and dressing quite severe welts on the balls of my feet. It is unusual for me to get in such a condition; I have covered some 900 miles so far this year, walking through Scotland and England on rough paths, but here I am, having walked sixty-odd miles on level sandy tracks with blisters! I should have asked my daughter to bring my walking boots. It doesn't make sense, and I curse my decision to use untested shoes. My machine-like walking ego is punctured, but a trivial circumstance compared to my brother's bedridden condition.

She packs up and is ready to go, a *carpe diem* person, like her father. We stride out along the seawall to view the saltmarsh landscape of Scolt Head, the tide slowly ebbing to reveal a fractal-like network of mud creeks. Marshland leads to a wide sandy dune-fringed beach at Holkham. Enormous skies with lazy distant cumulus clouds brew early in the day, like *The Simpsons'* opening credits. Pinewoods anchor the shifting sands as we join a cycle track into Wells-next-the-Sea, stopping at the lifeboat station for lunch.

My blisters are painful, beyond a point where stubborn progress is wise. I know I will have to bail out, but do not tell my daughter just yet. She is striding purposefully along the tideline path to Blakeney on tracks that could not be more joyful to walk along otherwise. I buy two ice cream cones, and we sit together on a bench. She can already see in my eyes what is coming, her emotional radar being so much more powerful than mine.

'Could we catch the bus back to the car?' I ask.

'Of course, Dad. Is it your blisters?'

'I'm so sorry, it's only sixteen miles to Cromer, but I just don't think I'll make it.'

'That's OK. Let's get you home.'

We climb the village street to catch the coastal bus service, which takes us past the landscape we walked, back to Holme. It is a relief to be sitting in the passenger seat as she drives me home. Google Maps suggests an arrival time that is five minutes short of our local fish and chip shop closing time. Rather than speed up, we leave it to chance and drop into a long conversation. I am learning from her wisdom and youthful insight. She wants to know about my early life and my brother.

* * *

In the intervening weeks, after the blisters heal, I walk a familiar three-mile circuit around Burnham Beeches, just north of Slough, to the west of London. This protected woodland is a marvel. I have been exploring the paths for thirty years and have yet to discover all its wonders. It occurs to me, after a quick mental calculation, that I have perhaps covered 4,000 miles in this woodland, more than the combined length of my forty-year ambition. Every time I go there, it is different, as the seasons change. The roe deer and muntjac pass through, buzzards and woodpeckers make new noises, vast mounds of wood ants appear and disappear. More than anything, the trees change colour and shed leaves: greens and golden hues and fallen leaves that turn to mulch. The greatest pleasure is to walk after a fresh snowfall when navigation is a challenge; the paths have vanished. My long walks are mere snapshots in time. I have only visited one path along each long-distance trail (with some exceptions), whereas this walk is more immersive and complete with an added dimension of the seasons. Perhaps I do not need to travel so far, but just study what is on my doorstep. On a good day, the experience of completing a circuit is as pleasurable as any high mountain pass or coastal cliff walk.

My blisters have recovered enough for sixteen miles, so I am back a few weeks later with my wife and younger daughter. We enjoy symbolic ice creams together, just as I did a few weeks earlier with my elder daughter, and I put on my boots for the final stretch. They will have a mischievous day somewhere as I climb on the seawall and head out towards the neck of Blakeney Point. The marsh reeds sing their whispering harmonies; marsh harriers hunt in the distance, their unwavering gaze noting every movement and opportunity. I reach the shoreline and watch the little terns and their attendant black-headed gulls patrol the shore.

Now I have long stretches of shingle beach to walk – a high tide covering any sandy shoreline path. I peek over the shingle bank at intervals, seeking more straightforward inland tracks, but I have to resign myself to the crunch-crunch-crunch of shifting pebbles for six miles into Sheringham. I stop briefly at sunken Second World War pillboxes, their foundations undermined by winter storms. The graffiti is worn clean, unable to cope with the seaside elements.

It is a relief to reach the clifftop path leading into Sheringham. I ascend to a lookout station on the golf course, which offers views of the North Sea and the vast arrays of offshore wind turbines. It is time for a rest, but there is no cafe or tea room. I continue on the cliff path again, walking to Beeston Bump, another viewpoint. After navigating through a few caravan parks, I arrive at West Runton Gap, and a cafe that looks perfect. I stay for a good lunch. I have just polished off another slice of cake when a conversation starts up in the cafe between two dog walkers.

'I've just found a dead robin on the path,' she announces.

'Poor thing,' he replies, and after a short pause, 'I found a dead seagull on the beach last week, feathers everywhere.'

'My husband, Billy, found an owl, fallen out of the tree. Rats had got to it, what a horrible mess!' She is upping the stakes. Not to be outdone the man in the flat cap continues:

'Dead seal, smelt awful, washed up on the beach. I had a job keeping the dogs away from it, innards everywhere; must have been a shark!'

There is a silence that continues for a few moments as she contemplates her reply. You can see her mind working to deliver a *coup de grâce*. Then it comes:

'A dead dinosaur came out of the cliffs last month!' she states calmly.

I should not have been sipping my tea as she said this, for the explosion of laughter into the mug is difficult to conceal. Before he can respond, the waitress confirms the story.

'That's right, Jill, they appear all the time after the storms. There are a lot of fossils in the area, you know.'

The conversation finished, I stand to leave. I had no possible means of entering the competition. The man and his dog rise too; his scraggy mutt is keen to get on to the beach to sniff out something substantial – a new legendary find.

I can now see the pier at Cromer, my final destination. I half expect my emotions to surface, but they do not. Perhaps they have been processed over the past few hours as I walked those final miles. I feel a deep satisfaction at having completed nine-teen iconic long-distance trails. Still, it is a feeling of content-ment rather than achievement, or maybe I feel survivor's guilt in the context of my family circumstances. Glancing up at the last acorn signpost it reads, 'Norfolk Coast Path – Hunstanton 47 miles'. Opposite this sign is another, that reads, 'Sea Palling 18 miles'. To my dismay, it has an acorn symbol too. This sign marks the England Coast Path, a new National Trail under construction, so I know that my task is incomplete. Is this a metaphor for my life? I am not yet ready to die?

'Hey, Dad!' my daughter shouts, then gives me a big hug. 'Well done. Any blisters?' My wife joins in; tears are welling in my eyes and theirs too.

Our emotions in check, we walk back to the van and stay a night at the campsite for a barbecue and a few beers. My daughter starts sketching the scene of my arrival from a picture taken on her smart-phone. A few weeks later, she completes an abstract painting, a personal token that marks the conclusion of my endeavours, a souvenir as precious as any I possess.

'Which path was the best?' I am often asked.

'Why do you do this?' is usually the second question.

My first answer has to be 'all of them'. By this, I mean the entire experience of all the big trails as one continuous journey: the good times and the bad, the stunning diversity of landscapes and people, the fact that these pleasures drew me into walking them all after those first steps I took as a fifteen-year-old. The satisfaction I derive from walking is more with a sense of purpose than the thought of a destination; I value the motion of walking more than a daily goal. It gets under your skin and into your blood – an addictive pleasure and utterly joyful.

Why do I do it? The answer is simple, but I distilled the response from many emotions of the mind and heart. The young woman in Scotland was right.

It makes me happy.

Total mileage: 3,023 miles

NOTES

1   Reproduced by kind permission of the Estate of George Sassoon, via Barbara Levy Literary Agency.

2   Reproduced by kind permission of Dan Maier, via Curtis Brown literary and talent agency.

3   The poem was carved by Joseph Tubbs on a beech tree at Wittenham Clumps in 1844 and 1845.

4   Reproduced by kind permission of Faber & Faber.

5   Reproduced by kind permission of Ian McMillan.

6   'The Rain Stone' is one of the Stanza Stones poems. It was published in *Sandettie Light Vessel Automatic* (2019) by Simon Armitage and is reproduced by kind permission of Faber & Faber.

7   Reproduced by kind permission of Faber & Faber.

8   Reproduced by kind permission of the Battle of Britain Memorial Trust CIO.

9   Reproduced by kind permission of John Wedgwood Clarke.

10   Ibid.

11   Ibid.

12   Ibid.

13   Ibid.

14   Reproduced by kind permission of Ian McMillan.

15   Reproduced by kind permission of Tom Bryan.

16   Unable to trace copyright holder.

17   Reproduced from *A Norfolk Songline* by kind permission of Hugh Lupton. This wonderful book is available from *hughlupton.co.uk*

18   Ibid.

ACKNOWLEDGEMENTS

To all my friends and colleagues who have generously given their time to support my ambitions to write a book. Their patience, understanding, guidance and wisdom have played a major part on my journey and it is only through their support that I completed my first manuscript. Special mentions to Jackie, Carolyn, Clare, Ron, Tony, Fiona, Carole, Nigel and John. If I have forgotten anyone, I owe you a pint.

Along the trails, I came across wonderful poetry and art, which helped me understand the environment and my journey, stimulating thoughts and reflection as I walked ahead. I made a note of many poems, and later research confirmed the authors and artists. Many have been generous in giving permission to reproduce their work in this book, to illustrate the emotions and feelings of walking. Special mentions go to Dan Maier for his midlife-crisis shipping forecast, which I spent days trying to recite; John Wedgwood Clarke, whose poetry is carved on many benches along the Yorkshire Wolds Way; Hugh Lupton for the words on Tom Perkins' sculptures on the Peddars Way – words that resonated strongly with my connection to an ancestral home; Tom Bryan for his poem on Scottish weather; Ian McMillan for his words on the Pennine Way; and the words of William Walker, written after the Battle of Britain.

I have been unable to find the authors of some inscriptions and poetry, as hard as I have tried. Other works, still in copyright, are acknowledged elsewhere in the book. I am eternally grateful for all of these words, as they played in my mind, replacing the stresses and anxiety of daily routines with more profound thoughts. You have a lot of time when walking to reflect and contemplate the infinite. If I have a favourite, then I have to credit Sara Teasdale, who captured my state of mind along the top of the South Downs so clearly.

Lastly, I have to thank my publisher, Vertebrate Publishing, for starting my new career as an author; something I would not have believed possible just a few years ago.

FURTHER READING

www.nationaltrail.co.uk – official website for the National Trails of England and Wales: follow the acorn

www.scotlandsgreattrails.com – Scotland's equivalent for their Great Trails: follow the thistle

www.ldwa.org.uk – the Long Distance Walkers Association: a wonderful resource for many major trails, and they hand out certificates to members who have completed the trails described in this book

www.southwestcoastpath.org.uk – definitive resource for anyone walking the longest National Trail (until the England Coast Path is completed); essential guide book available from their webshop

www.walkhighlands.co.uk – detailed path information for Scottish trails; more than a lifetime of challenges

www.independenthostels.co.uk for many beautiful and unique hostels not conforming to a national style, yet *www.yha.org.uk* have many great hostels in beautiful locations

www.trailplanner.co.uk – my website and blog for walking and cycling adventures *www.stanfords.co.uk* – map shop that has been the start of many adventures

www.ordnancesurvey.co.uk – walking in the UK without an Ordnance Survey map is almost unthinkable

www.mwis.org.uk for mountain weather information service, or *www.metoffice.gov.uk* for weather forecast, or inshore forecast for coastal paths

www.v-publishing.co.uk for walking guides and new maps for many of these trails, or *www.harveymaps.co.uk* for tough, light, waterproof maps

ABOUT THE AUTHOR

Martyn Howe is a freelance technology consultant with a passion for long-distance walking. In 2016, he realised a lifelong ambition to walk nineteen iconic trails in England, Scotland and Wales. In total, these walks covered some 3,000 miles over 153 days, taking him through some of the most wonderful and diverse landscapes in the world.

Martyn's love of adventure doesn't begin and end with the English and Welsh National Trails and Scottish Great Trails: he has also cycled 1,400 miles around the British Isles, camping out each night; and recently his wanderlust has guided him around 6,500 miles of Atlantic and North Sea coastline. His website *www.trailplanner.co.uk* contains more information on his walks, cycle rides and campervan tours. *Tales from the Big Trails* is his first book.